GOD AMONG US

Edward Schillebeeckx

GOD AMONG US

The Gospel Proclaimed

CROSSROAD · NEW YORK

1983

The Crossroad Publishing Company
575 Lexington Avenue, New York, NY 10022

Translated by John Bowden from the Dutch
Evangelie Verhalen
published 1982 by Uitgeverij H. Nelissen B.V., Baarn

© Uitgeverij H. Nelissen B.V. 1982

Translation © John Bowden 1983

Printed in the United States of America

Library of Congress Cataloging in Publication Data

Schillebeeckx, Edward, 1914-
God among us.

Translation of: Evangelie verhalen.
1. Catholic Church—Sermons. 2. Sermons, English—
Translations from Dutch. 3. Sermons, Dutch—Translations
into English.   I. Title.
BX1756.S353E8313   1983   252'.02   82-23575
ISBN 0-8245-0575-1

To Tony Nelissen
and my brother Dominican Bas Brink,
who in their sickness entrust themselves
to the merciful arms of God

Contents

The sermons, lectures and articles contained in this book were originally published as follows (in some cases the title has been changed):

    1 *TGL (=Tijdschrift voor Geestelijk Leven)* 37, 1981, 512-6
          (homily)
    2 *De Bazuin,* Christmas 1970
    3 *De Bazuin,* Christmas 1972
    4 *Relief* 40, 1972, 9-17 (homily)
    5 *Schrift* 25, 1973, 68-72
    6 *Relief* 40 (1972), 9-17 (homily)
    7 *TGL* 20 (1973), 145-55 (homily)
    8 Unpublished homily 1978
    9 Relief 48, 1978, 65-7 (homily)
   10 Unpublished homily 1979
   11 Unpublished homily 1979
   12 Unpublished homily 1981
   13 *De Bazuin,* 9 April 1976, Vol.59, pp.4f.

14 Unpublished homily 1982
15 On the occasion of my honorary doctorate at Louvain, 1974; see *De Bazuin,* 1 March 1974, Vol.57, no.9.
16 *TGL* 34, 1978, 5-23
17 *TGL* 35, 1979, 451-73
18 *Getuigenis* 18, 1974, 289-294
19 *De Bazuin,* 28 March 1975
20 *TGL* 28, 1972, 435-51
21 *De Bazuin,* 2 July 1972
22 Unpublished homily 1974
23 Unpublished homily 1970
24 *Concilium* 155, 1982, 23-31
25 *TGL* 37, 1981, no.6, 652-68 (Amsterdam India Festival)
26 *TGL* 36, 1980, 356-62 (homily)
27 *TGL* 35, 1979, 645-57 (article)
28 *TGL* 37, 1981, 40-8 (homily)
29 *TGL* 37, 1981, 512-8 (homily on the occasion of two fiftieth anniversaries of religious profession and one fortieth anniversary of ordination to the priesthood)
30 Unpublished homily 1981
31 *Concilium* 139, 1980, 10-21
32 *De Bazuin,* 29 October 1972
33 *Relief* 48, 1980, no.12, 369-76 (Homily on the Seven Hundredth Feast of Albertus Magnus)
34 Lecture to Dutch Dominicans (published in duplicated form), 1974
35 Text of speech as delivered on 17 September 1982

To the Reader

I have often been asked to expound the basic themes of my big books Jesus and Christ for a wider public and in a simple way. I would very much like to, but I shall only be in a position to do so after the publication of my third book about Jesus: *Christ and his Church* (which I hope will be within a year).

At the same time I have been urged to collect together some of the sermons which I have given in various places. These are interpretations of passages of scripture in the Sunday liturgy in which the theologian ('forgetting' his theology) speaks as a preacher. Despite a thematic selection, these sermons are quite random; many of them were given when it was my turn to preside at the eucharist of the Albertinum in Nijmegen, where I live.

As well as sermons I have included some short articles which have been published in journals for spirituality and which themselves often go back to sermons, and also a couple of lectures.

What binds together you, the reader, and me the most has its roots in the stories about the gospels that we tell to one another.

Edward Schillebeeckx OP

I

The Way to Freedom

1

The Forerunner   (Mark 1.1-8)

Only a few verses from the lengthy prologue to the Gospel of Mark
have been read in today's liturgy: just those verses which relate to
Jesus' forerunner, John the Baptist. It is sometimes a good thing to
pause for a moment at this preliminary stage of Christian redemption.

We should see this first part of Mark's prologue as being rather like
something from one of Vondel's biblical plays: before the drama begins,
a messenger, an 'angelos', sometimes a real angel, appears on the stage.
The messenger comes to present the main character in the play to the
audience. He himself plays no further part in the action. Having
announced the coming drama, this figure vanishes from the stage, often
even for good. Sometimes he returns during the course of the action to
give the audience information about what has happened meanwhile
off-stage, or to tell them things of which the other characters are so far
ignorant but which the audience need to know if they are to be able to
follow the action properly. Thus although this messenger is a subordinate figure, he is of real importance. The play is not about him, though
he appears first; that can lead to misunderstanding, because all the
attention is first directed towards him. He himself tries to prevent this
misunderstanding by telling us that the drama which is about to begin
is about someone else: 'someone who is stronger, greater than he is'(see
Mark 1.7).

In today's story from the Gospel of Mark, John the Baptist is this
'angelos', messenger and forerunner. He introduces the chief character
in the story: Jesus of Nazareth. Moreover he explains to the public, his
readers, who this Jesus really is. The performers – the disciples and the
other Jews – are still ignorant of this at this stage in the story. The
tension in the story is in fact produced by the fact that they are
ignorant, whereas the audience is aware of what is going on. So the
messenger seeks to prepare the audience for the entry of the main

character, whose secret he reveals to them beforehand. Afterwards this messenger disappears from the stage, in Mark literally and definitively (Mark.1.1-14; he appears simply in a flash-back in 6.14-29; 9.11-13).

To understand this short passage properly, and also to grasp what it means for us, above all now in the season of Advent, we need to see that it is in fact made up of a web of all kinds of reminiscences of Old Testament texts: Exodus (23.20), Malachi (3.1; 4.5-6) and Isaiah (40.1-11). These texts prompted all kinds of messianic expectations in the time of Jesus. For the Jews it was a time of crisis. But they looked for a new Moses and a new liberation. This expectation was bound up with the coming appearance of a Moses-like messenger, bringing good news, who would first proclaim aloud the approaching event of liberation. In the meantime this messenger was already identified with the prophet Elijah, who had been taken up to heaven but would one day return again. All these expectations come together in these first verses of Mark. But Mark presents the real event, the heart of the message, the historical event of Jesus, in terms of an account in what is known as Second Isaiah (Isaiah 40), a work by an unknown prophet from the end of the Babylonian captivity. We have just heard that text and it is essential for our understanding of Mark's prologue.

Like the beginning of Mark's Gospel, Isaiah 40, too, is a prologue. In both cases a messenger is sent from God who must 'cry out' in a loud voice that the liberation of the humiliated and oppressed people is at hand. It will happen at any moment, indeed it is already in process of happening.

In this Isaiah's prologue it is striking that the prophet deliberately conceals himself behind his message. He is unimportant; the only important thing is what he has to say: the message of God's approaching liberation. The first of a series of commands that the prophet must cry out to all the people 'in a loud voice' is, 'Prepare a way in the wilderness', so that the people, freed from the captivity in Babylon, can make their triumphant way home through the wilderness to Jerusalem, to the land of their fathers. This series of 'cries' makes you feel that the great liberation from Babylon is actually happening; these cries are actually setting in motion the process of liberation. The good news excites people everywhere; even Jerusalem, far away, hears it and has to pass on the tidings (Isa.40.9) that a new exodus is taking place under the leadership of a new Moses. The news goes around everywhere. The cries build up to the last loud prophetic shout: 'Depart, depart, go out thence!'(Isa.52.11), away from the servitude of Babylon, through the wilderness, and back home to freedom. In these dynamic texts you can see the captives beginning to set out, the same kind of experience that we now have when we hear the 'cries' of Ernesto Cardenal or Pablo Neruda.

In fact, though, the way to freedom runs through the wilderness. Hence the first message is that the people must prepare a way, more accurately a street, straight through the wilderness. In both Isaiah and Mark this is what the people have to do first of all.

To understand what is meant here by what we may find the bizarre idea of a 'street through the wilderness', we must have a fair idea of what life was like for the anonymous prophet who has taken the name of Isaiah, living in Babylon. From Babylonian hymns and from archaeological evidence we know that 'the boulevard', the high street or main street in Babylon, exercised an enormous fascination on the mass of people. It was rather like the Champs Elysées in Paris, leading to the Arc de Triomphe, or the Via Vittorio Emmanuele in Rome, leading to the colossal, pretentious monument to the king. The Lenin-, Marx- and Eisenhower-allees all lead up to great monumental buildings. So Isaiah too wants a 'highway for the Lord', running through the wilderness and leading to the temple in Jerusalem, which was to be rebuilt. In Babylon the streets bearing the names of gods or the resounding names of great kings, memorials to former victories, to jubilation and triumph,were also the place where every year colossal, majestic statues of gods were carried along in colourful state cavalcades and religious processions for all the world to see: the greatest show on earth! The Jewish exiles, including our prophet 'Isaiah', had watched this pagan demonstration of power sadly every year, but nevertheless fell under its bewitching spell. In it they felt the living power of Babylon.

Nevertheless, Isaiah presented precisely this picture of the pagan triumphal route to the Jews, not as a street for Babylonian gods but as the 'Lord's street', 'a straight road for our God' the Lord (40.3), called 'the highway of Yahweh'. 'Where God shows his glory', the prophet adds, and also, 'for all to see'. However – and this is the secret key to the whole account – Israel's God is no Babylonian god, and Jews were forbidden to make images. God's glory is not revealed in splendid cavalcades on great streets or in processions with imposing effigies, but only in everyday history, and above all in the event of the liberation of his people from slavery, through the difficult journey through the wilderness, back to 'the freedom of Zion'. That, Isaiah says, is the way in which 'God's glory is made manifest'(40.5a) and 'revealed to all'(40.5b). God's power conquers through weakness; barren wilderness is what his people go through to their final liberation. God's honour and glory do not consist in his own pomp or in colourful triumphal cavalcades to his own glorification. His honour and renown, his glory, is the welfare and the deliverance of his people; that is where the God of Israel finds his prestige. So the whole world will see that the humiliated and disheartened people are raised up by God and exalted because Israel's God remains faithful to his promises. That is where his jealous honour is to be found; in the exaltation of the insignificant, the poor and the lowly – those who are oppressed.

Thus building a way through the wilderness is the prior condition for the homecoming of Israel in freedom, just as Moses once had to go through the wilderness with his people to arrive at their home in the promised land. In his prologue Mark renders this by saying, 'Repent, for God is at hand'(1.15): deliverance is imminent.

Although it is somewhat disguised by the influence of other traditions, Isaiah's 'picture of the street' was taken over by Mark. After Moses and Isaiah, John the Baptist is the third to announce the now definitive exodus from servitude. That is Mark's 'good' news, his message of victory or conquest. Like the Second Isaiah, John the Baptist also wants to keep in the background. He is the lesser one, and his message is concerned with someone stronger: the approach of God in Jesus of Nazareth. He may not even be the humble disciple of Jesus. It was the privilege of a rabbi's pupil to help his master put on his shoes, but this man will not even do that. John the Baptist is simply the angel or messenger who went before Moses in the journey through the wilderness (Ex.23.20; 32.34; 33.2); he is at the same time simply the prophet Elijah who had to come as the forerunner of the messianic deliverer(Mal.3.1,21).

In this, John the Baptist, like the prophet 'Isaiah', also has something to say about making ready a way-for-the-Lord. However, misled by a wrongly punctuated and therefore incorrect Greek translation of the Old Testament, Mark does not speak of a 'street through the wilderness', but of 'one calling in the wilderness'. Still, this is no bad thing; it even turns out well in the end, since as a result the forerunner is identified as the prophet Elijah from the Second Book of Kings (II Kings 1.8) and given as it were a geographical setting: very near the edge of the wilderness, where John preached (Mark 1.4), and near the Jordan, where he baptized (1.5): there the forerunner brings the good tidings about Jesus of Nazareth. And despite the incorrect translation, Mark, exactly in the spirit of Isaiah, makes Jesus himself build a way through the wilderness: in this Gospel Jesus' career begins with his testing in the wilderness: the way of God. The liberator, the one who brings the people home, must also himself travel the way of our human suffering. The work of liberation, 'the way of God', costs blood and tears and does not lead down the broad boulevards of Babylonian gods.

In Christianity, Mark's message tells us today, we are indeed concerned with liberation. But as in the first deliverance from Egypt under Moses, in the second exodus from Babylon, and finally, in the definitive deliverance brought about by Jesus, for us the 'work of liberation' means going through the wilderness: that is the way in which we can be certain that God goes with us and that we are not risking some solitary adventure with an ideological 'God with us'. We may leave open the question whether consistent Christian action may ever get us into prison. At all events, our work of liberation is not a smooth, obvious triumphal course in Babylonian style. Given the geography of our world, the *condition humaine* of our human existence, we shall in fact have constantly to keep going through the wilderness if we are to bring about some liberation for others and to taste something of the savour of liberation for ourselves.

Finally, what is striking about both the book of Isaiah and Mark – and this is their last message for today – is that neither of these prophet-forerunners calls himself a liberator and that their own personalities disappear behind the message of liberation-through-another. They both feel themselves to be useless servants, however necessary they may be, because it will have struck you that in this prologue to Mark our attention is drawn to the historical appearance of Jesus in our world by a third person: an eccentrically dressed young man with the 'hair shirt' characteristic of a prophet (cf. Zech.13.4) and the 'leather girdle' typical of Elijah (II Kings 1.7-8): in other words a fool. By contrast, Jesus, the all-important figure, makes an unobtrusive appearance, in the usual clothes of the ordinary person of his time. You could very well pass him by, had there not been this unusal man to point a finger at him. Jesus' coming to and among us is so unobtrusive that he could remain unknown in our history were we not constantly, time and again, endlessly, to proclaim him and point a finger to him (perhaps being rejected by the world, like the Baptist, as crazy). That is the reason why our Dominican order exists and it is also the task for our ministry and for all Christians in their lives: to do what the prophet Isaiah and what John the Baptist did. For God is always a God who is to come – that is his name and nature – always in a different and a new way according to the different circumstances in which we live. He therefore always needs humble and yet daring forerunners. Even now. That is today's Advent message.

2

God 'who visits his people'
(Christmas)

Historically we know nothing about the circumstances and the place of Jesus' birth. By contrast, what Matthew and Luke say in their account of this birth is in fact 'gospel', not a report of facts but an evangelical – if you like, theological – reflection on the beginnings of the man Jesus in the light of the end of his life and the church's confession of him as the Christ.

He was given the name Jesus, a common first name in those days (see e.g. Col.4.11). On that day perhaps a number of children were born in Palestine who were given the name Jesus. Our Jesus was one of the many; his birth remained unnoticed, completely anonymous, an ordinary everyday birth, a joy only for those who were directly affected by it: Mary, Joseph and probably some acquaintances.

That is in fact the original 'Christmas event', in its historical anonymity and inaccessibility. We know nothing of the other Jesuses and the other babies who were born on that day. However, for many people Jesus the son of Mary is still the most real thing in their lives. His name is still proclaimed and confessed, remembered and called on today. It cannot be a coincidence that this happened to this Jesus, and not to those many others.

The birth of a human being is always the beginning of a new possibility in our history. This new person is still open in all directions: the course he or she will take cannot be predicted or estimated. The birth of a human being is the possibility of a new and completely surprising love, but also the possibility of new grief and evil in the world; a possibility of new hope but also the possibility of new despair: 'What will become of this child?', Luke makes people ponder (1.66) at the birth of John who will later be called the Baptist. Tacitly or in an outspoken way, this is the worldly-wise wondering of so many parents, who look at their baby in its cradle, still unconscious of all this, and then look into each other's eyes questioningly , not in order to get an answer, but to catch hopeful or sorrowful reactions.

What in fact is to be the story of this new person who has entered our history? He or she appears on the stage when the story has already been going a long time. It begins for each of us as it did for Abraham: 'Abraham went out, not knowing where he was to go'(Heb.11.8). But despite all the disillusionments which characterize the story that we have entered, human beings seem to live in hope. There is always more hope than we can ever grasp from the story. Therefore the question of something new, something better, rightly comes up at the birth of any person. Nevertheless, he or she has to discover self and others through a history that has already taken place and through the story of mankind that is going the rounds. He or she will have to find their own identity within the story that has already begun, the story that is told to them and into which they grow, so that finally they can begin to play their own personal role in it. How will they pick up the thread of that story? What twist will they give to it? Or will the story pass them by, without their making any contribution to it? Will they fail to hear the *cri de coeur* which others hear and which startles them out of their lethargy?

Jesus appeared right in the middle of Israel's story, which was experienced as a story of God's concern for mankind. It was also a story of a God who was serious about his identity. Over the course of centuries of history this story had already taken shape and form, but nowhere yet was there any suggestion as to how it would finally turn out.

While he was growing up, Jesus deliberately took up the thread of Israel's story. The whole of his life history, the way in which he acted and the reaction of his contemporaries within Palestine, should make it possible for us to see what the new possibility would be in his case. Above all in the last years of his life his sudden public appearance made outsiders whisper and mutter – in longing or in doubt – 'Could it be he?' People felt there was a connection between Israel's story and what was expressed in him. However, he himself rejected all allusions to an earthly messiahship. He did not recognize the voice of Israel's messianic story in the messianic figures that were expected at that time. Furthermore, John's head had already fallen because people kept muttering about something like 'the coming state' in connection with him, and the Romans were over-sensitive about Jewish messianic movements which also wanted to cast off the Roman yoke. Jesus evidently wanted to say something before he too lost his life – in whatever way that might be. Or was he so filled with the one whom he called the Father that he was never concerned about his own person and only thought of his calling and his mission for others? 'Why do you call me good? Only the Father is good.' That can be said only by someone who is so obviously good that he is not even conscious of being good. And precisely that will betray his identity.

A group of people had put unconditional trust in him, though they were clumsy, weak and swayed by their own existing ideas as just ordinary people. They did this because something remarkable and new seemed to emerge in his relationship with God, whom he called his Father. It was so remarkable that at one particular point these rather uneducated fishermen raised a question about which they must have wondered, 'Teach us to pray' – clearly to be understood as 'like you do'. This remarkable aspect of Jesus' life was also expressed in an almost untiring care for his fellow men and in his championship of the weak against the powerful. He did all this in the perspective of a phrase which was very well known, indeed magic, in Israel, the kingdom of God: God's rule as the kingdom in which God's will is done on earth as it is in heaven, i.e. without any master-servant relationships.

They did not always understand this. Not even his stories. Above all he told parables. Sometimes they understood them, and then they felt happy. Most of the time, however, there was misunderstanding. Whenever this misunderstanding concerned God, his Father, Jesus could react abruptly and sharply, as any one might react when the peson he or she loved most was concerned.

Only when Jesus had died, in a brief climax of conflicts which cost him his life, were the eyes of his closest followers opened – after what was at first complete disillusionment. In fact their experience came as a revelation. They described it as really having their eyes opened; the Greek word used all through the New Testament is *ophthe*: it was revealed to them, they now 'saw' it, their eyes were opened. He was the guarantee for the renewal of their lives. Now they understood how Jesus had taken up the thread of Israel's story and given it such an unexpected and incalculable twist that they were amazed that they had not seen it before either through what this God had revealed already in the Bible (the Tanach or our Old Testament), or through what Jesus said and did when he was still among them. This Jesus was alive, with God', and they now experienced his presence in their midst, in the renewal which he had brought about in their lives. They had to take all kinds of key terms from the Old Testament to be able to express to some extent their impressions and the image that had been stamped on them by their encounters with Jesus. Their terms included Son of David, Messiah, Servant of God, Son of God, the Holy One of God, the Righteous One, the Son of Man. No one of the titles that they used was in itself enough to express their experience. They were all needed, and even then they stilll broke to pieces on the image that Jesus himself had imprinted on them, simply by being himself, in his actions and his prayers.

God had indeed visited his people, as the Semites put it: the *kabod* of God himself, his invisible glory and splendour, shone out visibly on Jesus' countenance for anyone who looked to Jesus in trust, who actively saw and listened to him (II Cor.4.6). To begin with they had imagined this splendour too narrowly, in either petty or pretentious human terms, and therefore had been unable to see it. It is not so obvious that God's omnipotence should show itself in the helplessness of a disarming love. People think of power and splendour in different terms. After first completely bowling them over, the crucifixion had made them understand this, almost despite themselves. So they ascribed their new insight, the opening of their eyes, to the 'power from on high', the work of the divine spirit, which had been the strength of Jesus' life, as they now could clearly understand.

When the Christians looked back on their dealings with Jesus before his death, everything took on its proper meaning, just as we too sometimes revise our opinion of someone on the basis of an event which opens our eyes and makes us say, 'Oh, that's what he was like!' We knew it really, but without that happening we would never have thought of putting things in that way. Now what we really knew unexpectedly takes on its proper setting: it is completely new, but really we could have known it all the time. Only when they looked back in this way did the Christian believers hear the angelic song of jubilation over the birthplace of Jesus: 'Glory to God in the highest, and peace on earth to mankind.' That is, God's heavenly glory is visibly present in peace among men now that Jesus himself is present among us.In a kind of flashback the Christians made this song ring out above an event which had taken place about thirty years before in an anonymous silence, so silent that the historical details can no longer be ascertained and one can only begin to talk about the anonymous beginning of Jesus' life in terms of its end. The angels in fact made their appearance when after the resurrection of Jesus believers celebrated in their assemblies their trust in Jesus and thus as it were mobilized all that was real to them, to present it to God with their praise and thanks for the gift which had been given to them in Jesus. Then nothing was too much. Angels, stars, wise men from the east, 'astrologers', but also simple people and shepherds, everything and everyone was summoned to offer praise to God.

At the same time, people felt that this Jesus must inevitably be a stumbling block for the powerful of the earth, people who seem only to be put off by other people's goodness and therefore become aggressive. When pure goodness appears, without the sentimentality of mediaeval views of the crib, all the opposing forces of the earth do in fact join together: 'They come to search for the child, to destroy him' (Matt.2.13). Love is disarming. That is, people can be won over by it, or, it makes those who are evil even worse. The theme of the massacre of the innocents in Bethlehem has more human truth than the historian can ever discover. Faced with love which shows itself to be unarmed – and not knowing that it is love – the human reaction is either unconditional surrender or panic fear which will do anything to strengthen its own position of power, even to the point of killing all young children who are two years old and younger (Matt.2.16). Any threat, possible or imagined, is exterminated.

Love in fact becomes the definition of heaven and hell, already on earth in the midst of our history, and therefore for ever. The first generation of Christians understood this well when, in the light of Jesus' life, death and resurrection they meditated on the beginning of that life: the birth of Jesus. 'Legend is the metaphysics of reality.' Human birth, life and death are in fact accessible only in a story, and not in theory or 'theology'.

Over against Gnosticism, speculation and what is not story, the church has summed up the story of the gospel in its creed: 'I believe in Jesus.' 'I believe in Jesus as the Christ, as the only-begotten Son, as the Lord.' Of the many titles in which the New Testament tried to put into words what Jesus meant for the first Christians, the creed retained only these three: 'the Christ, the only-beloved Son, our Lord'. But the subject of these three predicates remains the same: Jesus. I believe in Jesus of Nazareth; one of our kind might and could manifest who God himself is, in person, for all of us. This child is indeed a gift of the Holy Spirit (Matt.1.20), God-with-us (Matt.1.23). Christmas Day is the feast of God's humanity.

Whenever God visits his people, as biblical language puts it so picturesquely and with all kinds of nuances (which can only be brought out by an examination of our own consciences), transformations do indeed take place, of the kind which we can see above all among the first Christians. After about twenty centuries we Christians seem to be over-familiar with God's visitation. That is why it happens so imperceptibly in our churches. Furthermore, in his ways and purposes which can never be defined precisely in our human terms, God seems to have introduced a process of 'getting us out of bad habits' which we (rather short-sightedly) have begun to call 'secularization' or 'the death of God'. In this process God evidently wants to make his Christians once again receptive and sensitive towards 'God who visits his people', for the salvation of all.

3

'All Jerusalem was Afraid'
(Matt.2.3)

According to the way the Gospel of Matthew sees things, when the birth of Jesus was made known something remarkable happened: 'Herod the king and all Jerusalem with him were afraid' (Matt.2.3). The king was afraid; the Greek word used in the New Testament has all kinds of nuances: he became excited; dismay, agitation and bewilderment overcame him; he was in confusion, in anguish, all over the place, in short, he was shattered. 'And all Jerusalem with him'; this clearly means everyone who exercised authority in Jerusalem under the watchful eye of the Romans: 'the high priests and the scribes'(Matt.2.4). Here the birth of Jesus, the first Christmas, is evidently presented quite blatantly as a threat to the establishment, to the ruling powers, to all those who exercise authority over their fellow-men, at least in contrast to God's authority, that is, those responsible for a rule which does not liberate people for freedom. 'The appearance of goodness and the God concerned for mankind' (see Titus 3.4) – the feast of Christmas – thus becomes the beginning of an event which is expected to turn our history on its head and overthrow conditions which restrict and enslave people. It is as though everything in a position of human power unfailingly feels the threat from Jesus. Such a Jesus discloses human beings to themselves and reveals their consciences so that they either put up opposition or repent.

Our conventional celebration of Christmas is in sharp contrast to the particular Christian view expressed in this verse of Matthew. Criticism of Christmas celebrations is familiar enough: the idyllic sentimentality of the middle-class Christian family. Perhaps looking for an excuse, it organizes a day of peaceful brotherliness with the obligatory number of annual Christmas reconciliations, at least for this day. But at the same time this is a festival of false peace: outside, bombs fall on one people; unrest, tension and uneasiness, injustice prevail; and not far from us even Christians carry out terrorist attacks against one another every day, perhaps with one day's break so that both sides can celebrate the Christian festival of Christmas. Commentators and theologians make their own contribution to the discontent over our celebration of Christmas: the infancy narratives in Matthew and Luke cannot and may not be regarded as a kind of eye-witness account of historical events as they actually happened; rather, they are made-up stories giving a retrospective interpretation in the light of Jesus' later life and execution, and the higher calling of the resurrection. Finally, in our society the festival of Jesus' birth is culturally bound up with an earlier, old Germanic winter festival with domestic, fireside celebrations by the burning hearth and the evergreen fir tree, a comforting relic of the summer that is past and also a hope of natural warmth to come. To fill the cup of discontent to overflowing for our critical age, in Western society Christmas is the climax of consumer purchasing. Whether celebrated in a Christian or a secular way, it is a peak of the carefully planned present-industry, a peak of all our prosperity at the expense of the hunger of two-thirds of the world's population.

This is fair criticism. We can no longer celebrate Christmas 'innocently'. But quite apart from its grimness (which also, of course, underestimates deep human feelings), this criticism also misses the threat to be found in Matthew's interpretation of the Christmas festival, and it also misses the unfathomable gift that the birth of Jesus, from God, is in fact meant to be. The criticism shames the way in which we make Christmas private and middle-class; it does not criticize Christmas, but us. It is directed to the wrong quarter.

That gives us something to think about. For the believing Christian, the birth of Jesus is the real beginning of salvation, that is, of a concern to bring renewal to the bloody course of our history, coming to life and taking personal form in that history. The birth of this man is a first great step towards what the Bible calls the coming 'commonwealth of God', though it uses old monarchical terms and calls it the kingdom of God: the liberating love of God in the realm of mankind. This is a new happening in which hope is experienced by those who were without hope; it brings life for those who were condemned to death. Law — commandments and prohibitions — becomes gospel, good news; promise becomes fulfilment; strangers become members of the family; 'the blind see and the lame walk and the poor receive joyful news' (Matt.11.5; Luke 7.22). The poor must be satisfied now, straightaway: 'Give us today our daily bread', not, 'Patience, patience! All will be well in due course.' The lame must be able to walk and the blind must be able to see now, straightaway. Our Christmas festival recalls the birth of a man who during his lifetime was to be so mindful of the history of human suffering and to see it so intensively as an over-filled repository of grief and pain, unreconciled and unliberated and without future, that he felt that a limit had now been reached. Something definitively new would have to happen.

This dream has often been dreamed, in the depths of intolerable suffering. But now it is actually happening, through the astonishing new life-style of this man. 'The time is fulfilled, the kingdom of God is at hand.' History itself, our old human history, takes on a new orientation. Its course is changed.

That means that we, people who make history, must be prepared to have our own course changed. The kingdom of God calls for *metanoia,* that is, a radical change in existing circumstances: in our own hearts and what conditions them, in our human institutions and structures. Salvation is given to people (to whom else?), but to particular people, whose personal identity is also formed or broken by social and political conditions, institutions and structures, which may be good or may be bad. We need to take seriously the biblical message of salvation for men and women, though without being tied to the 'biblical' conceptions of what a person really is.

'All Jerusalem was afraid' of the birth of this Jesus. As we celebrate and recall the festival of Christmas and what it means to us today, that means that Jesus' birth is a threat of a judgment on our perverse heart (which has no room for our fellow human beings) and on our structures and institutions in so far as they enslave and bruise people, shattering their identity instead of giving them true freedom.

So more than ever these days we need the Christian celebration of Christmas, which for us is at the same time a festival when we penitently say 'my fault', because we aren't really liberating Christians. It is a festival of repentance, but nevertheless primarily a grateful celebration of what makes our repentance possible: God as our future, the God who comes in our history, the bringer of salvation that finds a footing in the world of our human experience, however sporadically and regionally and because of our neglect – almost in a discriminatory way. But despite our guilt Christmas remains a joyful remembrance of the origin of the well-grounded hope of a new history that will renew us; not an alibi for what we make of it, but a stimulus towards a new life-style which brings liberation.

Instead of being a one-sided hope for ourselves, Christmas must become the festival of hope for others, the festival of our effective hope for those without hope. To celebrate Christmas, then, means to allow ourselves to be steeped in the fact that suffering, meaninglessness, evil, the sin of the world lie deeper than natural, individual and collective abuses might suggest. But at the same time it means realizing in faith that the possibility of salvation, meaning and grace in our history is also greater than the visible forms of salvation might suggest. Where people are already healed or begin to be made whole we have only the start, the sign of complete salvation to come. Finally, Christmas means the hope of what to us is an unfathomable link between our Christian life-style, which is new and brings renewal, and the salvation that is promised to us. 'You shall renew the face of the earth.' As long as there is a brother, a fellow human being has not been 'freed', I myself am not free. Dostoevsky felt that in his *The Brothers Karamazov,* and so did the agnostic Bertrand Russell. To meditate openly about Christmas, indeed simply to celebrate Christmas openly, can perhaps make us realize that 'Christian identity' consists in identifying ourselves with others. That is to say, it consists in having the courage to listen to the message of the kingdom of God not from the perspective of a prosperous position and an already warm nest, but above all with the ears of people who are oppressed, wronged and written off, poor and persecuted; and to ask ourselves how the message of God's salvation and liberation in and through Jesus would sound then. If we did that, then like Jerusalem, perhaps all our man-made institutions and structures would be afraid, as would any heart that did not dare to experience this, the other man's way of listening to the Christian message.

No longer being able to celebrate Christmas because we direct our criticism to the wrong quarter means putting the clock back about 1972 years: already at that time there was 'no room for him' in Bethlehem; no possibility of celebrating Christmas.

We need Christmas very much indeed, because salvation – man's well-being, disclosed in Jesus – cannot and may not be understood only in the light of the Risen One. It must also be understood in the light of the earthly Jesus from before Easter, in the light of his appearance as man and in the light of his message of the coming kingdom of God which enters our history precisely through a life-style like that of Jesus. For this life-style was approved by God when he gave Jesus a personal future after his death as a pledge for our justified expectation and concern for the future.

It always strikes me that anyone who looks in the New Testament for the identity of Jesus is always directed to someone else, to his fellow human beings ('what you have done for the least of these my brothers you have done for me', Matt.25.40) and to his God ('Philip, he who has seen me has seen the Father', John 14.9). Jesus always finds his own identity outside himself, in other people. This relieves him of the burden of having to affirm himself, that burden and constraint of which we are well aware: being worried about our own identity. Therefore, because he is freed from himself, he can live a liberating life for others, right to the end. His identity was solidarity with the least among us, with all of us, people without freedom who are looking for it, and who can only be born in love and by being accepted by others. Is not our life empty unless we mean something to others and others mean a great deal to us?

In the light of this I sometimes think that while there are doubtless many other factors, the present identity crisis among Christians, above all among priests and religious, arises from the way in which they search desperately for their own identity instead of identifying themselves with others and in so doing also finding an identity that satisfies them psychologically, unsought and in addition. I am struck by the fact that in the New Testament Jesus' identity is not a problem for Jesus himself but only for his followers. Perhaps that is not so much because his identity was crystal clear to himself, but because he simply did not think about it. Jesus did not apply any 'christological titles' to himself; he was caught up wholly in God's cause, salvation for humankind – the cause of humanity. He quietly allows what others say of him, under his spell, to go over his head. For the crowd he was a prophet, and after his purification of the temple, which played on the imagination of the Jews, he was hailed by them as Messiah. For the humble people round Lake Galilee he was the wonder-worker who had compassion on their suffering and who alleviated their distress, if need be with miracles. For the more well-to-do hosts who invited him into their homes to sit at their tables he was the subtle narrator of parables. For others he was the vigorous debater who checkmated his opponents in controversies. For the probably much smaller circle of faithful followers he was above all else the man who called God his 'Abba', which made such a surprising impression on them that they felt that he had to be seen as a special 'son of God'. For everyone, no matter what their position or to what group they belonged, it was at all events clear that a 'power went out from him'. Depending on their own disposition and needs anyone in his presence felt the significance of this power – even those who were not well-disposed towards him: they regarded it as the power of Beelzebub.

By his behaviour and attitude and the authority that went out from him, which are so difficult to define, Jesus himself in fact called to life the manifold impressions which people had when in his presence. So he allowed himself to be named by others as they wished, depending on the salvation that they found in him, though he did not accept these names uncritically. He rejects any one-sided identification; he sometimes refuses to perform miracles because he is not a bizarre wonder-worker who can conjure up marvellous acts; although he is 'Master' and a wise teacher, he retains his freedom over against the conventional interpretations of the 'Masters', indeed even over against the Law. For him the criterion is not the Law but 'man's well-being' ; and he knows that this is also God's own deepest concern. He does not allow exclusive claims to be made for him by any particular group. Paul shows in his own way of life that he understood Jesus very well in this respect: 'All for all' (I Cor.9.19-23).

These many possibilities in Jesus make him a mystery, an unfathomable secret that already dictates the attempts of the Gospels, with their many pictures of Jesus, to identify him and bring him into being. The mysterious 'phenomenon of Jesus' is not a creation of the first Christian generations, but is rooted in Jesus' own behaviour – his sayings, his actions and his silences. It is rooted in his over-definite complexity and flexible ambiguity. All this, moreover, is put completely in the shade by his ignominious execution – the most profound mystery of his devotion to humankind as 'God's cause' and the equally profound mystery of the repeated meaninglessness of the history which human beings make.

This mystery of the life of Jesus – and it is a mystery for us as it was for them – seems to be concentrated in the fact that he spoke of God and man in such a way that any person and any human grouping could understand him in their own language, with their own need of salvation and desire for happiness. He had a message for anyone who was receptive to him. In this Jesus 'God's cause' and 'man's cause' virtually coincide. He conveys that to us paradoxically, and thus in an incredibly acute and appropriate way. He asks us 'first to seek the kingdom of God' but that seems to mean, 'help the poor, clothe the naked, give a glass of water to the thirsty...'(Matt.25.31-46), for those are the criteria on the basis of which God will make his final judgment. What was then possible only on an inter-personal basis must now in addition come about through the political and social dimension of *caritas*. That is therefore at least the beginning of the kingdom of God. God's light seems to burn on earth only with the oil of our lives – of righteousness and love.

This mystery of the man Jesus, God's parable and man's paradigm, cannot be summed up in one formula. The church did what it could, given the historically-conditioned questions that were posed. But the mystery can never be eliminated nor can it ever be put fully into words. Praxis will make Jesus alive among us. As a mystery, he is therefore never the exclusive possession of Christians. He is 'common property'. 'He spoke in all openness' is the way in which the Gospels make him defend himself at the time of his trial. He is not in fact there just for an 'in-group', even if they call themselves Christians. Although he may hold us, Christians, enthralled, we cannot lay any exclusive claim to him: he is 'manifest', there for all. Precisely because of that we all need to learn to spell out the secret of this mysterious life – Africans and Europeans, Asians and Americans — as the power which makes meaningful life possible.

Perhaps there are those among us whose life-style is such that we feel drawn to say: these people are so amazingly good, so incredibly new as people, that we must ask, 'Where does this quality come from?' Such a provocative experience has only one answer: 'Why do you call me good? Only the Father is good.' Those are Christians who have understood the mystery of Jesus. People like that (and sometimes we may find them among those who are not Christians) can and may celebrate Christmas festively and exuberantly. In their shade, we can then honestly join in the celebration in a rather more modest way.

4

Magnificat: A Toast to God

'I will call upon his name as long as I live' (Ps.104)

Once when I was in Rome I saw an instrument hanging on the wall. I was told that it was the famous Aeolian harp. It is a delicate stringed instrument, which is fastened outside on a wall; at the slightest breath of wind the strings begin to sing – just. This is an image of God's grace, which plays imperceptibly on the still sounding-board of the human heart. That is what prayer is. This image of Christian prayer is evocative, but at the same time it is misleading because it is over-simple. I want to try to fill out the content of this imagery on the basis of the Magnificat, to try to give it more inner meaning.

Whenever one expectant mother pays a visit to another, they inevitably talk about their children-to-be. According to Luke's Gospel, Mary, who is pregnant, pays a visit to a certain Elizabeth (herself in her sixth month). The coming birth of a new child is always the beginning of a 'new possibility' in our human history: a new future is in the making. This is what sparks off the conversation.

Both mothers were pious Jewish women 'of the land', believers who looked for the coming of 'the Lord', of which their national and religious history was so full. Jewish religion is a religion of the God who is to come, of a God who brings salvation, liberation and deliverance in history.

Of course within such a view of history the coming birth of a child takes on a special significance. Any child is regarded by a pious Jewish woman or man as a direct gift from God, a gift to which the only possible response is a Magnificat, high praise of God, in gratitude to the one who does such mighty things. The Old Testament, the history of Mary's own people, gives various instances of Magnificats sung by expectant mothers. I Samuel 2.1-10, Hannah's Magnificat over the birth of her child Samuel, is a typical example. In fact, something like this will have been the state of mind, the Magnificat, of any pious Jewish mother. The expression of this grateful praise to God follows a basic general pattern which sometimes nevertheless takes on new content in the light of each particular situation. However, for each Jewish mother the Magnificat is the secret of her own life, the secret of herself, an experience which remains hidden from others. The specific content of Mary's Magnificat, as the thanks of a mother to God, is also unknown to us, since the content given to it in the Magnificat that we find in the Bible has been supplied by the evangelist Luke himself. This he did as a Christian, i.e. in the light of his knowledge, in faith, of the life and death of Jesus which already lay in the past, and in the light of the Christian witness that this Jesus indeed lives with God, as God's right hand in the active concern which God has for all humankind. Luke therefore makes the content of Mary's Magnificat a reflective, prayerful meditation in which the basic structure of all authentic Christian prayer clearly comes to the fore.

'I thank him from the bottom of my heart,
and none of his gracious deeds will I forget'(Ps 86.12).

The Magnificat is first of all a grateful hymn of praise to the glory of God, i.e. praise of God purely and simply because he is what he is: a living God. 'My soul glorifies the Lord, my spirit rejoices in God, my saviour.' This prayer comes from the depth of the psyche and the pneuma, that is, the praise arises from the innermost depths of the person praying: the one who prays is transformed completely and utterly into thanks and praise. This is no superficial welling-up. The person who prays is affected to the very marrow; she or he cannot help this praise. It is too much for them to be able to put into words. We human beings know this on the anniversaries of having been married, of having been a priest, for so many years; of having served faithfully for so many years or having been so many years in a religious order. Our words of gratitude fall short. Our feelings come from a depth which even the person giving thanks can no longer fathom.

In the Magnificat which Luke attributes to Mary there are two reasons for this depth. God is addressed here as 'my Yeshua', my saviour. Mary praises God who has given her Yeshua, Jesus. In a pious person this immediately arouses the feeling 'I didn't deserve it', in short, the feeling of unworthiness: 'He looks on his servant in her lowliness'. Such a divine gift to a simple person, one of many, only increases the gratitude. Luke interrupts Mary's prayer, as it were, at this point. In so doing he betrays the fact that he himself is at prayer, for he knows from Israel's long experience that God always chooses what is of no account and that because of this choice, that is for ever impressed upon mankind's grateful remembrance: 'Hencefore all ages will call me blessed. The Almighty works marvels for me.'

Just as Yahweh freed Israel, a people of no account, humiliated by their servitude in Egypt (Deut.10.22), so that all nations praise their good fortune (Malachi 3.12), so now we remember, says Luke, the mighty things that Yahweh did in Mary. And we shall continue to remember them. From this we learn at the same time that a personal prayer is never completely new, something that has never been said before, but adopts and gives a new personal shape to prayers which others have already prayed before us. Prayer is praying in a tradition of prayer.

The consequences of this tradition can also be seen in the Magnificat. Prayer is not just grateful praise of what God does for me; it is always also anamnesis, remembrance. The gracious act of God which people praise and for which they literally offer their congratulations is never in isolation. It must be seen in a wider context of never-ending gracious activity.

Therefore in the Magnificat there follows the great anamnesis of God: a proud remembrance of what God has done in the past. Here the Magnificat specifically recalls only two categories of people: on the one hand there is God's constant yet ever new mercy on all the faithful or God-fearers who are nonentities in the eyes of the world, who do not or cannot make their voices heard, because they are always drowned by others. On the other there is God's mercy on all Israel, the *'ebed Yahweh,* all suffering Israel as the son of God or God's most faithful servant. God's gracious deeds to both these categories of people are remembered with gratitude. For the person who prays knows that through God's mighty arm the nonentities are always lifted up, raised, indeed exalted to God: 'His mercy is from age to age, on those who fear him. He puts forth his arm in strength and scatters the proud-hearted. He casts the mighty from their thrones and raises the lowly. He fills the starving with good things, sends the rich away empty.' God does not seem to like earthly powers as the pious Israelites had experienced them in reality.

By means of this great remembrance, the believer who prays puts God's gracious act, of which the person who prays is himself the recipient, within the perspective of a more comprehensive saving event in which all others are involved. The prayer directs concern away from our own persons, and places everything within the wider context of a history which stands under God's promise: 'He protects Israel, his servant, remembering his mercy, the mercy promised to our fathers, to Abraham and his sons for ever.'

Thus the Magnificat becomes grateful praise for God's great promise of salvation, which may come to govern our lives. The great things which God has done for me move into the supreme collective event of promise and saving act. Prayer, however personal, however deeply it comes from a person's heart and spirit, is nevertheless only Christian prayer when this personal prayer is actively taken up into the perspective of the promise and saving history which are for all men and which transcend the purely personal dimension. This Christian characteristic removes all individualism from prayer and at the same time gives it a broader undercurrent: as it were the whole of history issues in Christian prayer.

Therefore the believer who prays not only can recall God's former gracious deeds, but has the Christian courage to remind God himself of them. Reminding God in this way plays a central role in Jewish prayer, and above all in the Old Testament. The Magnificat says: 'He protects Israel, his servant, remembering his mercy.'

Furthermore, in many Jewish-Christian prayers God's own recollection of former goodness was rightly regarded as the foundation and legitimation of what we now call intercessory prayer or petition. This was so taken for granted that it made Jesus' disciples ask him, 'Lord, teach us a *tephillah* as John also taught his disciples a *tephillah'* (Luke 11.1). That is, Lord, teach us how to frame an intercession, a petition. Thereupon Jesus taught them the Our Father. God's own recollection of former gracious actions legitimates our intercession. God's recollection is his creative faithfulness through history. This assurance of faith is expressed attractively and disarmingly in Hannah's song of thanksgiving as a Magnificat to God for the birth of Samuel: 'There is no rock like our God' (I Sam.2.2). Prayer is man's answer to this: grateful congratulations to God. So prayer always has something of a celebration about it; sooner or later it calls for liturgical consummation or expression, communal congratulations which all those who want to recall God's gracious acts want to offer to God. I do not believe that prayer does not make sense because God knows everything. Nor do I believe that communal prayer simply serves to strengthen, edify and admonish the brethren and lead to human togetherness. Prayer is not solely, or even primarily, concerned with finding support for ourselves or others: it is concerned with God. For God is just as appreciative of congratulations and celebrations as we tend to be. I believe in a very real interplay of action and reaction between God and mankind, though as human beings and believers we scarcely understand just what this way of reacting, of truly being affected and touched, would be like in the case of God himself. Human lovers too are well aware that they love each other. Their 'I love you', said over and over again, has no value as information. But does that mean that there is no point in repeating it often? ' Le coeur a des raisons, que la raison ne connait pas.' 'The heart has reasons that reason does not know about.' That is prayer. I ought really to stop there. But consideration in prayer of the Magnificat in the context of the first two chapters of the Gospel of Luke has a great deal to tell us about the nature of Christian prayer, above all when that prayer, like the Magnificat, still has such an Old Testament flavour. It is not for nothing that it is Luke who calls Mary the *symballousa* (2.19), i.e. the one who meditates. She tries to bring together these divergent things in her heart and to trace the golden thread of salvation in what happens to Jesus and to her. Our English translations put it rather flatly: 'She kept it in her heart.' What is meant, however, is a prayerful reflection which seeks to draw out the saving significance of ordinary events in our lives. Luke himself goes some way in that direction.

The Magnificat, a song of praise uttered to God by an expectant mother, is ultimately so completely taken up into a thanksgiving to God for the whole of the history of salvation that prayerful reflection on it arrives at the insight that this history is held in tension between a beginning and an end. In the Magnificat Mary is the eschatological, i.e. the final, personification of Israel, whereas Abraham, 'the father of all believers', is the protological, i.e. the first, personification of that same Israel. Between these two poles lies the whole of Israel's history, which has grown old in the longing for and expectation of the final coming of God's liberation. In the course of the infancy narratives, Luke therefore brings on to the stage four very old people: Zechariah and Elisabeth, Simeon and the old prophetess Hannah. They are intended as types of Israel watching down the ages, almost tired of watching and looking for final deliverance. But now that God is at last definitively visiting his people in Jesus of Nazareth, these old men and women can sing their Nunc Dimittis: the new covenant has begun, permanently, and now at least everything can be different.

A piece of Christian dogmatics is here distilled into a prayer. On closer inspection we should put it in a different way: it is really the meditative prayer which calls this dogmatics into life. At all events, the saving action of God in history and reflection in prayer belong intrinsically together. Without recognition in prayer, our history can hardly be called salvation history, and without salvation history, prayer becomes purely a human projection without any foundation.

Therefore it is as though prayer is a harmonious accompaniment to God's own saving actions, the resonance of them in our spirits and in our hearts.

Furthermore, it appears that God's saving action itself calls our prayer to life. Theologians talk of this experience in a rather abstract way when they say that God has the priority in prayer and that prayer is a grace, more an initiative from God than from men. God first loved us (I John 4.10). But this grace does not drop down straight from heaven. It comes to us in a very specific way from history, at least for the believer who knows where to look for it. Therefore prayer is never an introvert action. Certainly it is a matter of concentration, but it is concentration on those cardinal points of our human history in which the action of God is distilled into a provocative presence.

Praying is therefore *pati divina,* experiencing the divine, not in the (Neo-)Platonic sense, which is the context from which the word in fact comes, but in the Jewish-Christian sense: being open to the visitation, the coming of God into our history; letting the kingdom of God come. The Gospel of Mark has found just the right term for this: you can enter the kingdom of God 'like a child' (10.15). The child is the model for the believer, not because of its still naive, uncritical view of the world (though that is the way in which the term is explained by some people in 'orthodox' reaction to modern man come of age), but because of the child's capacity to be able to accept a gift without ulterior motives or calculations – as it were without guile. That is why the child is a model for us. The kingdom of God, grace, we ourselves, are pure gift: gifts which ask to be accepted as they are by children. The child shows its gratitude by being utterly caught up in its gift without any false shame, by being actively involved and fascinated by it. And that is what gifts are for, at least if we do not want to give them in a Pharisaic fashion.

However, the child has also to learn to say an extra thank-you: in that respect it is naturally still naive. As grown-up people, Christians, who are to be childlike in the world, we must therefore detach ourselves now and then from our fascination with all the gifts around us, i.e. with our own life, to say an extra thank-you. That is what prayer is: the extra thank-you to God in a life which in its entirety is pure gift, and which we experience as such every day by enjoying its good things. The Magnificat teaches us the need for this extra thank-you. For Jewish-Christian thanksgiving and praise (*berakah*), of which this prayer gives us an example, always begins with 'Blessed' or 'Praised' be God.

In every Jewish-Christian prayer, God himself is the one who is praised (*baruch*) as the source of blessings or gracious deeds. This is so up to and including the eucharistic prayer, which always begins with a 'eucharistia', i.e. 'We praise and thank you', and it is the same with the Magnificat: 'My soul glorifies the Lord'. God is the one who is praised, the one to whom the congratulations are offered. This means that our thanksgiving and praise to God belongs to our definition of God. In the Jewish-Christian tradition of prayer, the fact that God himself is praised, becomes a property, a qualification of God himself. A God about whom people keep silent is ultimately not God at all. To live *etsi Deus non daretur,* i.e. to live a completely self-centred life, as though

God did not exist, is ultimately impossible. The person who prays teaches us that. So belief without prayer is not Christian belief.

We can never identify prayer completely with our Christian life, with our daily work, or our concern for our fellow men, though this concern is nevertheless the practice of the love of God and is therefore indeed prayer in action. To misunderstand this last point makes all explicit prayer into an ideology. Yet we may not forget that God, who takes his identity seriously, naturally – by definition – asks that he should be mentioned explicitly, at least now and then. Of course in our own Christian past we have often spoken perversely about God in such a horrific way, commiting murder in his name and on ships with the name Jesus on their flags dragging away black slaves like cattle to white countries, that we must respect those who would rather keep quiet about him – at least for a while. But despite this guilt, we believers cannot in the end keep quiet about God. Sullied though his name may be, we must talk about him: in prayer – for in addition to our self-made meaninglessness there is also a good deal of given meaning in our lives.

To live in a world full of gifts, without anyone ever getting up and saying 'Thank you' out loud, sealing this with a kiss, is – as I am sure you will agree – prose without the poetry of life. Prayer is poetry – the kiss – in the prosaic life of the person who believes in God. We cannot leave something of that kind out of our lives.

5

Jesus' Story of God

It is often difficult for us, modern people, familiar with the demands of the historical sciences, to understand a 'narrative culture'. One illustration of this is the story of Jonah who spent three days and three nights in the belly of a whale. The ancient church fathers already had difficulty with this story, but in our own time failure to understand it sometimes goes to ridiculous lengths. After a great deal of learned research, one scholar came to the conclusion that in his flight Jonah in fact went into hiding in some kind of pub or little café known as 'The Whale' – 'In The Whale'. Evidently we have lost our 'narrative innocence'! Many cultures have a story about a man who is swallowed by a large fish. That particular story can be used to express all kinds of deep truths about life. Jonah's prayer (Jonah 2.2-10) shows why this popular folk-tale, known in many cultures, was taken up into the Old Testament. God does not abandon his people, however hopeless the situation is. That is expressed in the prayer of Jonah in the belly of the whale, surrounded by the all-engulfing primal waters – a crazy situation of utter helplessness and despair. Such a story can be repeated endlessly. It contains, in concentrated form, all kinds of existential experience accumulated over a long history by people who know the savage power of water. However, when the Old Testament takes up this story, known from elsewhere in antiquity, an extremely hopeless situation is brought within the context of Jonah's very direct prayer.

In this way a new story is born: the story of unconditional trust in Yahweh's helping presence. Later this story will be told yet again. But any repetition of it is completely new; Christians take up the Old Testament story of Jonah once again, and connect it in a completely new way with Jesus' death and resurrection. Such a story has endless possibilities. It is told afresh each time; it remains itself and constantly becomes something different.

The New Testament, which tells us about Jesus, is also set in a 'narrative culture', not in a culture like ours, which has replaced narrative innocence with historical sciences. However, *we* cannot neglect either the one or the other. For us, modern men and women, 'the story' – even the story of Jesus – is only a good thing to listen to when we have arrived at a second primitive state, a second narrative innocence; that is, when we have passed through historical scholarship and criticism and thus returned to a 'narrative innocence' which can itself then act as a critical force on scholarship and criticism.

So remembering the narrative culture of antiquity, we must first of all approach the Gospels with the question: what do these Gospels really seek to convey, for example when they describe the miracles of Jesus? Only then can we look for the hard historical core in their stories. The historical question is certainly not unimportant, but it is just part of a greater whole.

Jesus is a parable, and he *tells* parables. Only parables can 'expound' a parable. Why?

The telling of a parable, the actual fact of a parable, is a remarkable phenomenon. Usually it involves a paradox, a shock effect. On rare occasions this is a consequence of our Western failure to understand the Eastern commonplaces in these parables. The parable of the sower has a farmer who is evidently off his head: he sows the seed not only on the field but also on rocky ground, in places where thorns grow, and even down the middle of the path. People in the East would immediately understand why, and it would not shock them in any way. What I mean is deliberate shock-effects. The workers who come at the last hour get just as much as those who have toiled all day: this not only shocks our social sense but also shocked that of the people who were listening to the parable at the time. The five so-called foolish brides-maids seem the more attractive characters to us; young people who hear the story immediately dub the five other ones, the 'wise' ones who refuse to help their companions, 'selfish', and that's what they were even then. A parable is always focussed on a 'scandal': at least a paradox or something unusual. A parable often stands things on their head; it seeks to break through our conventional understanding and existence. By virtue of an inbuilt element of 'alienation' and 'surprise', connected with an ordinary everyday event, it seeks to make the listener begin to think. You are not roused every night to help a stranger in need over a particularly difficult matter. And you do not regularly lose a sheep or a coin. Yet I, too, am confronted here and now in the parable. It forces me to think. Parables are 'brain-teasers'. The familiar event is set against an unfamiliar background and as a result the commonplace begins to become a stimulus. It shakes us.

The purpose of a parable is to force us to look at our own life, at what we do and what happens to us, at our own world, from another perspective. Parables disclose different new possibilities of life in contrast to our conventional actions; they give us a chance to experience life in a new way. Parables have a practical and critical force which prompts us to seek a renewal of life and society. Although they are drawn from familiar things and events in everyday life, by the inclusion of a scandalous, surprising or paradoxical element they begin to challenge our spontaneous judgments and behaviour. The good Samaritan doesn't just help; he evidently does some mad things as well: he goes on foot so that the wounded person can ride; he takes him to an inn and returns a couple of days later; he himself pays the cost of the stay and promises to take care of all future expenses (Luke 10.33-35). And in a deliberately provocative way, in the retelling of the story this helpful man is made a Samaritan, while two clergymen (a levite and a priest) pass by without heeding. There is an element of existential seriousness in the everyday character of this parable. Within the concrete, human life of our world it conceals a deeper appeal. Parables do not just point to another world beyond this one, but to a new possibility in this world, our world: to a real possibility of beginning to see and experience life and the world in quite a different way from the usual one. By conventional standards the good Samaritan did rather too much good! And yet, that is precisely why the parable is told: for the surprising, 'excessive' mercy of the 'good shepherd' (in Hebrew the word for neighbour, *re'*, is close to the word for shepherd, *ro'e*, which sounds almost the same, so that perhaps this was originally a parable of the good shepherd, an image to put the leaders of the people to shame). The new world disclosed by the story opens up a perspective on a particular possibility of life for those listening to the parable now. In the world of the parables of Jesus people do not live and judge as they do in our ordinary, routine everyday world. With the exception of three parables (the rich miser; the rich man and Lazarus; and the Pharisee and the publican), all Jesus' parables are 'worldly'. God is never mentioned in them. And yet, anyone who listens to them knows that through these stories he or she is confronted with God's saving actions in Jesus. This is the way God acts, and you can see that from the actions of Jesus himself. That is, if you look with a heart which is prepared to repent.

The parable therefore remains 'in the air' so long as the listener does not decide for or against the new possibility of living which is opened up in it – and in the end that means deciding for or against Jesus of Nazareth. Will the listener also enter the new world? He is given the choice between two models of life. Will he accept the new 'logic of grace and mercy' and bring about a radical change in his own life? In the end Jesus and his world are 'expressed' in the parables which open up a new world, a world in which there are only grace and love, and a world which seeks to criticize and change our human history of suffering, which is the result of short-sighted actions. It is also striking that time in the parables does not have a chronological significance. That does not mean that the story is timeless or above time. On the contrary, a relationship to the hearer's present is always a crucial part of the story: this appeal to the audience is presented essentially through telling or listening to the parable. There are no problems of translation or reinterpretation: I myself, here and now, must come clean and say whether I too recognize the new possibility of life as my own. Therefore a parable does not need a speaker to comment on it; it does not need an exposition 'from elsewhere', an interpretation. The parable itself interprets our life, our existence, our actions. At most, the telling of a second or third parable, rather than an argument, can make clear the sense of a parable – sometimes through continually new paradoxical shock-effects and disconcerting questioning of our ordinary, everyday, conformist behaviour.

Jesus himself is a parable: his person, his stories and his actions. Furthermore, his life is marked out by a consistent 'shock effect'. The Gospel of Mark makes that quite clear. In 2.1-3.5 it collects together five shocking stories, isolated actions of Jesus as a result of which those around him are forced to determine their attitude towards him: the healing of a paralysed man whose sins he forgives (2.1-12); Jesus eating with a publican, someone who collects money and tolls for the Romans (2.13-17); Jesus' defence of his disciples who do not fast while Jesus is with them (2.18-22); his explanation of the behaviour of his disciples who are plucking ears of corn on the sabbath (2.23-28); and finally, as a climax Jesus himself heals on the sabbath the withered hand of a man without hope (3.1-5). The reaction of the leaders follows immediately: ' The Pharisees went out, and immediately held counsel with the Herodians against him, how to destroy him'(3.6; see also the context of Matt.12.14 and John 5.18). Not many people understand the story that Jesus himself represents, the story that is also understood by those who are ready to receive the helping presence of God in his life-style (Matt.13.11). But the parable is so provocative as to make a neutral attitude towards it impossible; unless someone is open to the story they will only find the behaviour of Jesus incomprehensible (Mark 4.11-12), scandalous, and against the Law (Mark 6.23, see Matt.11.6; 15.9). People have to make up their minds, because the story of Jesus does not just disclose a new and different possibility of living but subjects our own, actual, much-cherished attitudes to devastating criticism. Simply out of a concern for self-preservation some people therefore rejected the parable of Jesus; they found it apocryphal and heterodox

– a danger to their own established habits. The execution of Jesus on the cross is ultimately an intrinsic consequence of this failure to understand the living parable of God.

In his concern for man and his history of suffering, for publicans and sinners, for the poor, the lame and the blind, for the dispossessed and those alienated from themselves by 'evil spirits', Jesus is a living parable of God: this is the way in which God looks on mankind. The story of God is told in the story of Jesus. It is God himself who in the life story of Jesus discloses to us a new world, another way of experiencing reality and another life-style: so the New Testament story about Jesus is an answer of the first Christians to the story of Jesus himself. Therefore all the life-stories of Jesus come alive again in the life or the story of the church itself. The church becomes a community in which those who have opened themselves to the critical force of the parable of Jesus' life tell stories round a shared table. In this way we too can listen to Jesus' story today. We are simply asked whether we will stake our life on it.

Someone might ask: but is that in fact the case? Did God's mercy really appear among us in Jesus? That question is really addressed in the wrong direction, because that is precisely the question that we are asked when we listen to the story of Jesus and the story about him. No one – neither historians nor scholars nor even the first Christians – can answer this question for us. As we hear the parable, we are confronted with the question whether we will stake our lives on it. There are more than enough pointers in the gospel stories to indicate the presence of an awareness of the interval between the experience, in faith, of the power of the crucified Jesus, now risen and present in the community, and their recollections of involvement with him during the days of his earthly life. That is extremely important. As a result, in the story told about Jesus in the gospel and the church, enough still comes over of the authentic story of Jesus himself, the story that Jesus of Nazareth was; indeed we have the essentials. So we can now listen to the question 'Who do you say that I am?' (Mark 8.29) as a question addressed to ourselves.

The response by which Christians confess Jesus as the Christ – that is, recognize God's story in his human story – cannot be achieved through exegesis; it is not a kind of conclusion drawn from a thorough analysis of the texts (however necessary this may be to get behind them to the true story of Jesus). The mediated presence of the offer of God's mercy – characteristic of any story and especially of the parable – is even more concentrated and compressed in Jesus than anywhere else, both in what he conceals and in what he discloses. Nowhere was the concealment in the communication so improbably great: people could put this Jesus to death in the name of orthodox religion. But nowhere is God's immediate presence so tangibly present for those who encounter him openly, with a sense of self-criticism; the church tradition even ventured to call him 'truly God'. Humanity, the life story of this man Jesus, thus becomes the unique chance by which God's immediate presence becomes accessible to those who are willing to undergo this self-critical *metanoia* or repentance. Anyone who puts themselves at risk can still, now, listen to the story of Jesus in such a way that in it they recognize the great parable of God himself, and at the same time the paradigm of our humanity as men and women. Here is a new, unheard-of possibility of existence, thanks to the God who is concerned for humankind. But part of the plot – the intrigue – of this Jesus story is that its shocking freedom becomes a scandal for those who take offence at it (Luke 7.23) while at the same time it is liberating freedom, salvation, for those who venture to entrust themselves to its mystery.

Thus people must spontaneously take up the story of and about Jesus himself, tell it out, and make their own life-style a repetition of the parable which is nevertheless new. For parables do not end with a moralizing sentence, but extend the dynamics of the story (whether implicitly or explicitly), with a perspective on to a new story: 'Go and do likewise'(Luke 10.37).

6

Jesus the Prophet

In 1953, when young hippies were not as yet a typical phenomenon, and long before Martin Luther King cried out 'I have a dream', the American-French visionary Jack Kerouac wrote the following: 'I have a dream: I see a revolution of young people, setting out with rucksacks, thousands and millions of young Americans, leaving their own home and society and climbing mountains to pray; they love one another...and through their friendliness and their unexpected and surprising actions, they ceaselessly present to the whole world the vision of eternal freedom.'

Did this prophet predict the future which since then has become a concrete reality among us? Or did he not rather feel so intensely in his own heart and life that our society, under the exclusive domination of a technological economy, was intolerable that a kind of irresistible longing for freedom came alive in him, a liberation to which he then gave symbolic, old-fashioned expression in terms of breathing freely in the open air and a carefree, pre-industrial country existence? At any rate, Kerouac sensed how not only for himself but also for many others our concrete, developed social structures have become an alienating, stifling burden, an affliction, and that his longing for freedom which is not under threat must therefore inevitably become a collective experience of many people, a new movement. So he sees the young people fleeing from our society; he already sees them setting out as in a new exodus, a multitude on the march, a few possessions hurriedly gathered together, rucksacks on their backs, in search of the idyll of liberating freedom. In 1953 he already saw them, the Jesus people and the Western Zen Buddhists, setting out from our society for the hills: to sing there, to love and to be quiet, to dream and to pray.

Other prophets, like Martin Luther King, from a similar experience of the history of human suffering, arrived at a prophetic vision of a new and better world, a world of freedom, but in their case it was a better world for which much hard work was needed , and for which a great many hearts first had to be changed.

Obviously prophets do not look into the future. Rather, a prophet sees the history of human suffering. In the course of history he sees accumulated suffering which in his own time, and in his own person, has met with a peak of awareness. Suffering has a critical and distinctive force of its own which prompts renewing action. Indirectly and negatively this forces in on the prophet the conviction that things can and must and shall be different. Indirectly, the experience of contrast makes him aware of the possibility of coming freedom. He sees freedom already, as in a vision: it is near. It is about to happen. In this way a prophecy is born and a prophet arises. For prophets do arise, stand up, like a judge who is about to pass final judgment.

Prophets, who are also called seers, are people who see this. They see through their time, the negative features of it, and from what they see they put into words in a visionary way the possibility of positive developments: what should and must happen, a great vision which on the one hand works above all as a catalyst and on the other hand leads to hostility, imprisonment and even death, because many people feel themselves unmasked by it. Prophets are a sign of contradiction; for what they say can never be verified rationally.

In this eucharist of our student church we are going to celebrate Jesus as prophet and reflect on his prophetic message.

Against the background of the two different modern prophetic tendencies which I mentioned earlier, and which divide believers from one another, those of Kerouac and Luther King, one question becomes extremely important for us Christians. What is the nature of the prophetic vision of Jesus of Nazareth which stands at the beginning of Christianity? For Jesus, too, was a prophet.

According to scripture he is 'the prophet of the end-time', i.e. the man who so intensely recalls the history of human suffering and sees it in such concentrated form as an excessive accumulation of hurt and unrelieved suffering that he is convinced that the measure is so full that something definitively new just has to happen. The Gospel of Mark says, 'The time is fulfilled and the kingdom of God is at hand' (Mark 1.15). The Indian god Shiva had the same experience: things cannot continue to go on as they are doing. So this god dances this world to pieces, in order to begin with a completely new creation, and...has to experience the same thing all over again! On the basis of similar experiences the prophet Jesus nevertheless arrived at a completely

different vision: that of the radical renewal and definitive reorientation
of our own human history.

The scriptures sum up the prophetic vision of Jesus like this. 'Repent,
for the kingdom of God is at hand' (Matt.4.17). In other words: People,
turn from your ways, otherwise you will bring about the downfall of
your own world. However, despite everything, things can, must and
shall be completely different: on the basis of a new community with
God. This is just about to happen. Jesus' time must have been used to
such prophecies, for shortly beforehand another prophet had arisen,
John, who had emphasized his message by administering a baptism,
and similarly proclaimed: 'Repent, God's kingdom is at hand'
(Matt.3.2). However, in contrast to the grim tone of John the ascetic,
who had threatened an imminent and disastrous divine judgment upon
this people, Jesus came with a message of salvation and mercy:
salvation is near. Now liberation, salvation and redemption are coming.
However, he was no simpleton of the proverbial kind, believing that
when the need is greatest, salvation is at hand. He had something of
the seriousness, the threat, of John about him too. In a moment of
prophetic disillusionment about the stubbornness which people could
show, he cried out: 'Jerusalem, would that even today you knew the
things that make for peace!'(Luke 19.42). For this prophet, Jerusalem,
the priestly city, the city of Zion's temple, Israel's pride and consolation,
was the symbol of misunderstanding, of misunderstanding of the signs
of the time and therefore God's own ways. Although he loved the holy
city, for him it was in fact anti-prophecy, the place where people
sacrificed calves and bulls, very precisely, with a complicated ritual,
while inwardly supposing themselves to be better than others. They
knew no sacrifice of love or mercy, and imposed a yoke of oppressive
regulations above all upon poor men.

From the Mount of Olives you could see it: the temple of Jerusalem,
an extremely complex site, a hundred yards broad by a hundred yards
long. Only about twenty years before Jesus' birth people had started to
rebuild it. Some years before his birth the work was finished, at least so
that the temple could be used. The work of embellishing it went on all
through Jesus' life. The temple was eventually completed in 64, just six
years before it was finally destroyed by the Romans.

One evening, when Jesus was on the Mount of Olives with some of
his followers, one of them said, 'Look, Master, what a fantastic
building!'(Mark 13.1). All the expectations of the Old Testament are
concentrated in this Jewish enthusiasm. But Jesus answered sorrow-
fully, at the same time drily and threateningly: 'Not one stone of this
temple will be left standing on another'(Mark 13.2). Later this
prophetic musing would be one of the most telling charges at the trial
of Jesus: 'This man said that he would destroy the temple.'

What, then, precisely was the prophetic message, the vision of this prophet? It was the vision of a life of righteousness and love, of mercy and freedom, expressed in what was then a universally recognized symbol, the rule of God. The kingdom of God had for long been the symbol of all that liberation meant: it was essentially 'Good news for the poor' (Isa.61.1; see Isa.52.7). The question was, what is to be understood as true liberation? For Jesus, the answer was what it had been earlier for the great Old Testament prophets: a human community of peace, where swords were beaten into ploughshares (Micah 4.1-5), and where the wolf, the lamb and the lion lived together in peace (Isa.11.6), because men did not rule over their fellows, but God lived in communion with everyone. For Jesus, the specific content of the rule of God – we would say the community of God – was embodied in his own actions and conduct. But sometimes Jesus himself sketched out the broad outline of the kingdom of God. This community of God is present where his name is hallowed and his will is done, where people have enough, even a surplus, and where guilt is forgiven (Matt.6.9bff.; Luke 11.2bff.). If you challenge that, allow the simple people to get worked up about this utopia, and compel them to keep silent, then, 'The very stones will cry out' (Luke 19.40): so Jesus prophesies. What for him is so self-evident that if necessary even the stones would bear witness, some leaders of this people cannot see for looking. The people themselves, the oppressed and the over-burdened, those who were bowed down by society, who could not live a holy life because they did not even have enough to live on, found that what Jesus said revived a hope which had long been quenched: the rule of God would bring them, the poor, in particular, abundance and riches (Matt.5.3-12). This prophet does not want to take anything from the rich; politics do not interest him unless they foster injustice; he simply wants to give an abundant reward to all: both those who have worked from the first hour and those who have worked from the last. For them the rule of God means the unmasking of human society, of enslaving rule of men over men. And that has political relevance. For Jesus, the rule of God is a matter of de-theocratizing. Human society must always respond in the light of the rule of God which never enslaves or oppresses but brings freedom, and thus relieve any suffering which is caused by human powers. Through the prophetic recollection of the accumulated suffering in human history, Jesus knows how human rule over fellow men in fact pollutes and enslaves. By contrast, when God begins to rule, all these yokes fall away: 'You weep now, but then you will laugh'. Jesus' message is in fact a message of freedom and liberation from yokes. He constantly sees the threatening danger of the power of men and demons over other men: power is the heart of and the reason for the human history of suffering. He does not seek to correct this power situation in detail; he is concerned with a definitive total prophecy: in place of a rule by power he wants to put a divine ordering, the rule of God, for that implies freed men without alienation. That is Jesus' prophetic vision.

Furthermore, this vision is already beginning to be fulfilled in Jesus' prophecies and actions: 'The blind see and the lame walk (the lepers are cleansed and the deaf hear)...and the good news is proclaimed to the poor' (Matt.11.5; Luke 7.22). The kingdom of God proclaimed by this prophet is clearly not for later: the human history of suffering must come to an end now; now the lame must be able to walk, the blind see and the poor be satisfied. 'Give us *today* our daily bread.' Not, 'Patience, patience, all will be well later.' Jesus is a prophet who constantly illustrates the meaning of his message in action. Where he appears, people are restored to themselves, freed from their bonds, so that in turn they can give themselves to one another...and to God. 'Go and do likewise', this prophet repeats after a parable or a story in which he confronts his contemporaries with utopian demands which are evidently humanly impossible. 'When you arrange a dinner, invite the poor and maimed, the lame and the blind', he tells them, in visions which see the kingdom of God realized, just as Isaiah and Micah saw the wolf and the lamb quietly grazing side by side. In the prophet Jesus we have a manifestation of radical discontent with the actual course of human affairs: what now happens among you is not *shalom,* not peace, not freedom. That is not the rule of God, a rule which knows of no yoke. Mark well: Jesus always speaks of human liberation and in so doing indirectly shows what God means for us. He seldom mentions God directly; he does so almost exclusively through human experiences. Later, Paul will explain Jesus' message at length when he speaks of the 'freedom of the children of God', heresy for any established religion. Yet precisely that is the rule of God which Jesus proclaims. This prophet was constantly talking about being enslaved or being lost. In prophetic fashion he speaks about a lost coin, a lost sheep, a lost son. As proof of it all we have his preference for dealing with those who according to 'the Law and the traditions of the fathers', i.e. according to the current divinely legitimated norms, were social and religious outcasts. He extended table fellowship to 'publicans and sinners'. He attached particular importance to those people who were written off in social and religious terms and no longer counted in fashionable society. He showed that they were also important to God, since fellowship of this kind, eating together, has a religious significance above all in the East. There is no schizophrenia here between the divine and the human. Nevertheless, religious fellowship with sinners was an intolerable transgression of all social and religious bounds, even there at that time. In that respect Jesus was 'heretical'. This did not escape the watchful

eye of the religious leaders. The word went round: 'He is a friend of
publicans and sinners'(Matt.11.9; see Mark 2.15ff.); 'He welcomes
sinners and eats with them'(Luke 15.2). The age-old accusation against
all the prophets was also made against Jesus: 'He leads the people
astray'(John 7.12). In their hearts those in power who oppressed the
people felt that Jesus was unmasking them, above all when this prophet,
in one of his fiery and strident outbursts which had led some people to
say that he was off his head, had called the leaders of his people
'whitewashed sepulchres'. They were outwardly correct and never
wrong, but inwardly there was nothing but decay and corruption.
Above all, in such loaded imagery we can see what makes a person
really a prophet, makes him appear with a new message, proves as it
were the origin of the prophecy. This was Jesus' experience of contrast.
On the one hand was his communion with the living God whom he
experienced as being so intimately near, who set him free, and whose
loving concern he saw even in the astonishing beauty of 'the lilies of the
field' and in the trivial appearance of a sparrow. On the other hand was
the inauthentic servitude which inflicted hurt and smart, which caused
unnecessary suffering and introduced oppression and slavery into our
human history, or to 'this generation', as Jesus often put it. By that he
meant 'down to this last generation', for things had always been like
this. In Jesus, mysticism and the liberation of the world come from one
and the same source: his experience of contrast between the living God
and the history of human suffering. The layman from Israel – for that
is what Jesus was – without any official title, for he was not a Jewish
priest, nor a scribe or rabbi, nor a theologian or community leader, but
simply a carpenter's son – saw through the evil of his own time and of
all times. When he saw the crowd looking for him, he often lamented
over them: 'a sheep without a shepherd' – that was his people. That
was also Jesus' grief. He took pity on the oppressed, but incessantly
launched prophetic attacks on their leaders. In a saying of Jesus which
is historically authentic, as exegetes term it, we hear: 'This generation
will be responsible for the blood shed from the blood of Abel to the
blood of Zechariah' (Luke 11.51). This prophet, Jesus, was driven by
the disturbing remembrance of the history of suffering experienced by
mankind which has still not been overcome in this generation now alive.
People are still attacked and enslaved by others: in human terms there
is no rule of God, no freedom. Prophets who draw attention to that are
rejected as spoilsports. The Christian community saw this clearly when
it made Jesus say: 'Jerusalem, Jerusalem, who kills the prophets and
stones those who are sent to you. How often would I have gathered
your children together, as a hen gathers her chickens together under
her wings. But you would not' (Matt.23.37). The Gospel of Luke puts
it sharply: 'As it was in the days of Noah, so will it be in the days of

the Son of man. They ate and drank...until the day when Noah entered the ark, and the flood came and destroyed them all' (Luke 17.27).

Jesus believes unconditionally in his prophetic message, but at the same time he seems to fear a repetition of the well-known fate of prophets: they are neutralized by being treated as visionaries, or removed in accordance with the rules of the power game. But a true prophet, like Jesus, does not allow himself to be robbed of authentic experiences by any authority whatsoever, even if it costs him his life. A prophet is a believer-without-a-loss-of-reality; by definition, he is someone who is not an ideologist. The religious prophet is the great exegete or expounder of humanity and in this he is an expounder of God. But a prophet does not interpret history and his own time with a Socratic detachment, like a cultural philosopher, but with a practical and critical concern, i.e. to mobilize his contemporaries to new actions which will bring renewal. 'Hypocrites,' Jesus cries out: 'you know how to interpret the appearance of earth and sky; but why do you not know how to interpret the present time?' (Luke 12.56). As a prophet he sees what anyone can see and should have seen, whereas those who seek to trap him remain blind. Furthermore, Jesus himself performs actions which make others see and think, but still they do not see the signs of the times; and he himself will not perform sheer acts of power to compel them to see: such compulsion would be domination and not the rule of God. Jesus wants to make people act responsibly and to call them to life. He does not really proclaim the end of the world. He seems to share this view with many of his contemporaries, but that is not the point of his prophetic message. Given his particular situation, he seeks to call men to heightened responsibility, to freedom, love and righteousness. That is his prophetic message; the other proclamation, the end of the world, is usually taken for granted. In concrete terms this means that the end of history is already at hand and still people have not changed it for the better. Therefore Jesus' prophetic message remains firmly and immovably provocative, even if its presupposition, the approaching end of the world, seems to be mistaken. That simply shows how much as a prophet this man was a truly authentic being of his time, despite or precisely in his universal message. He prophesied as a child of his time: 'Truly I say to you that there are some standing here who will not taste death until they have seen that the kingdom of God has come in power' (Mark 9.1; 13.30). Barely a year later Jesus died, in fact in a small corner of the world; Rome and Palestine had forgotten the event soon afterwards. Only Tacitus and Pliny, Roman historians, had anything to say about a certain criminal Jesus who was executed by Pontius Pilate for his 'pernicious superstition', and the Flavian friend of Rome, the Jewish historian Josephus, simply said that

Jesus was executed for witchcraft. There is always something ambiguous in and about a prophet. He remains a sign of contradiction.

But perhaps Jesus' mistaken supposition that the end of the world was approaching conceals a story with a double basis. On the one hand any prophet is so convinced of the urgency of his message that he is certain that it must and can and therefore will be realized today, immediately, and not tomorrow, unless mankind is completely mad. Because of the structure of the prophetic message and its origin in experience, future and present essentially flow into each other. Prophetic speech is utopian speech which calls forth the strength for direct action. Anyone who believes in utopia sees it already coming. It also emerges from the prophet Isaiah that prophets want to speed things up. On the other hand, and this is what gives Jesus' message its double basis, there seems to be more in Jesus than simply the breakthrough of a prophetic insight in his own time. In what according to biblical interpreters is a historically authentic saying of Jesus, we read, above all in the Gospel of Luke, the following prophetic promise of Jesus: 'Truly I say to you: every one who acknowledges me before men, the Son of man also will acknowledge (in the end time) before the heavenly court' (Luke 12.8). The end, the last chance of salvation that God gives us, is Jesus of Nazareth himself: anyone who confesses him now will (in the end) be confessed and recognized by God. That is the authoritative promise which Jesus gives to anyone who accepts his prophetic message. We can either accept this promise which Jesus gives in trust, or we can reject it. The unique thing about this prophet is that as well as his prophetic personality there is the conviction that people's attitude towards him is decisive for our definitive chances of life and our fortunes. The person and his message as it were coincide. So the first Christians could just as well speak of the 'kingdom of Jesus' (cf. Matt.16.28) as of the kingdom of God (cf. Mark 9.1): Jesus is the Lord.

Before everything was over Jesus would utter his greatest, completely unexpected prophecy. This time, not in a prophetic word, for people had silenced his word through violence, but in a prophetic action in which it is left to us to interpret the prophecy. Like other prophets, down to today, he was killed. Of course the violent death of a prophet can fix the memory of his message even more clearly. Perhaps. Probably in a modern society with means of communication like radio and television. Not in a corner of the world between about 28 and 34 by our way of reckoning time. Thus the significance of the death of this prophet seems to lie elsewhere. Jesus proclaimed the kingdom of God and himself inaugurated it during his lifetime; where he appeared, there was an experience of liberation. His appearance was an appearance which created communication, liberating men and bringing them healing, so that they again had time and strength to give themselves to one another and to God. However, this prophet who created communication had to undergo what in and of itself disrupts all communication radically and for good and makes it impossible. Death finally declared his vision of the universal rule of God as such to be an ideology. For Jesus was not like one of those false prophets about whom the prophet Micah had already said: 'They lean upon the Lord and say, "Is not the Lord in the midst of us? No evil shall come upon us?"' (Micah 3.11) Jesus did not have such a cheap view of God. Evil overcame Jesus: he was executed. Trust in God can be confronted with hopeless situations which put God in question, above all when everything fails and there is no demonstrable ground for hope anywhere in history. Empirically and historically, death, above all the execution of Jesus, is in fact the radical contradiction of his promise that with him the kingdom of God had begun and that anyone who confessed him would be acknowledged by God. After Good Friday, world history continued its usual course as though nothing had happened, as is the case after the death of any human being. At the same time the death of Jesus puts the legitimacy of his message in doubt: is his prophetic message an ideology, human wishful thinking, or is it a divine message? That was the last prophetic appeal, the definitive challenge of Jesus, the prophet of eschatological salvation, to his people. His death is a prophecy in which the ambiguity of the prophetic is stood on its head. It is in the nature of an open prophecy which only we who survive can respond to with an interpretation, whether by rejecting his prophecy as invalid, or assenting to it, which we can only do in a response which is itself prophetic. This last is what Christians did in the conviction that this man was right, despite the contradiction of death. That is, despite all appearances, Jesus' prophetic message about the imminence of the kingdom of God was not contradicted by his death. But to assert this is itself a new, a believing, already a Christian, prophecy.

If Jesus' message is still valid, this means that in Jesus the kingdom of God must have established itself even in his death. In other words, in that case Jesus' death is the defeat of all non-godly rules and powers and, at the profoundest level, of the rule of death itself. In that case, all taboos, all demons, all ties, all fate, are overcome. The rule of God, and not death, has the last word. Christian belief in Jesus' resurrection, in his life with God in our midst, is the ultimate consequence of continuing to believe in his prophetic message. The resurrection is not the legitimation or verification of this message, nor the basis of Christian faith: we do not legitimate a point of faith, viz. faith in the message of Jesus, with another point of faith, our belief in his resurrection. Despite Jesus' death, Christian faith is a matter of belief in his prophetic message and promise. And this is possible only through a new prophecy.

Through the prophetic character of the response of believers to the
prophetic challenge of Jesus' death, Christians are themselves essentially a people of prophets. That is how the earliest Christian church
already saw it. These first Christians experienced the event of Pentecost
in their communities as an outpouring of the spirit of prophecy over the
whole people, as the fulfilment of the old prophecy of Joel (Acts 2.1-
13; Joel 3.1-2). The first prophetic appearance of the Christian
community is in the presentation of the prophetic message of Jesus'
resurrection. Christians are prophets who continue to proclaim the
powerlessness of all human and demonic powers and rules which
enslave and oppress men and whose final means of representation is
death, the attack on life. Therefore within the dimensions of our earthly
history believers must continue to ensure that these powers are in fact
made powerless. Christian belief is possible only in the form of a
continued prophetic handing down of Jesus' message of the liberating
rule of God with its intrinsic appeal to responsible and liberating
action, but in the explicit awareness that Jesus himself is the permanent
focal point of his own prophecy, the kingdom of God: 'Jesus is the
Lord': he is the living one.

Therefore the church of Christ is a church of mysticism and a church
of human liberation. In Jesus, mysticism and the liberation of the world
came from one and the same source: his experience of contrast between
the living God and the history of human suffering. Mysticism, liturgy
and worship without an essential concern for liberation and the
improvement of the world amount to pseudo-mysticism: 'Why do you
call me Lord, Lord if you do not do what I say... Depart from me all
you workers of iniquity' (Luke 6.46 with 13.27, both from the source
Q). On the other hand, a church concerned with liberation and the
improvement of the world which has no mysticism is only half a church
– for not only is God's rule the liberating source of all liberation, but in
addition we have to overcome subtle forms and causes of oppression
which cannot be discovered without mysticism and the experience of
God. Moreover, human beings are impotent to plan and to make a free
future simply by means of scientific analysis and technological planning,
because such a future is not entirely within our power.

If today, after about twenty centuries of Christian and church life, we
look back on the prophecy of Jesus and the person of this prophet,
Jesus the Christ, there is, finally, something else that we must take to
heart.

At the time when Jesus emerged as a prophet, the all-important
thing was the critical and utopian force and content of his message of
the liberating rule of God as a stimulus to action, although trust in the
person of the prophet himself in no way stood outside that. Now, in the

Jesus Christ of the churches, the concern is almost exclusively with the person of the prophet, while we are silent about his message, often misunderstand it and distort it while nevertheless calling ourselves Christians, the followers of Jesus. Jesus has become exclusively the object of worship, often a kind of icon from which the features of the prophet have been obliterated. The critical and provocative aspects of this prophetic voice of liberation, which arouse and mobilize men and women, seem to be lost in the smoke of the incense of our worship. Certainly I believe in Jesus as the Son of God and I do not want to leave you in any uncertainty, even over the use of this ambiguous word 'the Son'. At the same time I believe in what Chalcedon wanted to preserve when this great Council said: One and the same person, i.e. Jesus of Nazareth, is truly man and truly God. Otherwise I would not be standing here by a liturgical altar. But precisely as a Christian I must also point to the threatening danger of an exclusive and wholesale divinization of the man Jesus. Such a divinization not only distorts the fundamental direction of the revelation which – precisely because we as human beings really do not know God – has shown us who he is and how he acts, above all in the appearance of a human being. In this human form, specifically in his prophetic word and actions, we can come to know who God is and how he acts. Apart from Jesus we would not know this, nor could we sense it. Furthermore, a mistaken conception of Jesus' divinity runs the risk of radically neutralizing the critical force of his historical prophetic message, as a stimulus to action, the message of a prophet who spoke so powerfully about the liberating utopia of the rule of God on earth and acted in such a way that religious and secular authorities which tormented and enslaved others, feeling themselves to be compromised in their positions, removed him from the scene. Furthermore it also neutralizes that core of his message which is critical of the church. Jesus did not proclaim any teaching, any doctrine; he issued a summons to responsible action, to repentance, in the light of the approaching rule of God which would consist in liberating freedom and *shalom* for all. I am afraid that with the sharp edge of our confessions of faith about Jesus we sometimes blunt the force of his prophecy. A prophet does not repeat the old traditions unimaginatively, but works on tomorrow's new traditions. One-sided divinization of Jesus, i.e. an interpretation which points exclusively towards his divine side, is in fact a historical nuisance; it spoils things and deflects a seditious recollection of a provocative prophecy from our history. One could say that it is also a way of putting a prophet in cold storage, of shunting him into a siding. In Jesus' message, 'First seek the kingdom of God' all too clearly meant: live on the basis of the experiences of the contrast between God and the history of human suffering; help to realize the kingdom of God here on earth. The rule of God is not a matter of the overpowering of the world, this time by God himself. 'No, Assyria shall not save us, we will not ride upon horses; and we will say no more "Our God" to the work of our hands. For in them the orphan (the downcast and oppressed) finds mercy. Then I, Yahweh, will heal their faithlessness, I will love them freely.' So runs an ancient prophecy of Hosea (14.4-5). The rule of God (the word itself sounds theocratic) is the disarming appearance in this world of the love of God in the form of human, peace-making love which does not dominate but which liberates and serves, which provides critical prophetic opposition, that is, active opposition, to everything that makes universal *shalom* impossible, in the world and in the churches. It overcomes these, the dictates and the weakness on the one hand of our own hearts and on the other hand of the stubborn but equally fragile structures in which we live. Both despotic and repressive powers are involved in a dialectic interrelationship: and they can only be overcome in a dialectical way. Repent! For the kingdom of God is at hand!

7

The Free Man Jesus and his Conflict
(Mark 2.18-22)

Mark 2.18 'Now John's disciples and the Pharisees were fasting; and people came and said to him, "Why do John's disciples and the disciples of the Pharisees fast,but your disciples do not fast?"

19a And Jesus said to them, "Can the wedding guests fast while the bridegroom is with them?

b As long as they have the bridegroom with them, they cannot fast.

20 The days will come, when the bridegroom is taken away from them, and then they will fast in that day.

21 No one sews a piece of unshrunk cloth on an old garment; if he does, the patch tears away from it, the new from the old, and a worse tear is made.

22 And no one puts new wine into old wineskins; if he does, the wine will burst the skins, and the wine is lost, and so are the skins; but new wine is for fresh skins" (Mark 2.18-22).

I want you to join me in listening carefully to the *religious message,* that is the good news from God (Mark 1.14), that Mark is giving us in this gospel story. If we take into account the history of the origin of this text, we see that it is told in such a way that in it we can still listen to a recollection of the earthly life of Jesus, i.e. of the joyful and liberating character of the encounter with Jesus of Nazareth. It is precisely through this that we are given the possibility of approaching the unfathomable mystery of Jesus' freedom.

Mark 2.18-19a

In order to *understand* the complete message of the final text we must
first dig for the message which goes back directly to faithful reminiscences of disciples who, on the basis of their belief in the crucified
Jesus, now risen, looked back on their experience with him when he
was still among them on earth. We find these reminiscences in verses
18 and 19a.

The Christians remembered the reaction of Jesus to the impact
which John the Baptist made on his contemporaries as a strict ascetic.
By contrast, Jesus gave the impression of being 'an eater and drinker'
and moreover one who, scandalously, even ate and drank with publicans
and sinners (Mark 2.16). People played off the two prophets against
each other so that they did not have to listen to either of them. The
Gospel of Matthew saw the situation acutely; Matthew says: 'You are
like children sitting in the market places and calling to their playmates:
"We piped to you, and you did not dance; we wailed and you did not
mourn." For John came neither eating nor drinking, and they say, "He
has a demon"; the Son of man came eating and drinking, and they say,
"Behold, a glutton and a drunkard, a friend of tax collectors and
sinners!".'. Here Matthew sketches out (11.16-18) what it was really all
about. All the freedom of Jesus' life-style and that of his followers is
here brought into the discussion; not so much the question of fasting or
not fasting as the problem of ecclesiastical casuistry. The question lies
deeper.

Jesus answers this attack briefly and well: 'Friends (or guests) of the
bridegroom do not fast while the bridegroom is with them' (19a). Or,
in our Western way of putting it: you don't fast during a party; people
come to a party to have a good time. Obvious, you might say. But the
answer of Jesus is not so trite or obvious, for the simple reason that
there is no question of a marriage feast. Granted, Jesus' answer begins
from the idea of the obvious every-day experience that people do not
fast on a wedding day. But he did not have to be Christ to make such
a trite remark as: 'There's a time for everything: fasting at one time
and feasting at another.' There is more behind it than that.

Nor, however, is it the intention of this gospel pericope to proclaim
Jesus' departure in principle from the Jewish obligation to fast. Jesus
nowhere condemns the fasting of the disciples of John, and of course it
is clear that he held the temple, sabbath rest and the synagogue in
great esteem, as he did the Jewish fast days. In fact he sees the Law as
a sign of God's grace and mercy to the Jews, for their salvation. But it
is not for their condemnation! Here is a first clear indication. Jesus
notes how often people entrench themselves behind the letter of the
Law and in so doing rob its deepest concern, God's mercy upon men, of

its force. Through what is actually done, Law and sabbath are alienated
from their deepest intent and become an intolerable, crushing burden
for ordinary people. Jesus sees the obligations of the Law in the light of
a God who is concerned for humanity (Titus 3.4). In his view, human
happiness, salvation and well being are the criterion for all norms, laws
and institutions. Law must be the manifestation of God's mercy.

Against this background, the good news that Jesus brings begins
suddenly to shine through: in place of the Law there now comes the
specific person of Jesus as the manifestation of God's mercy, at least
for those who are prepared to perceive in the life-style of Jesus the
helping nearness of God (Matt.13.11). Anyone who is not prepared for
that, the neutral bystander, the one who swears solely by the Law, does
not see the saving presence. On the contrary, he sees only the
incomprehensible (Mark 4.11-12), indeed scandalous behaviour of
Jesus and his followers (Mark 6.2-3; see Matt.11.6; 15.12), which goes
against the Law.

The question raised here is: Yes or no? Do you trust me? It is a
matter of a decision for or against Jesus. Those who give him that trust
do so in the conviction that in Jesus God's own concern for men has
been manifested. As this Jesus is fully alive among his disciples, there
is every reason for those who trust in Jesus alone to be happy. So don't
think of fasting! Thus the heart of the story is that this Jesus, the
tangible manifestation of God's mercy with men, is here, present and
alive among his disciples. It is good and right that the disciples of John
the Baptist should fast – not a bad word is to be said about that. But if
Jesus' disciples were now to fast that would be a misunderstanding of
the specific situation, viz. the presence of salvation in the living person
of Jesus of Nazareth. The gathering of the disciples with this man
Jesus is essentially a festive one, prepared by Jesus himself, a saving
community. Moreover the time Jesus spent among men who still either
misunderstood him or followed him with unconditional enthusiasm is a
very special time. Jesus' presence then becomes a living dispensation
from fasting or mourning.

From this it already becomes clear that Jesus never lives on the
basis of abstractions or general norms: he always sees people in their
own very specific situations. That is why he can prove so surprising, so
disconcerting to his fellow men, in a deeply human way. Although his
disciples did not always understand precisely what he meant, it was in
any case certain that they were so devoted to their master, their Jesus,
that they adored him. They knew that in him they had a gift, a present
from God to us! If you are so under the spell of someone while he is
present and alive, you cannot mourn and fast and play the ascetic. It is
striking that in this pericope about fasting it is not once said that Jesus
himself does not fast; this is an accusation which is made about Jesus'

disciples (v.18). Jesus defends their conduct and gives an answer: 'What else do you expect? Salvation is among them.' That is clearly a challenge and a provocation: to recognize him or to reject him as a gift from God. One has to respond to such a provocation. In this and in all the gospel stories, the question is: 'Who do you say that I am?' This question is also directed to us by the present story. And it is meant as good news. Do we still experience the presence of Jesus as something that makes us feast exuberantly in the presence of the bridegroom? While John's call to repentance was essentially bound up with an ascetic penitential practice, Jesus' call to repentance seems to be essentially bound up with table fellowship: eating and drinking with him, an event in which his disciples were in fact already able to experience the eschatological, i.e. the decisive and definitive, advent of God's mercy, as a living presence. Believing in this Jesus is joyful trust in God. That is no time for fasting.

Mark 19b-20

In the meantime, though, I can hear your objections and doubts. That may have been the case for the disciples of Jesus when he was alive, but what about us, now that Jesus is dead? The first Christians also had the same objections, and vv.19b and 20 are evidence of this. (That is the second stage in the tradition of the first remembrance of the days when Jesus was alive.) However, the Christian community which recalled these words after the death of Jesus and handed them on faithfully saw themselves presented with a serious problem. They felt that now he was dead, table fellowship, a joyful meeting with him, was no longer possible. What then? Hence the later insertion of vv.19b and 20; they are a kind of subsequent meditation by the Christian community. In it the Christian community related the old words of Jesus to their own new situation now he was absent. They felt Jesus' words spontaneously, and said: 'As long as they have the bridegroom among them they cannot fast. However, the days will come when the bridegroom is taken away from them and then, at that time, they will fast.' These are no longer Jesus' own words, but a reflection of Christians on the fact that now Jesus has gone away. This emerges touchingly from the way in which the old memories of the disciples' life with Jesus during his earthly days are expressed. These Christians felt acutely the difference between now and then. The text puts this movingly: when Jesus was still with them – we are told – they *could* not fast, they were not in a position to, because of the living presence of Jesus. That the disciples did not fast then was not a kind of legal dispensation from fasting but an existential matter: they couldn't do anything but not fast. These words betray something of the enchantment and power which were exercised by the living Jesus of Nazareth.

The Christian tradition preserved this remembrance very carefully –
without this enchantment Christianity of course would never have
become a historical fact.   But there is also the first reaction, the other
side of the coin. Then follows the sober reflection: now, in our situation,
this Jesus has been taken from among us. Jesus is dead. Now we fast,
now we mourn, since that is what is called for. In these verses the
situation is clearly determined by the contrast between joy and
mourning, presence and absence.It emerges not only from this pericope
but from more than one event in the Gospels (see e.g. Acts 1.1;
Phil.1.23; John 16.16-24) that historically it was not the case that the
joy of Easter was as universal in primitive Christianity as Luke
supposed some three generations later, in his Acts of the Apostles
(2.46). The fact that Jesus had been taken from among them could not
be explained away. Of course they longed desperately for his return;
but in the meantime to begin with they felt orphaned and abandoned,
and fasted in their sorrow. However, v.20 is not an indication of a kind
of rule for fasting in the early church. It goes deeper than that. Just as
the disciples could not fast when Jesus was still with them – how could
they?- so now they have to fast, for sorrow. In other words, they cannot
eat because they are so sad. That is obviously the tenor of vv.19b, 20.

And yet! In this somewhat sorrowful meditation an element of new
hope emerges. Looking back on their fellowship with Jesus in the days
when he was still alive opened up a perspective on the community with
the returning Christ which was still to come and had not yet happened.
For the striking thing is that whereas in the previous, earlier recollection
the expressions 'the bridegroom' and 'the wedding feast' were simply
metaphors and similitudes, in the second version, which looks back on
the past, they become something more. Here Jesus, christologically, *is*
the bridegroom of the church. That is what he is and that is what he
remains, even now (see Matt.25.1-13; Rev.22.17; II Cor.11.2;
Eph.5.21-33). Although he has been removed from our history, he is
coming back.

Whenever people reflect more closely on this reality, fasting after
Jesus' death takes on a new significance. The consequence of this new
relationship with God in and through Jesus, already suggested by
Mark's Gospel, will be expressed later in explicit form only in the
Gospel of Matthew (Matt.6.16-18).

In the Old Testament (I Kings 21.27; Neh.9.1; Esther 4.3; Isa.58.5;
Jonah 3.5; Daniel 9.3) and also among the disciples of John, fasting
was a sign of sorrow over sin. But thanks to Jesus, for Christians,
fasting became a sign of thanksgiving for the new direction given
through God: Christians who fast, says Matthew, anoint their heads
and wash their faces. Their fasting is not a sombre and grudging
occupation, but fasting as though they were not fasting. No one sees it

and no one knows it; Christians fast for their Father who sees in secret (Matt.6.l6-l8). Sadly, this distinction – a distinction of mentality – in the Christian way of fasting was soon externalized and formalized in church life. For about twenty years later the Didache (8.1), a writing from the early church, obliges Christians to fast on Wednesdays and Fridays in contrast to the Jews, who fast on Mondays and Thursdays. It seems difficult to remain really free in terms of the gospel!

Mark's composition: Mark 2.18-22
So we come lastly to the composition of Mark himself: the final text of the pericope as we now have it in the Gospel of Mark[1] roughly about thirty years after the original event. It is evident from vv.21-22 that the point of the whole of this pericope is the fundamental opposition between old and new: no young wine in old skins, no new unshrunk cloth on an old shrunk garment. Mark himself adds these two images to the story, but they are clearly attached only loosely to it. Still, they reveal the intention of the story as a whole. For Mark it is not just a matter of 'the old' pattern of fasting practised by the disciples of John and the Pharisees as compared with 'the new' development that the disciples of Jesus do not fast: for in this narrowed perspective the addition of the last two verses would make little sense. Mark is concerned with the completely new phenomenon of freedom, as this had been manifested in Jesus. The freedom of Jesus and his disciples is something completely new, which according to Mark's Gospel has come into the world with Jesus. The pericope about fasting is only one example of this. For this story follows directly on the pericope about 'plucking ears of corn on the sabbath' (2.23-28), and after it there is the story of a healing by Jesus, actually on the sabbath day (3.1-5). Moreover, this pericope about fasting is preceded by two similarly scandalous recollections of acts of Jesus: Jesus eats with a publican, someone who collects money for the Roman forces of occupation (2.13-17) and, blasphemously – as some bystanders cry out (2.7) – he forgives the sins of a paralysed man whom he cures (2.1-13); and only God or a priest in the name of God can declare this. These provocative facts of the freedom of the layman Jesus, which Mark deliberately brings together here, form the central theme of the whole of this context. It then comes to a conclusion with the words, '...they sought to do away with Jesus' (Mark 3.6). The powerful could not accept this. So here Jesus is characterized by Mark as a free man whose sovereign freedom was never used to his own advantage but to the advantage of others, specifically as an expression of God's free and loving concern for men. Such surprising freedom of a man towards the Law and the sabbath, albeit out of respect for the Law and the sabbath, which were actually being misused, to the detriment of God's saving purposes and

therefore against men, instead of serving them and liberating them, was a thorn in the flesh of all those who were unable to see in Jesus' life-style a parable of God's helping concern towards those who for personal and social reasons have little freedom. Therefore they sought to kill him. Such human freedom-in-the-service-of-others, seeking the liberation above all of those who for whatever reason are not free, cannot be reconciled with what the Gospel of Mark calls 'the old'. We might say that it is irreconcilable with the familiar history of human suffering which was regarded officially as the norm among the masses for whom the leaders of the people had no eye and no concern. In Mark 8.2, we read: ' I have compassion on this crowd, on these people'. But this compassion on the crowd, on the man in the street, on the *'am ha-'ares* — the lame and the blind, the publicans and the sinners (for at this time sickness, disease and misery were synonymous, implicitly or explicitly, with sin), this compassion on the ordinary person, who in his particular situation and because of it was not usually in a position to keep the law with its traditional patriarchal, casuistic interpretations and therefore was already discriminated against officially in both society and religion, this compassion shown by Jesus for all these people, was at the same time an accusation directed against the actual human government of the time and was therefore highly seditious. The incidental dispute over what was in itself a marginal phenomenon of religious life (certainly in earliest Christianity), namely whether or not to fast, is taken up by the Gospel of Mark into the wider perspective of the freedom expressed in the whole of the life of Jesus, which was liberating for some people but shocking for others. It is simply one example of that. According to the Gospel of Mark, the pericope about the fact that Jesus' disciples do not fast, the charges which Jesus answered by vigorously defending his disciples, is simply one of the many drops of water which in the eyes of the leaders of the religious and social administration filled their cup to overflowing. This pericope, five short verses, is one link in the explosive chain of Jesus' life, which through his freedom, with its appeal to God's freedom and mercy, ended in his being condemned to death, an execution in the name of the God of the powers of this earth who served themselves instead of serving the many. But this God was – thank God – not the God and Father of Jesus. That is Mark's good news for us all.

In fact, from a small, almost a border incident in the life of Jesus, whether or not his disciples should fast, Mark is able to give a masterly portrait of the new element that has appeared in Jesus: trust in Jesus which is nevertheless highly personal. Mark's message is that with Jesus a radical new change has come about in our history, to the consternation of those who are offended by him, but to the salvation of those who entrust themselves to the mystery of this man Jesus – Jesus whom his disciples rightly therefore began to call 'the Son of God'. Mark makes this confession of trust all the more piquant by putting it, as a first confession of faith, on the lips of a pagan Roman soldier, who sees how Jesus dies on the cross. Not Peter, who has fled, but this pagan is the one who according to the Gospel of Mark says, 'Truly this man was the Son of God'(Mark 15.39). No status, not even membership of the people of God – and we might add to that, not even membership of the church – guarantees that people have truly understood the spirit of Jesus' liberating freedom, in obedience to the will of the Father. What Mark calls 'God's good news'(Mark 1.14) – is indeed a joyful message which for the moment frees us from sorrowing and fasting purely and simply because we are happy in knowing that God is with us in Jesus Christ! Emmanuel!

8

Friend, Go up Higher
(Luke 14.1,7-14; Sirach 3.17f., 28f.)

On a first, superficial examination, the readings for today, from Sirach and the Gospel of Luke, suggest the same kind of almost trivial middle-class popular wisdom. If you are invited to a meal, don't go straight up to the head of the table and sit down; if you do the host may say to you, 'Sorry, this lady or this gentleman has precedence .' Look for less important places at table, and then perhaps the host will say, 'Friend, I can't let you sit there – come up here.'

Each of us will recognize here our own middle-class practices, perhaps what we ourselves do and what happens to us. All this is part of human life. But what are such middle-class calculations doing in the Bible? Is middle-class morality being suggested to us as a guide to life? Or should we understand the story in quite a different way, more profoundly and more spiritually, rather than in the obvious sense? In that case is the Bible using a kind of secret language? I don't believe so. The New Testament, and perhaps Jesus himself, takes middle-class wisdom at its word. God in fact acts just like the host – no differently. The immediate concern is less with the behaviour of the guests than with what the host does. Jesus teaches us to speak about God, the host, within the context of ordinary human experiences. Christ is the presence of God in this world, but under the sign of weakness and the cross, of helplessness and failure, humiliation and death. Our own particular world, characterized – or rather distorted — by painful humiliations, is and remains God's creation, the world with which God is concerned. 'However small and weak I be, God has raised me up. With a sweep of his arm the proud and the great are removed. He casts them down from their thrones and raises up the humble.' All this Old Testament spirituality is summed up in today's readings, but they are then illuminated all the more brightly by the Easter exaltation of the humiliated Jesus. God treats Jesus – and us – in the same way as the host in the parable: he cares for those who are humiliated and turns away the proud. We see that fully only in the death and resurrection of Jesus. In stories which anyone can understand, today's readings provide the essence of what we might call distinctive Christianity, specifically the way in which God deals with people. Here we have as it were the thought-form and at the same time the life-style which is characteristic of Christianity: any hopeful affirmation also contains a painful, humiliating radical negation: those who exalt themselves will be humiliated and those who are humiliated will be exalted. That is often the case in human life. Jesus and the Christians take up precisely this trivial fact to make clear to us something of God's own attitude towards people. We should not be misled by the way in which this is expressed in terms of reward and prestige. Luke himself breaks through that pattern: we must not invite the rich to our tables but the poor, because the rich simply repay the compliment by inviting us back: the poor can't do that. Only then is it evident what being good is.

In accepting that it is impossible for us to be able to bring our own life history and that of the whole of mankind to a good end, we confess that God, and God alone, through Jesus, can exalt our history from its humiliated condition through Jesus. The gospel teaches us that we only prevail, i.e. arrive at a deeper level of communication, in the humble recognition of our failings, in being disoriented. Not just any conceptual faith, but above all the Christian praxis of faith, hope and love, must first go through the experience of suffering and humiliation if they are to be on the same wavelength as Jesus' life, death and resurrection. God seems to have a predilection for those who do not belong to the elite or to the religious clan. So Luke weaves a second parable into his story, as he often does: 'If you give a banquet, invite the poor, the maimed, the crippled and the blind.' But who does that? Nobody – apart from the community of God, the church in its celebration of the eucharist. That is the only table to which not only friends and relatives are invited but also cripples, the blind, the maimed and the oppressed. We can come to it in wheelchairs, with a broken and tormented heart; even our enemies may come. Here we already experience a vision of the future in which all those who are humiliated and discriminated against are exalted; here there is no longer any distinction between Jew and non-Jew, as the reading from Hebrews tells us with the utmost solemnity. Here we come together for the 'panegyric', the feast, the gathering which the people of the future share with one another. In the game which makes up the liturgy we experience what does not in fact happen in our daily life in the world – even in a monastery. We experience what we cannot fully achieve, much as we would want to. In the liturgy we therefore confess that our love for one another is actually a pure gift of God. Precisely because reconciliation has come near to us in Jesus, in recollection, and in hope, we begin to suffer because the world is not yet redeemed. The liturgy thus provokes us to act outside the liturgy in accordance with this vision of the coming kingdom of God among us, celebrated here symbolically in anticipation, because we cannot make it a reality. At the same time what we do here in the liturgy subjects what we do outside the liturgy to severe criticism. Despite all our good intentions, outside the liturgy we shall fail in our task. And because of our circumstances and because of ourselves we are simply not in a position to succeed. To recognize this in penitence is already to be open to what is possible through grace, through the work of God in us.

So we have moved from the middle-class table to what the gospel calls the eschatological banquet, where without any failure in communication everyone may sit in the place of honour.

We have just heard Sirach rightly say: 'The mind of the intelligent man will ponder a parable, and an attentive ear is the desire of the wise man (the one who tells parables)': so convinced is he of the wisdom that the parable seeks to convey to us. He who has ears to hear, let him understand.

9

The Light of the Body is the Eye
(Matt.5.13-26)

Matthew's train of thought is very clear: the light of the body is the eye (6.22). If your eye is clear – gives light – then all your being is light. Now you don't light a lamp and then hide it away somewhere, under a bowl or a chair, or behind a massive set of scales – those used for weighing corn (in a simple Jewish living room these were the most obvious places where you might lose something that you were looking for). You put a light on top of something, in full view, so that it lights everything and everyone in the room. Now you Christians, you are the light of the world. So you are not to remain hidden somewhere; you have to be where the world, where people, can see you. That is the simple message of Matthew's story for today.

In contrast to Mark and Luke, who derive quite different, moral lessons from the old popular Jewish wisdom or the proverb of the 'light on the lampstand', Matthew puts this popular wisdom into the context of his great Sermon on the Mount. And then something quite special emerges from it.

During his lifetime the disciples had asked Jesus: 'Lord, what will happen to us when the final kingdom comes?' However, in Matthew's church the situation had meanwhile changed. The question then became: 'Lord, how are we to live as Christians in the midst of this world?' Remembering Jesus' inspiration and many different indications, Matthew responds to this question with his Sermon on the Mount. This Sermon on the Mount is put in the context of beatitudes on the poor, the oppressed and those who weep – the great Old Testament 'Isaianic' prophecy which Jesus had made his own: 'Yahweh has anointed me, he has sent me to bring good news to the poor, to proclaim liberty to the captives...to comfort all who mourn, to give them the mantle of praise instead of a faint spirit' (Isa. 61.1-3). A message for the poor, the oppressed, those who weep: that is the heart of the Sermon on the Mount, the basic law of Christianity, the new morality. The content of the good news for the poor is 'the news of your salvation, that now God is beginning to reign' (Isa.52.7); that is, righteousness and love are now beginning to dwell among men. For that, 'I, Yahweh, have called you as a light to the world'(Isa.42.6).

In this great passage of Isaiah the popular wisdom about the 'light on the lampstand' in Matthew takes on an unsuspected deep signifi- cance in terms of prophecy and the gospel. But in that case we must bring these two texts in Matthew together: only if we ourselves are utterly and completely transparent, will we be a light for the world – provided that we do not go off and hide! Given the context (6.19-21, 24), Matthew means the clearness of the eye, the lamp of the body to be an undivided heart, a simple gaze directed wholly towards God; for the particular word which he uses here directs us towards the undivided love of God which we find in the Old Testament: 'with all your heart and all your soul and all your mind and all your strength'(Deut.6.5). In other words, as the light on the lampstand, our place in the world is not somewhere behind walls or under corn scales where we hide ourselves so that the world cannot see us. Our place is in the world, so that everyone can see us: in the world, but with a clear gaze which is directed towards God.

Thus this pericope in Matthew asks us two straight questions. 1. Are we not living in such a way that the world can no longer see our light? Are we a light hidden under the corn scales? 2. Are we a light for our fellow human beings – is there among us something of that same concern for our fellow human beings as was to be found among the first disciples – a concern which can only be understood as transparency towards God and not simply the expression of a fortuitously extravert temperament? Is our eye clear and our heart undivided? These are questions for which the church gives us a period of forty days to formulate our answers, conscientiously testing our life-style by them. In today's first reading we heard: 'Then your light shall shine forth...and Yahweh will guide you continually'(Isa.58.7-11).

To assert that Christians are the light of the world, the salt of the earth, may sound elitist. One might think that Jesus himself would never have put it literally like that. For what we do know with certainty about Jesus is his almost crude opposition to any kind of elitist Qumran mentality, the mentality of religious people who in an exclusive way 'know themselves to be chosen by God' and then tell others – imagining themselves to be lights for them – what they think really matters. Such people in the time of Jesus called themselves the 'sons of light', and therefore regarded others as the 'sons of darkness'. For Jesus, however, the coming of the kingdom of God means the manifestation of God's love for everyone – Jews, Samaritans and Gentiles. Now that can best be expressed precisely by the metaphor of light: God, who makes the sun, his light, shine upon all, both good and evil. Furthermore, for Matthew the important thing is not the light itself but everything and everyone that is lit by it. As he puts it, 'so that the lamp gives light to all those who are in the house'(5.15b). Thanks to your light, others can find one another.

We have all been here already for about half an hour: has any of you thought for a moment about the lights above us? They give us light, so that we have been able to see one another, communicate, be together and act together, for that half hour. In the same way, says Matthew, you too are the light of the world. Perhaps no one will think of you in particular while your presence among people is bringing them together. Perhaps some kind of religious intuition – or is it just a coincidence – has provided for today's second reading the beginning of I Corinthians 2.1-5. Paul, the great light of the Gentiles, stammers, as did once the prophet Jeremiah: 'I felt weak, nervous and anxious.' True prophets, those who bear the light, are never triumphalist prophets: for the most part they are are reluctant, and rebel against their mission and calling. One might ask whether we do not play the prophet all too readily and enthusiastically, when in fact we have nothing new to say, nothing against the grain, but simply give a thin religious coating to some or all of this world's prophecies (not that they are necessarily unimportant).

My dear brothers, in the bull of Pope Honorius which gave official approval to our *familia dominicana,* there is an explicit reference to this pericope in Matthew: you are the salt of the earth, the light of the world. This may be a further reason for us in the coming time of fasting, to reflect more deeply on this brief text from Matthew. How far are we making anything of it? If we do that, as the first reading puts it, 'Then your light will shine forth as the day and your wounds will quickly heal' (Isa.58.10).

10

A Glass of Water for a Fellow Human Being
(Matt.25.31-46)

The gospel to which we have just listened presents us with the Last Judgment: the real end. In the form of a country shepherd's story (to which we find it very difficult to attune ourselves) we are given a religious vision of the future. However, if we look more closely at Matthew's composition of this vision it is striking that it can really also be seen as a retrospect. Matthew simply tells us who Jesus has been – someone who spoke in the midst of our history about the divinity of God – expressed in the Jewish concepts of that time with the words kingdom of God; moreover a man who had acted in the spirit of this God, i.e. had accomplished the works of the kingdom of God. He had gone about doing good in the service of people in need, the outcasts, for whom he opened up communication. What Jesus said and did is projected into the future by Matthew as a standard for the Last Judgment. Even he cannot say more about the future; but he knows that in Jesus the divinity of God appeared as the achievement of more humanity between fellow human beings: giving a glass of water to thirsty people in the desert, their lips chapped by the desert drought; providing clothing as protection in the day against the searing heat and in the night against the sudden bitter cold (that's the way things are in Palestine). He attempted, then, to fulfil everyday needs, in situations in which the most insignificant people suffer the most. So Matthew's story of the Last Judgment is evidently focussed on purely human concerns; indeed, it seems even to be atheistic, since the name of God is not mentioned in it except when the matter is settled: 'Come, blessed ones of the Father'. The key here is the needy person, the person in distress. Our attitude towards these people, the humble and the needy, is what is at stake in the last Judgment, i.e. it is the standard, the criterion by which the significance and content of our life is to be judged. The main criterion is therefore not whether we have lauded and praised God liturgically as the king of the universe, or have supported the church and its organizations. No, the question in the judgment is simply: Have we – personally or structurally – helped those in need? This need not simply be a matter of people in the abstract, all those who belong to the human race. Rather, it is a matter of our attitude towards the lowly and the insignificant, the oppressed, those in any kind of need, whether material or spiritual; the neighbour who may be distant or close, who is in any kind of need, who lacks something, perhaps a bit of your own life that you love and find indispensable.

So at first sight there is nothing Christian about Mark's story. The story itself stresses this, since the club that we call 'Christian' is left out of account: this is the judgment on *panta ta ethne,* i.e. all peoples, without any distinction between the people of God and Gentiles (25.32). All will be judged on the giving of a glass of water, not from the surplus out of a water tank – which is something that people in the desert would never have heard of then – but out of the little remaining in a few water bottles. The physical conditions envisaged here are more critical. This is precisely the situation that Matthew has in mind in his vision of the end of all things. The end of all things is to be found in the midst of our daily life.

And yet! On closer inspection this is still the external aspect of Matthew's story; even this is not the specifically Christian element that he has in view. His vision of the Judgment is anything but atheistic, despite all the modern so-called 'Christian atheism'. Matthew has not forgotten what he had said a few pages earlier: ' What reward do you have? Do not Gentiles do the same?' (Matt.5.46). Furthermore, we find all kinds of literature from the same period – from pre-Christian Judaism, Egypt and neighbouring countries, in which what people should do as humane beings is described with just the same imagery: giving a glass of water, clothing the naked, visiting those in prison. So this is ancient Eastern, very human experiential wisdom, though even there it is not just something that is taken for granted.

However, anyone who hears only this in Matthew's account misses the real point with which he is particularly concerned, on the basis of the remembrance in his community of Jesus' own proclamation of the divinity of God as salvation of and for insignificant, oppressed people. For what we do not find in Jewish and Egyptian texts comes into the foreground in Matthew, namely the identification of the judge of the end time, who makes the judgment, with the lowly person in need: 'Inasmuch as you have done it for one of the least of these you have done it for *me'*(25.40). *Me,* that is the Son of man who is mentioned at the beginning of the story: 'The Son of man comes in his glory surrounded by his angels (the corona of the eschatological court of judgment), and will take his place on the judgment seat, before which all nations will be summoned.' By means of this identification of the final judge with the lowly person in need Matthew interprets the Christian significance of giving loving help to the needy in a very special way. He does this in a twofold sense. First of all, it is the oppressed of the world who will judge us by the standard of the suffering which has been inflicted on them. That is perhaps why the final judgment on those who find themselves on the wrong side (Hebrews called it the left hand side) is such a harsh one: 'Depart from me, you cursed ones'. They have kept so accursedly far from these needy people during their lifetime that one can now well understand their reaction. However, such an identification is perverse. The lowly person is at the same time the Son of man who utters the judgment. And for Matthew this is Jesus, the Christ who identifies himself with the lowly, with any member of the human race, all the sons and daughters of men. To take the side of those in need is to follow God himself, God as he has shown his deepest compassion towards humanity in Jesus. 'He loved us when we lowly Christians were still in misery' (see Rom.5.10). God's concern for man becomes the criterion, the standard and at the same time the boundless measure of oùr concern for the needy. This boundless sensitivity towards human needs only develops fully out of a personal experience of God's own gracious 'Yes' to all men: 'Yes, you may live', the expression of God's being, described by theologians as 'justification through grace', a learned phrase for God's love for mankind. This divine boundlessness is not so obvious to us human beings; it transcends what we call co-humanity. Of course it is obvious to all those who have experienced God's mercy themselves, in other words to religious men and women; it is also the test of the authenticity of our liturgical prayer, which praises Jesus as Lord of the universe.

This boundlessness becomes clear from the first reading to which we listened in this celebration, that from Ezekiel. The prophet asserts that people who by virtue of their office are made shepherds and pastors of the needy in our society are in fact letting them come to grief. For that reason God pronounces his judgment. 'I the Lord will myself look after my sheep and care for them.' God is more human than any human being. With the Gospel of John we can say: 'God so loved the world.' I believe that we human beings find it difficult to understand the love of God for all men who are in want, who fail, and are oppressed. It *is* impossible to understand; but the great vision of the Last Judgment which Matthew sets before our eyes shows us something of the unshakeable and incomprehensible love of God for man. This also explains the harshness in the divine judgment on all those who in whatever way ensnare fellow human beings or hurt them to the depths of their souls, even if this is simply as a result of doing nothing. At that very point we come up against the sensitive concern of God for what is closest to his heart: human beings, and above all human beings in need. According to Vondel and all kinds of apocryphal writings, even angels were offended by this love of God for man. Finally, Jesus, whom we may call his only-beloved son, is also a man like you and me – except that he is more human. Human love, as the liturgy teaches us today, is a religious happening.

There is just one more thing I want to say to end with. We may not detach the story of the Last Judgment according to Matthew from the whole of what we are told in the Old and New Testaments. If we do, we risk reading into this text a cruelty which is alien to it. Furthermore, the preference for the needy should not make us forget the others. In Ezekiel we heard, ' I the Lord will myself look after my sheep and care for them'; after that there follows not only, 'I will bring back the lost and stray sheep, bind up the wounded and strengthen the sick', but also, 'I will look after the fat and the strong sheep'. The Good Shepherd does not leave the ninety-nine healthy sheep in the lurch. Where this is said elsewhere in scripture, it is only a way of stressing a total concern for the lost sheep. In Christian terms, you cannot deny deeply emotional feelings for the ninety-nine remaining sheep for the sake of the one lost sheep. Christianity is thus a *complexio oppositorum,* that is, a very complex, evidently contradictory and yet simple matter, but it calls for creative imagination in which priority for the needy and the lowly does not result in any inhumanity towards the ninety-nine fat sheep, even if in our society these are only one third of the world's population. What must happen as a result, I don't exactly know. However, I gather from the readings for today that the call for a partisan predilection for people in need must be reconciled with solidarity with the equally precarious men and women represented by the 'fat and strong beasts' among us, as Ezekiel put it, without distracting attention from this partisan concern. The readings are not a law book, but critical reminiscences of already old and proven experience of religious people. They summon us to combine, with some creativity, concern for the oppressed with a universal compassion on all human beings, even on those who have made a mess of their humanity. I believe – and I say this with some hesitation – that at the last judgment perhaps everyone will stand on the right hand side of the Son of Man: 'Come, all you beloved people, blessed of the Father, for despite all your inhumanity you once gave a glass of water when I was in need. Come!'

'For he himself has gone before,
Faithful shepherd is his name.'

11

'Not On Your Life!'
(John 13; Maundy Thursday)

The first reading is taken from 'Joseph and Asenath', a Jewish romance composed among the Jewish Diaspora in Egypt, and dating from the end of the first or beginning of the second century. It incorporates some features from the book of Genesis, and is about Asenath, the daughter of Potiphera, priest of On (Gen.41.45), whom Joseph married in Egypt and who bore him two sons, Manasseh and Ephraim (Gen.41.50-52).

'Blessed be the Lord the God of Joseph,' said Potiphera the father of Asenath. He called a servant and said to him, 'Make haste to prepare the banqueting room and make ready a sumptuous meal, for Joseph, the mighty one of God, is coming to visit us today' (3.4-6)...

Later in the day a young slave ran up to Asenath and called out, 'See, the Lord Joseph is already standing at the gates.' Asenath hastened with seven slave girls to meet Joseph. Then she said to him, 'Come, my lord, and enter our house.' She led him by the right hand and brought him inside. Joseph took his place on a chair which Potiphera, Asenath's father, had shown him. Thereupon Asenath herself went to get water and girded herself to wash Joseph's feet. But Joseph got up again and said, 'No, not you! Let one of the slave girls wash my feet!' But Asenath persisted and said, 'No , Lord, for my hands are your hands and your feet are my feet. If I wash your feet, it is the same as if you were to wash your feet.' And while Joseph continued to make a show of resistance, she washed his feet (20.1-3).
    Later, the Pharaoh blessed their marriage. He took two golden

crowns and set them on their heads with the words, ' May the Most High bless you and cause you to multiply.' He gave them a great feast – seven days long (21.4).

Joseph gave her two sons, Manasseh and his brother Ephraim (21.8).

Now before the feast of the Passover, when Jesus knew that his hour had come to depart out of this world to the Father, having loved his own who were in the world, he loved them to the end. And during supper, when the devil had already put it into the heart of Judas Iscariot, Simon's son, to betray him, Jesus, knowing that the Father had given all things into his hands, and that he had come from God and was going to God, rose from supper, laid aside his garments, and girded himself with a towel. Then he poured water into a basin, and began to wash the disciples' feet, and to wipe them with the towel with which he was girded. He came to Simon Peter; and Peter said to him, 'Lord, do you wash my feet?' Jesus answered him, 'What I am doing you do not know now, but afterward you will understand.' Peter said to him,'You shall never wash my feet.' Jesus answered him, 'If I do not wash you, you have no part in me.' Simon Peter said to him, 'Lord, not my feet only but also my hands and my head!' Jesus said to him, 'He who has bathed does not need to wash, except for his feet, but he is clean all over; and you are clean, but not all of you.' For he knew who was to betray him; that was why he said, 'You are not all clean.'

When he had washed their feet, and taken his garments, and resumed his place, he said to them, 'Do you know what I have done to you? You call me Teacher and Lord; and you are right, for so I am. If I then, your Lord and teacher, have washed your feet, you also ought to wash one another's feet. For I have given you an example, that you also should do as I have done to you. Truly, truly I say to you, a servant is not greater than his master; nor is he who is sent greater than him who sent him. If you know these things, blessed are you if you do them...I tell you this now, before it takes place, that when it does take place you may believe that I am he. Truly, truly, I say to you, he who receives any one whom I send receives me; and he who receives me receives him who sent me' (John 13).

In the dusty Near East, people went barefoot in sandals. So washing feet was the order of the day. The two stories about a footwashing, and in each case the considerate refusal to accept it, show the Jewish spirit at its best. The differences are nevertheless fundamental.

According to rabbinic literature (Strack-Billerbeck II, 557), the Jew

washed his dirty feet himself; but in a male culture this was also seen
by the rabbis as the duty of the wife towards her husband. So Asenath
was not doing anything special. The point of this story lies with Joseph,
the Jew who refuses to have his feet washed by a Gentile Egyptian
woman, who is going to become his wife. The sensitivity lies with the
Jew Joseph, but it is challenged by the love of the pagan woman: 'My
hands are your hands and your feet are my feet: I am you, you are me.'
Here we have the deepest and most sensitive love in the private sphere
of interpersonal relationships; the structures remain.

With Jesus we have something completely different. Rabbis who had
only to nod to be served by their disciples would not allow these
disciples to wash their master's feet: that was going too far. They either
washed their feet themselves, or had them washed by a servant or a
slave. Foot-washing was menial slaves' work, the kind of job that we
now have done by foreign workers, African or Asian. Furthermore,
Jesus reversed the relationships: he who, as John says, could rightly be
called 'Lord and Master', himself did the dirty work of the foreign
labourer. For Peter, who had already become accustomed to the
disarming goodness of his master from painful experience, this was
going too far. There are limits to crazy goodness. Impetuously and
spontaneously he categorically refused. You, wash my feet? Not on
your life!

In this story we should be able to see that Peter is protesting in the
name of hierarchical social order against the anarchic manner of Jesus,
which overthrows the social order and breaks through all the master-
servant relationships established in society. Without doubt Peter's
refusal can only be understood against a dominant social background
of rank and status and the rules of fashion which predominate as a
result. Otherwise John's story would not have had this shocking and
liberating significance. Against this background both Jesus' action and
Peter's refusal take on deep religious significance, and both have far
reaching social consequences as well.

John's story about Jesus washing the disciples' feet shows a development within Christian reflection on this way Jesus had of shocking
people. John in fact gives two interpretations, though they are both
interwoven. The earliest interpretation is that Jesus gave a model to his
disciples: in the Christian community there are not to be any master-
slave relationships. The three other evangelists make Jesus say, 'You
know that the lords of the Gentiles rule their subjects with an iron fist
and that the great abuse their power over them. This is not to be so
with you' (Matt.20.25-26). John makes this tangible in the footwashing
by one who may still be called in truth 'Lord and Master', the Son of
Man, the Word in the beginning with God. We may not suppress this
earlier interpretation by John's community in favour of the deeper,

authentically Johannine interpretation relating to Jesus' coming death. Of course the second interpretation is an extension of the first.

Jesus' reply to Peter's refusal is typical: 'Unless I wash your feet, it's all over between us.' John puts it rather more solemnly: 'You have no part in me', not without reason. The relationship with Jesus is decisive for what is always called Israel's portion and heritage: life. If Peter will not have his feet washed by Jesus, he will not live. Here John suggests very profound relationships. Here too we have the plot of the whole story, albeit within the old social view of rank and status. Peter's concern to have a part with Jesus was precisely the reason why he refused to have his feet washed: out of friendship and love for Jesus he refused this slave's work. He thought of his master in high and lofty terms. Without any hesitation he would have washed Jesus' feet: that was no problem. Nevertheless, when he heard Jesus mention a possible separation, this impetuous but unenlightened Peter made a complete U-turn: 'Then in that case wash my head and my hands as well.' This is the best indication that Peter still did not understand what Jesus was doing. Jesus understood very well. He knew that such a reversal of values could only be understood when 'the hour has come', that is, the hour of the death of the Son of man, the revelation of supreme greatness in the deepest humiliation. Jesus, recognized by his followers as Lord, was nevertheless doing slave's work. He wants his coming death to be interpreted as his last and greatest work: the service of a spiritual, exalted Lord and Master to earthly men. The footwashing is to prepare the disciples to see that Jesus' coming death is not a fiasco, but a work of liberation, because it reverses all values, even those which are established in society. Just as we heard in the Gospel of John on Palm Sunday that Jesus allowed himself to be hailed as king – 'I am a king too', he will say to Pilate – but makes his inaugural entrance on a lowly ass, so John wants to impress on us with the footwashing that this man executed on the cross is the true Kyrios, emperor or Lord, the one who is truly great, and not the Roman emperor in whose name Pilate had him crucified. True greatness, royal and human, the greatness of a Son of man, is at the same time both concealed and made manifest in the performing of 'a work': the work of a slave, an action which overthrows all accepted relationships. This is behaviour in accordance with the kingdom of God, not in accordance with the standards of this world and of our society. Footwashing and crucifixion belong together: this illustrates the helplessness of the great figures of this world, the rulers who can only manipulate their power by enslaving others, even by torture and execution, while in so doing they confess their own impotence. Their enslaving power is impotence: Jesus' liberating impotence is power, saving omnipotence. The second interpretation of the footwashing – the Johannine exegesis of Jesus' humiliation to the point of death on the cross (the cross of slaves and criminals) simply gives a more radical dimension to the first interpretation (the model of humility). To serve the lowly as 'master' is a demand 'to the death', a demand which, if we are to be Christians, must matter more to us than our own life and death. It is a conviction on which we must be prepared to stake our lives. That is why Jesus says to Peter: 'If I do not wash your feet, you have no part in me.' The reference to Jesus' death is thus not something which undermines our life or evacuates it of meaning; it is not a mystification or sacramentalizing which calls us away from the demands of politics and religion. It makes these demands more radical – so that we may then celebrate them in the eucharist.

So it is good for us to note that where in the other gospels we read the story of the eucharist, here John, mystic though he is, leaves it out, and in its place describes the way in which Jesus washes the disciples' feet. For we have often isolated the deepest significance of the eucharist, which in the New Testament is experienced as a service or diaconia towards others, and made it a mystery in itself, separating it from references to the actual realization in this world of those relationships and changes in relationship which Jesus wants to be realized precisely there – in this world.

In earlier days, on Maundy Thursday, during the all too empty symbolic washing of feet which were already clean, people sang the hymn *Ubi caritas et amor, Deus ibi est,* a hymn for which I sometimes pine. What it means is that God's rule is righteousness and love among men and not some pious sentimental happening. We know from all the prophets that love can make demands which are hard on those who do not love, while they are self-evident for those who do. Therefore perhaps we should not sing this hymn for the moment, so that we can take it up again joyfully when we have renewed the praxis of the kingdom of God. Perhaps it would also be a good thing (quite apart from other considerations) not to have any further symbolic footwashings, but rather, while celebrating the eucharist, to realize in modern situations, as Jesus did in his, what can be required of us, for example, by the fact that foreign workers are exploited like slaves. In that case the story of Jesus' washing of the disciples' feet can give us a clearer view of the particular, the specific consequences of acting in accordance with the demands of the kingdom of God among men and women, in modern situations.

As John says, there will always be people who 'lift up their heels' at those who act in accordance with the kingdom of God – a Jewish saying which means roughly the same as our 'stick out one's tongue at someone', the sign of disapproval of such behaviour which is not appropriate in our world or our society.

We may indeed celebrate, in advance, this Maundy Thursday eucharist because as Christians we have entered into the believing certainty that despite the powers of this world, the kingdom of God is still on its way – as in the spirit of the footwashing we become servants of humanity.

To end on Johannine lines I would like to put forward one other consideration: Jesus went so far as even to wash the feet of the one who informed on him and betrayed him – Judas. Here was no Grand Inquisitor coming forward with his anathemas but someone who even lovingly, though perhaps with inner bewilderment, performed the duties of a slave for his betrayer. For Jesus, even Judas belonged to the ecumene of mankind, to the salvation of whom God is committed in his messenger and prophet. The one among you who would be the greatest should keep in the background, but at all times should be prepared to spring up and help. Only in this way, says the Gospel of John, shall what is written in scripture be fulfilled among humanity.

12

This Sickness does not Lead to Death
(John 11)

In the Gospel of John this story concludes the first part, which is concerned with the seven signs performed by Jesus, and is the introduction to the second part, which tells of the real glorification of Jesus in his suffering, death and resurrection.

In passing, it is striking how John's Gospel visibly realizes the saying of John the Baptist in this story: 'He must increase and I must decrease' (3.30). Four times, in ever-shorter pericopes, the Gospel returns to John the Baptist, and shortly before this story of the resurrection of Lazarus, the Baptist is mentioned yet again and for the last time (10.41) in a short transitionary verse. Now that the Baptist has disappeared from the stage, Jesus' 'increase', his glorification, can now begin!

However, in the Fourth Gospel this increase on the part of Jesus takes on dramatic proportions. The story of Lazarus' death is inter-woven with the problems of Jesus' own life. This interlude (11.7-16) relates to a discussion between Jesus and the disciples, whether Jesus may go to Bethany, which is near Jerusalem. Shortly before this, people had wanted to stone him there (10.31). The disciples were quite glad that Jesus, having received the message that Lazarus was fatally ill, seemed to take this news simply as information and made no attempt to go in the direction of Jerusalem. When Jesus decided to go to Bethany two days later, one of the disciples said to him, with a touch of gallows humour, 'Shall we go too, to die with Jesus?' The Johannine Jesus was also aware of this. The death of Lazarus and the tangible certainty of Jesus' own approaching death have been woven together in this Gospel into a whole: the cause of Jesus has come to its end. Hence too the double emphasis on Jesus' delay, and his deep shock at the tomb of Lazarus. He was indeed showing brotherly sympathy with the bereavement of this dear family, but in addition, in Lazarus' death and his own approaching death, he experienced the increasing pressure of the powers of darkness. It is a special feature of the Fourth Gospel that it interprets the resurrection of Lazarus as the direct cause of Jesus' own death sentence. When 'the high priests and Pharisees heard what Jesus had done with Lazarus, they called a session of the Sanhedrin' (11.47) and, 'from that day forward they were resolved to kill him' (11.53). Jesus knows that the raising of Lazarus from the dead is his own death sentence. That is the real dramatic background to this story, which furthermore is to be found only in the Fourth Gospel.

Resurrection stories are well known from different early Christian traditions, but in the Johannine tradition one of these resurrection stories becomes a notable event and a piece of Johannine community catechetics which is ultimately included in the final redaction of the original Gospel.

Through a messenger Jesus receives news of a family where he had a *pied à terre:* Martha and Mary, whose brother was dying. After waiting for two days, Jesus went with his disciples to Bethany. When they arrived it seemed that Lazarus had already been buried for four days. That was a shock; it is as though someone were to come back from holiday to find that his father had been buried. It is said quite emphatically that Lazarus has been dead for four days. Many Jews held the popular conviction that after a person's death the soul hovered around the tomb for three days and that only on the fourth day did it disappear for good to the kingdom of the dead. Thus by the fourth day a pseudo-death was impossible. Jesus' hesitation about going to Bethany is just a literary device to allow Lazarus time to be dead for four days and to rule out the possibility of a pseudo-death. The seventh great sign of Jesus is in prospect, which, like the first, the miracle at Cana, is to reveal the glory of Jesus, i.e. his true being. From a human point of view there is no more hope for this dead man.

Martha says that, when she is the first to run to meet Jesus. 'Master, if you had been here my brother would not have died'(11.21). This is not a reproach, but expresses an infinite sadness, of the kind that we often find today with people who fasten on to some idea or sheer coincidence in connection with a beloved one, seriously ill, who dies: 'Doctor, if only you'd come a few hours earlier, perhaps...' and then they don't go on to finish the sentence. 'Perhaps!' Even those who survive are bound to die in the end, as an intimate relationship is broken off by death. This is literally what the second sister, Mary, says. However, there is a decisive difference in detail between what she says and what Martha says, and it is with that that the Gospel of John is concerned. Only Mary 'falls at Jesus' feet' as soon as she sees him (11.32); in the Fourth Gospel, falling on one's knees before Jesus is the sign of a high christological confession relating to Jesus. Implicitly Mary has arrived at the true Johannine faith in Jesus. By contrast, Martha believes in Jesus, but given the title by which she addresses him she is still thinking in early Jewish-Christian, low-christological terms about him. For her he is simply the messianic Son of God, 'he who comes into the world'(11.27). Martha still does not have a fully developed Johannine faith. She still does not realize that the word and the life itself has been made flesh and now already stands large as life before her. Jesus must first therefore make clear to her that the future in which she believes is already present, today; that it is a living reality. Martha believes, like most Jews of her time, in the general resurrection on the last day, but Jesus says to her, 'I am the resurrection', 'I am life'. 'Do you believe that?', he asks Martha. 'Do you believe in the exalted figure of the Johannine Jesus? Do you believe that what is eschatologically new is present here and now and is not just something that will come into the world, that furthermore it can be demonstrated directly, on the spot?' Tacitly, Mary had this experience when she fell on her knees before Jesus; that is why she does not need all this Johannine catechesis. So what we have here is in no way a contrast between a so-called contemplative Mary and a so-called active Martha, but the difference between what the Fourth Gospel calls on the one hand incomplete faith and on the other hand mature, high-christological Johannine faith: faith in the incarnate Word and Life 'from God'. God's glory is now already concealed in Jesus and can be revealed directly. Thus Martha too comes to mature faith: in terms of the great hymn of the Johannine prologue!

The actual event of the raising of Lazarus is told in a brief and matter-of-fact way, as an ongoing echo of what chapter 5.28 had confessed about the end time: 'The hour will come when all those who are in the tomb will hear his voice.' So with a loud voice Jesus summons Lazarus from the tomb. In the last resort the important thing about the event is not the dimension of miracle. In the Gospel of John of course the raising of Lazarus is not a 'work' of Jesus, but one of his 'signs', and this is something essentially different. Signs have a christological significance ; they presuppose faith and seek to bring people to the deeper faith of the Johannine community. To believe purely on the works that Jesus does is incomplete, half faith: belief in Jesus purely as God's prophet. Shortly before the resurrection the Gospel goes on to sum up all the themes that are of importance here in one more powerful way: Jesus as life; Jesus as the light of the world; the theme of faith and the theme of the glory of Jesus; that is, the manifesting of Jesus' unique communion with the Father. The nucleus of the story is therefore that Jesus restores physical life as a sign of his power to give eternal life, now already here on earth and at the same time as a promise of the resurrection on the last day. This is also the nucleus of the whole of the Fourth Gospel, now visibly illustrated by the incorporation of a recollection of one or other of the resurrection traditions within Johannine theology.

So in this Fourth Gospel, it comes about that Jesus' raising of Lazarus is interpreted as the cause of the execution of Jesus which follows soon after, and this resurrection is made into a dramatic paradox: Jesus' gift of life becomes the cause of his own death. Evidently the good may not be the light in this dark world; those who do the good make martyrs of themselves. But for John, this death is Jesus' glorification, as was said at the beginning of the story : 'This sickness does not lead to death but is for God's glory, so that the Son of God may be glorified through it'(11.4), i.e. so that the identity of Jesus may be truly recognized and confessed.

The resurrection of Lazarus is the last phase in the gradual glorification or the process of the manifestation of the mysterious identity of Jesus through his suffering, death and resurrection. These are mysteries which we shall begin to celebrate liturgically in the next two weeks.

13

God as a Loud Cry
(Mark 15.37; Matt.27.50)

For many people 'God' is not a friendly and cheering word. Perhaps they have lost not so much God himself as the human place, the context where he can be experienced meaningfully. Consequently they are repelled by the sight of 'charismatic phenomena', religious experiences among people who shout Alleluia at the periphery of a culture which has become meaningless. The sphere of spirituality, left unoccupied by the religious institutions, is rapidly being occupied in triumphalist fashion by these 'charismatics'. In this area which has been left open, God is celebrated and praised, thanked and lauded, in an atmosphere of total reconciliation and liberation, at great length, and in contradiction to everyday reality.

I may have put that rather crudely. For alas, one has to concede that in our one-track scientific and technical, functional culture every person is in fact an anonymous, replaceable pawn. The feeling of late antiquity, that of living under *ananke,* the compulsion of fate, dominated by demons and all kinds of heavenly and astral powers, may seem strange to many people today, all unsuspecting that in their own time they themselves live under a similar compulsion of fate. The game is played, not discussed, and within it every individual is purely a variable.

The compulsive attempts which we often see people making around us to prove themselves irreplaceable reflect how things in fact are. Within the game that is played, every person is a disposable object, a kind of waste product of a history which is thought of as a movement of constant progress. People are valued for their prestige and success, honoured for them both and then cast on one side, the sawdust of a historical process. Within the game that is played, people ask themselves lugubrious questions about those who are no longer productive, the sick and the old who are incapable of competing. Fatalism – an old experience in the East and in late antiquity – and the defensive mechanisms against it, have again become very modern.

At least we should recognize that in the cries of alleluia at the liberation to be found in all kinds of charismatic movements we have the refusal of people to remain an anonymous variable in the functional game of our Western society. People refuse to accept this picture of themselves which is forced on them. What should make us think is not first of all the supposed solution, but the *protest* expressed in it against the impoverishment and narrowing of our wealth of human experiences.

Collective explosions are never fortuitous. Being human is not a function of anything whatsoever, though people also have all kinds of functions and roles with which they identify themselves completely or partially, or against which they rebel.

Someone might ask whether I am in fact talking about Good Friday. Yes, indeed I am. I note that though Jesus' religious experience was never grim, it was not a permanent mood of alleluia, either. Only once, when the disciples returned enthusiastically from their first apostolic mission, and happily told Jesus that where they appeared the sick were healed and demons were driven out, did a mystical mood seize Jesus: he saw the power of evil cast down like a falling star, which is extinguished and fades to nothing (Luke 10.17-18). The purpose of his life was universal reconciliation. Here he saw a beginning of it: his message had an effect; evil gave way.

However, the New Testament tells us that Jesus died 'with a loud cry' (Mark 15.3; Matt.27.50, see also Heb.5.7). Against the background of a history of suffering and injustice and given the life-style of Jesus which identified itself in love with the suffering and wrong of others, so radically that for that very reason he was removed from society's game, the word God can hardly be expressed otherwise than in a loud cry of indignation which at the same time expresses hope for reconciliation. In this action, of which the message was an intrinsic element, do we not have the most sensitive point, at which religious experience becomes possible and fruitful? If we do, we also have a very clear indication of the way in which we can speak meaningfully about redemption and liberation.

Some theologians, like Rudolf Bultmann, thought that Jesus' suffering and death was a tragic historical misunderstanding. It showed that what Jesus proclaimed and did was irrelevant. It neutralized the radicalism of Jesus' message, supported by action consistent with it – and that opens the door to a sheer alleluia Christianity.

The New Testament thinks differently. Jesus' proclamation of what he called in his Jewish way the kingdom of God calls for a universal reconciliation in which all master-servant relationships disappear and all worldly ordinances which make this reconciliation impossible come under criticism, as does even the human heart. The kingdom of God is a reconciliation which abolishes all exclusiveness and precisely for that reason becomes universal by seeking to raise up the oppressed.

In view of the recalcitrance of our history the radicalism of Jesus' demand and his consistent action provoke an equally radical final solution as a counter-reaction: exclusion from the order which he put in question. The only way to achieve that was to remove him from the scene. Hence his crucifixion.

Thus Good Friday points to the unconditional character of Jesus' message and his life-style of universal reconciliation, excluding no one. This message, as an element of Jesus' action, was closer to his heart than the consequences of it for his own life. This of itself points to the definitive validity of any praxis of reconciliation; it is valid in and of itself, and not on the basis of any subsequent success that it may have. Without the radicalism of this message and this action, Jesus' death would not have become inevitable. His death is therefore neither a tragic coincidence nor a sorry combination of circumstances.

Not that Jesus sought his death. But where the radicalism of his caring identification with the suffering and the wrong inflicted on others knows no bounds and will not be deterred in any way, this world is dealt a fatal blow. In that case the world adopts even more radical opposition to the threat posed by love and the one posing the threat is immediately put out of the way.

Of course Jesus' disciples recognized this only afterwards, in what was their Easter experience. Then it dawned upon them as an unexpected grace that what counts is neither success nor failure nor misfortune – above all through the intervention of others – but the dream, the will and the action to bring about universal reconciliation without any privilege and exclusiveness, even if this happens only for an incomplete period of time which is in fact brought to a violent end, a flame which flares and dies, for just a few years, in a small corner of the world. In this 'useless' love, aware that as radical love it is worthwhile in itself and does not need to be measured by success, and therefore takes up its rejection into its loving radicalism, we are shown the true face of both man and God . True reconciliation is only present in the praxis of a self-giving love which excludes no one and therefore has a positive preference for all those who are outcast, and is universal precisely by virtue of that, despite and even in the limitations of a particular finite situation. Thus from a very limited and determined point it takes the world off its hinges.

Reconciliation and liberation are something more than a shift in power relationships, they are a new rule, only when they are meant to apply to everyone, albeit from a particular perspective of a historically incomplete situation. Reconciliation means identifying ourselves with what we are not, with people in a different position, with those other than ourselves; the others; those who are not ourselves; with the suffering and injustice experienced by others. Reconciliation is far from being an inner, climactic experience in which everything is already reconciled without the mediation or involvement of others.

History shows us quite clearly that in fact there is no universal reconciliation. History still lies open. But with the cross of Jesus we have the promise and the hoped-for victory. With him we also have the urgent need for the achievement of universal reconciliation, and the challenging power to achieve it. However, this reconciliation does still have to be achieved, and in our recalcitrant history it will always have the imprint of failure, suffering and death – and also of a love which is powerless in this world, but which never acknowledges defeat. It is a love which dares the 'useless'.

Human suffering in a world which is not yet redeemed, a suffering which impels us to action, can only be tolerated if Jesus' way of reconciliation, which revealed its radical character on Good Friday, becomes a living remembrance among us. As long as human beings try to use one another as means for their desires – economic, political, personal and even religious – the word God can only be used validly from a Christian point of view in criticism of those conditions which dishonour people, criticism which is backed up by appropriate action.

If living man is the fundamental symbol of God (and this is what the Jewish Christian tradition of experience may have taught us), then the place where human beings are dishonoured and oppressed, both in the depth of their own hearts and in an oppressive society, is at the same time the privileged place where (above all in our time) religious experience becomes possible in a life-style which seeks to give form to that symbol, to heal and restore it to itself: to express its deepest truth. And in that case religious experience is only possible wherever people find it in the depths of their relationships, or even in nature.

To know oneself to be reconciled *outside* this life-style (which is always incomplete), to feel oneself freed on the basis of a preaching which *announces* reconciliation – and this is all the more vigorous, oppressive and almost loveless the more the preacher can read scepticism or a failure to understand on the faces of those who listen to it – has nothing to do with what the New Testament means by the *grace* of the redemption in Jesus Christ or with the Christian experience of being *accepted by God* – the experience that we may live.

Above all in our time Christians should have the right to use the word God only where they find their identity through their identification with life which is still unreconciled and in their actual attempts at reconciliation. What is promised to us in the story which the church tells us about Jesus is that the real possibility of an experience of God is disclosed precisely in this praxis in conformity to the message of Jesus. Consequently the struggle against injustice and the praxis of reconciliation is the sphere where the mystical experience of God becomes possible and can show its credentials. Furthermore, because the one who can be experienced and known in this action of reconciliation is always greater than our actions and this experience, this very experience of God sometimes discloses a new and greater future to us as an intrinsic element of an action of reconciliation. Here we experience that though redemption is not within our power, God nevertheless gives a future to our actions.

Similarly, Jesus died and the conditions in which he died show us that our earthly life is the place where everything is definitively decided. Jesus died because of his radical respect for human life which is not reconciled and needs to be reconciled. That life may therefore seem to be stronger than death, which as a result becomes a pascha, an exodus. In this action of Jesus, which extends to the helplessness of his perfect love on the cross, we may hear God's confirmation: 'Yes, you may be. You may live.'

14

The Transfiguration of the Suffering
Son of God
(Mark 9.2-9)

In the Vatican Museum in Rome there is a picture by Raphael which portrays the three disciples coming down from the mount of eschatological glory after the glorious Transfiguration back to the prosaic world of the human valley of uncertainty and distress. It is an impressive painting. Intuitively, Raphael has felt what Mark really means by his story of the Transfiguration.

This story occurs in what can be called the heart of the Gospel of Mark (8.27-9.29). This section is really concerned with the right response to the question of Jesus' identity. In the passage which precedes this story Jesus had raised the question, 'Who do men say that I am?'(8.27). There follow three mistaken identifications of Jesus (8.27-28). Jesus is not John the Baptist, nor is he Elijah, nor is he even one of the many prophets. To the next question, what the disciples themselves think of him, Peter replies in the name of all of them: 'You are the Christ'(8.29). This is already a first identification, but for Mark it is still blurred; it is only partial. The perception expressed in this identification of Jesus as the Christ is like the sight of the blind man of Bethsaida just after his cure, in the story which immediately precedes this one. The man who has just been healed first sees people walking, but very vaguely: 'they look like trees'(8.24). To confess that Jesus is the messianic prophet is certainly a step in the right direction, but for Mark it is still only half an identification; it still leaves vague the deepest mystery of Jesus' identity. Mark wants people to see Jesus in sharper contours, that is, to identify him as the beloved Son of God. This is the revelation of God which through the Transfiguration story Mark wants to press home with the three disciples, Peter and the two brothers James and John. The messianic Jesus is God's own Son and therefore he has come not just for the Jews but for all men. The Gospel of Mark is concerned with the 'Gospel of Jesus, the Son of God'(1.1)

Mark sets the scene for this divine revelation of Jesus' deepest identity by a reference to contemporary Jewish expectations about the glory of the end-time. At that time first Moses, from the wilderness, and also Elijah, the forerunner who would announce God's final judgment, would appear on earth again. Just before the story of the Transfiguration, the Gospel has spoken about this coming final judgment by the Son of Man. The appearance of the two eschatological prophets, Elijah and Moses, was part of the Jewish expectation about the end-time (see also Rev.11.3,5-6). This context indicates that the story of the Transfiguration must be seen against an eschatological background. The story is meant to shed some light on what is about to happen. And this is only possible on the basis of Christian belief in the resurrection of Jesus – resurrection as the basis of the coming parousia of the Son of man. On the mount of the Transfiguration Jesus appears in brilliant white raiment: for Judaism and Christianity this was the symbol for the righteous who have already been taken up to God. Compared with the Gospel of Matthew, Mark is very sober. Matthew says of Jesus that 'his countenance shone like the sun' (Matt.17.2). Mark does not say anything directly about Jesus himself, except that he is wearing the white raiment of those who have been raised, whiter than any raiment has ever been. Then people hear a heavenly voice saying of this Jesus, 'This is my Son, my well beloved, listen to him'(9.7). The context is therefore clear; the story of the Transfiguration is set within the context of the expectation of the parousia of the Son of man, and this story is possible on the basis of Jesus' resurrection, indicated by the white garments which Jesus wears. The New Testament view of the risen Jesus and its testimony to him makes it possible to evoke an eschatological vision. Jesus the Son has a central position here.

But just as Mark makes Jesus immediately correct Peter's confession of him as the Christ – he is indeed Messiah but a suffering, persecuted Messiah (8.31-32) – so the story of the Transfiguration is also corrected immediately: this is evident from the conversation on the descent. Jesus is Son of God, indeed, but he is a son 'who will suffer many things and be despised'(9.12). Like the Christian concept of Messiah, so the Christian concept of Son of God is steeped in the idea of Jesus' tragic death: no one arrives at the recognition of Jesus as Messiah and as Son of God except at the same time by arriving at the discovery that this Messiah and Son *must suffer* before he can be transfigured, and by following the same course (8.24-38). Furthermore, the words 'My son, the well-beloved' at the same time recall the story of Isaac about to be sacrificed by Abraham. In that story, too, Isaac is repeatedly called 'my Son, the well-beloved' (Gen.22.2,12,16): Jesus is the 'new Isaac' who is not spared. Furthermore, Mark clearly shows that the three disciples understand nothing of this. Peter talks nonsense about three tents and Mark adds, 'he did not know what he was saying' (9.6). The Transfiguration can only be discussed and understood in the light of Jesus' resurrection from the dead. The three disciples also have to be silent about the event until Jesus is risen (9.9). They cannot discuss the event until they have grasped the relationship between cross and glorification. Elsewhere, too (5.37-43), where the same three disciples are witness to the resurrection of the daughter of a leader of the synagogue who has died, for the moment they are not allowed to talk about it: resurrection and glorification can also be understood in the wrong kind of way, in a premature alleluia mood. Any recognition of Jesus' identity as Son of God includes the loyal recognition of his suffering and death. Therefore this same Gospel of Mark only allows a man to confess that 'this man is truly Son of God'(Mark 15.39) at the crucifixion of Jesus, and then he is a heathen. People may not mention Jesus' identity outside his passion and execution. Whatever form the story of the Transfiguration may have taken before it found its way into the Gospel of Mark, for Mark himself this story is a staged message of the messianic 'necessity' for Jesus to suffer, precisely as Son of God, in order to be able to come to his glorification. Easter is the pasch, the exodus. Peter thought that glorification – God's dwelling among us, the God who pitches his tent among us – is possible without suffering and persecution. Only in the end-time will the description in the book of Revelation come true: 'Behold, the tabernacle of God is with men. He shall dwell among them. They shall be his people and he, God with us, will be their God'(Rev.21.3). In his enthusiasm Peter passed over an important stage in Jesus' career: his rejection and execution by his contemporaries. Immediately before the story of the transfiguration Mark puts Jesus' words: 'If anyone is ashamed of me...of him the Son of man will be ashamed when he comes in the glory of his Father surrounded by the holy angels'(8.38). Not to be ashamed of Jesus' messianic persecution and suffering, and even to take up his cross, is the condition for understanding the scene of the Transfiguration. For Jews, that the Messiah should suffer was unheard of, but in the last resort it was not inconceivable. However, that God's Son should be rejected and have to suffer went beyond all human imaginings, and this is the climax which Mark intends. This fact alone makes Christian belief possible even after Auschwitz.

What really comes first is not that we follow God in Jesus. In fact it is the other way round: in Jesus it is God who involves himself with our history of human suffering and identifies himself with the suffering of all mankind. Precisely for that reason, belief in Jesus as the Son of God is the entrance to a community in which the division between Jew and Gentile is transcended by God's universal mercy on all suffering humanity, whether or not they are of the household of faith. Finally, the story of the Transfiguration is in the last resort concerned with the transformation of human suffering into a realm where all tears are wiped away and forgotten and only garments washed white with suffering are worn. The story of the Transfiguration is as it were another Emmaus story: 'Did not the Messiah have to suffer all this to enter into his glory?'(Mark 24.26). After experiencing the Transfiguration, in the deeper meaning which Mark gives it, perhaps on their descent from the mountain in their conversation with Jesus as he speaks of his coming suffering, the three disciples could also say : 'Did not our hearts burn within us when he spoke with us on the way and disclosed the scriptures?' (Luke 24.32). For all his naive but always sympathetic misunderstanding, and despite his premature view of the three tents, Peter had still understood something of what was happening: 'Rabbi, it is good for us to be here'(9.5).

As the story stands in Mark, it is clearly a church catechesis, perhaps for the newly baptized. However, we do not know whether in its original version, in the first tradition of this story, the Transfiguration was also the expression of an actual experience of Jesus himself. We can only guess, though our guess may be well founded. Jesus' own career was not always clear to him from the start. Last Sunday we heard how after his baptism he was tempted – even though that baptism was an expression of a clear choice of vocation on the part of Jesus. Did it make sense to want to bring mankind to repentance? Was that not a hopeless task? Time and again people cause disaster and injustice, and the pictures in our newspapers bring this injustice brutally home to us every day. But Jesus then thinks of God's vote of confidence in our human history, not on the strength of that history but because God's being is the pure power of salvation which seeks the happiness and well-being of mankind. Mark's Transfiguration story lets us glimpse something of this, for it says, 'They, Moses and Elijah, talked with Jesus'(9.4). It was not Jesus who talked with them, but they who talked with Jesus: Jesus seems above all to be the one who listens. He meditated on the fortunes of prophets like Moses and Elijah. Elijah was hunted down by his own people and weary of life, wanted to throw in the sponge, but persevered nevertheless. Moses did so too, and so many others. Above all the dialogue with Elijah points to Jesus' growing self-understanding. Even for Jesus it is ultimately a matter of the responsible choice of the identity of his own way of life. Through contact with God the Father in prayer, by living on the basis of the legacy of the Jewish history of salvation and disaster, and by being himself rapidly confronted with opposition to his message and way of life from his own fellow believers, Jesus arrives at the insight that unlike Isaac he will not be spared. His way of life and his intimacy with the 'God of mankind' on man's behalf will also lead to the cross. In its basic origin, then, the story of the Transfiguration will go back to the complete breakthrough in Jesus' own self-understanding, namely that the choice of man's concern as God's concern brings with it persecution and even execution. Therefore Mark does not make the countenance of Jesus shine: there is no reason at all to rejoice over the necessity for the Messiah to suffer! Does not Jesus himself pray, 'Let this cup pass from me'(Mark 14.36)? Jesus' experience is also an experience for Christians to learn, prefigured by the three disciples who have much more difficulty than Jesus in understanding this fate.

In all probability the Gospel of Mark was written at a time of persecution for Christians. The 'white raiment' in the Book of Revelation is washed clean by the martyr-witnesses. According to Mark, that is Jesus' message for today.

II

Confessing Jesus

15

'You are the Light of the World'
(Luke 2.19-32)

I have had a hard struggle over what I should say to you today – not to do justice to my theological reputation (which is being celebrated today and for which I am grateful to my *alma mater* at Louvain) but in order to be able to bring you good news, *euangelion,* as a fellow believer (who as a theologian has a special responsibility all of his own). So I have been wondering how I should bring you the gospel, today's gospel: that of old Simeon, who was able to see in Jesus of Nazareth the light of the world.

Ours is a time when Western civilization is no longer seen as the whole world but as a small and often very pretentious part of the wider world of mankind, a wider world which suffers under Western pretensions and in particular Western practices. The claim of Christianity that 'Jesus is the light of the world' comes up against quite audible opposition: 'spiritual imperialism' is a charge which is constantly heard. The appeal to Jesus' universal significance, the claim that Jesus thus calls everyone to determine his or her own life, is in fact always mendacious, hurtful and ideological as long as we do not also take into account the specifically liberating behaviour of Christians, or the absence of such redemptive action.

We theologians have not been able to bridge the gulf between theory and practice: on the contrary, it has become broader and deeper. We have paid little or no attention to the questions which believers constantly raise, or have made them too little ours: we see more clearly than ever how the zeal for both human liberation and contemplative tranquillity is disappearing from our Christian brotherhood and is kindled *outside* our Christian churches, and we are not in a position to rekindle it again within them. To all appearances we are solely or principally active in banishing one another from the church in the name of Christ.

Here, at this moment, I know that we share this same concern; I know that despite all my theology I will fall short of giving expression to what binds us all together here as believers, people who are aware that God is concerned for his creation. All of us who have seen the film *Jesus Christ Superstar* have been struck by the way in which both old and young identify themselves with Judas, who struggles hard with the question who Jesus was, and with Mary Magdalene, who hesitates, caught in the tug-of-war between the *fascinosum* and the *tremendum*, between the attractive and the bewildering elements in Jesus. In that case we must come to terms with the question whether we are not too hasty in giving 'the church's' answer to their questions and fail to share the search for signs in Jesus of Nazareth which could direct the human call for liberation and salvation towards the Christian answer which points to a special saving action of God in Jesus. What makes it possible for us to join old Simeon in experiencing Jesus as 'the light of the world'?

For us, then, the essential problem is, how do we claim to find salvation in Jesus of Nazareth and what salvation do we find? If we are honest, we believers in fact recognize so many other factors which also bring us salvation, heal us and liberate us. There are many possibilities which restore human beings to themselves, so that they can be who they are, for others, and find liberation, redemption and joy, and ultimately peace there. Within this specific world of experience it becomes clear that only if we, believers, can also show experientially where we find salvation and healing in Jesus of Nazareth, will it also become meaningful (and even necessary) to go on to ask about the relationship between the man Jesus and the triune God, about Jesus as the Son of God – but not otherwise. In a world in which God himself has become lost to view, no Son of God can bring us to liberated humanity and thus to the living God. In such a world we need a man who has experienced being human to the core and who at the same time expresses God through words and deeds. If we want to respect God's saving purposes, then we must first of all criticize ourselves from the perspective of the man Jesus. God willed to encounter us in a human way so that in the end we would be able to find him. The answer to the question of the universality of Jesus, Christ, or the light of the world, discloses the true nature of man, to realize true humanity in a liberating way and in that to reveal the true countenance of God. To establish God's kingdom of peace is simply to experience truly the God who is concerned for humanity. In the end Jesus' identity can finally emerge from that: he is the personal manifestation of God's universal love for mankind, the Son of God. But in that case this must become a new personal discovery in the specific situation of our history of injustice, servitude and intolerance: 'For my eyes have seen – here and now,' says the old Simeon, 'your salvation, which you have prepared for all peoples, a light to lighten the Gentiles' (Luke 2.19-32). Can we and may we in fact say, 'My eyes have *now* seen your salvation?' Do we see amongst us, as Paul says, that Christians 'are an open letter from Christ, not on stone tablets but in and through their lives' (see II Cor.3-23)? Jesus' light burns in this world only with the oil of our lives, in very historical situations in which we do not so much cast liberating light as dim that light and even quench it.

We must not repeat this salvation parrot-fashion, but discover it anew, for we live in a different time from that of old Simeon. Compared with that of the New Testament, for the moment our own time has narrowed the religious conception of salvation. It has had to give a good deal of ground to other efficient organizations which bring salvation – with such visible and tangible success that they have led many people to give up the old familiar gospel comfort of Christian belief. That raises the question of what really contributes towards man's salvation, which is the crucial issue among today's problems. We see that it is possible with the help of science, technology and restructuring to remove all kinds of human alienations. At the same time, this effectiveness relates only to alienations which are essentially the consequence of physical, psychological and social conditioning – restrictions on human freedom, which can be lifted to a great extent through opposition coupled with knowledgable and active involvement. And in this we may see shreds of God's redemption. However, the question is whether there is not a deeper alienation in mankind, an alienation which in fact is essentially bound up with our finitude, with our involvement with our alienated nature, and finally with our personal and collective guilt and sin – the dirty hands of our human history which contains so much innocent suffering, injustice and oppression, and the cries of human and divine indignation. Mankind's liberation of itself, however urgent and necessary that may be, seems to be limited – really but unmistakably limited – unless it experiences itself as gift. The self-surrender of finite humanity must always be boundless. For the sake of one another we must stand apart from the pressure of our own identity. Complete liberation, redemption, salvation as wholeness seems impossible without the experience of acceptance and reconciliation.

The question, then, is whether the life and death of Jesus of Nazareth do not express precisely this deeper problem of life in a disarming way – in particular the question whether Jesus communicated in words and action a liberation which brings men and women freedom in Paul's sense: 'Brothers,' he says, 'you are called to freedom'(Gal.5.13). 'Christ has made us free to remain in freedom. So stand fast and do not let anyone lay a yoke of slavery upon you. So say I, Paul...'(Gal.5.1-2). We are redeemed for a humanity which can and may transcend itself and which, as Paul also says, 'through the power which works in us can accomplish infinitely more than we can ask or desire'(Eph.3.20).

What *is* God's message? What do we listen for in the life and the death of Jesus of Nazareth?

One of the most certain historical facts in the life of Jesus is that he expressed God through his message of the imminent kingdom of God, the rule of the God who is concerned for humanity. Jesus' whole life was a celebration of this rule of God and at the same time orthopraxis, i.e. action in accordance with this kingdom of God. The link between the rule of God and orthopraxis is so close that in this praxis Jesus could recognize the signs of the approach of the kingdom of God.

In the history of disaster and suffering in which Jesus stood, there was no basis or even occasion for finding anything which could explain meaningfully and in a way which would make sense the unconditional assurance of salvation which was such a characteristic of his message. For Jesus, such a hope, expressed in his proclamation of the nearness of God's liberation and mercy towards man, unmistakably has its basis in an experience of contrast. On the one hand there is the stubborn human history of disaster, disturbance, intolerance and unrighteousness, and on the other hand Jesus' own special experience of God, his *Abba* experience, his intimacy with the Father as the one concerned for good and opposed to evil, who will not acknowledge the superiority of evil and refuses to allow it the last word. On the basis of his *Abba* experience, Jesus could bring people the message of a hope which is not to be derived from our world history. Evidently one can say something about mankind, even the most important things that can be said about people, on the basis of a deep religious intimacy with God. The *Abba* experience of Jesus is an experience of God as a power of liberation and love for mankind, which says no to all that is evil and causes people pain. For Jesus, people are people for whom God cares.

Although attempts have been made to make Jesus simply the good man *par excellence,* the supreme example of humanity, we shall never recognize him if we simply remove or exclude from his life his special relationship with God. For it is precisely in this relationship that the meaning and the power of his message, his parables and his liberating life-style lie concealed, and it is with that in view that we are asked, 'Who do you say that I am?' Without the basis of Jesus' *Abba* experience, the *promise,* which can provide a basis for positive hope, falls to the ground and Christian hope is exchanged for a problematical utopia, the utopia of our closed-in humanity with its great expectations, illusions and desires, all without any reason for an absolute confidence.

Still, we have only half understood Jesus or have failed to understand him at all if we overlook the rest of what old Simeon says: 'Behold this child is destined for the fall and rise of many, to be a sign that is spoken against' (Luke 2.34). His person and his message were rejected: Jesus was executed.

Even in his death, Jesus is not narrowly concerned for his own identity and selfhood – his identity was to identify himself with mankind and with God's cause as the cause of mankind. That is what he lived for and that is what he died for. God is concerned for humanity, but in a world which is evidently not always itself concerned for humanity. As a result of this, God's love for mankind in Jesus takes on a colour for which we have already prepared the mix. However, in his love for mankind God transcends all our mixes and matches, without depriving us of our own finite autonomy. Historically, the course of Jesus' life does indeed end in failure, which cannot be explained either theoretically or practically. Seen within a purely human context, here we really come up against an ultimate fiasco, one more failure which takes its place in the growing series of executions of innocent people in our history of human suffering. It is a short-lived hope, which at the same time seems to confirm the feeling that many people find this unacceptable, though that feeling has a utopian character, given the particular character and dark force of our ongoing history as a history of human suffering. Events in the world at present strengthen this sorry experience in more than one part of the globe. Where does this not happen? We know nothing of the anonymous martyrs among us!

As a result of the life which preceded it, the death of Jesus, God's mystic and therefore the defender of mankind, presents us with a fundamental question about God. The only alternatives are: either we must say that God, the God of the approaching salvation-from-God proclaimed by Jesus, is an illusion, ultimately a utopian vision of Jesus; or, through this rejection and death of Jesus we are compelled to revise fundamentally our understanding of God, our own conceptions of God and our understanding of history, and give them up as invalid.The real nature of God only appears in the life and death of Jesus, doing so by disclosing a new perspective on the future: here is a future for those who from a human point of view know no future.

So I should like to end with the Christian confession of faith in which all this is summed up, not to impose it in an authoritarian way on others or to use it like the threat of an anathema to those who think differently, but as an expression of my Christian conviction of life, which can become a challenge to all those who are concerned for the

fortunes of mankind only through a matching praxis which brings
salvation, liberation and mutual happiness:

I believe in God, the Father; the omnipotence of love.
He is the Creator of heaven and earth;
the whole universe
with all its mysteries,
this earth on which we live, and the stars to which we travel.
He knows us from eternity, he never forgets
that we are made of the dust of the earth
and that one day we shall return again to it as dust.

I believe in Jesus Christ,
the only-beloved Son of God.
For love of all of us,
he has willed to share our history, our existence with us.
I believe that God also wanted to be our God in a human way.
He has dwelt as man among us,
a light in the darkness.
But the darkness did not overcome him.
We nailed him to the cross.
And he died and was buried.
But he trusted in God's final word,
and is risen, once and for all;
he said that he would prepare a place for us,
in his Father's house, where he now dwells.

I believe in the Holy Spirit,
who is the Lord and gives life.
And for the prophets among us,
he is language, power and fire.
I. believe that together we are all on a journey,
pilgrims called and gathered together,
to be God's holy people,
for I confess freedom from evil,
the task of bringing justice
and the courage to love.

I believe in eternal life,
in love that is stronger than death,
in a new heaven and a new earth.
And I believe that I may hope
for a life with God and with one another
for all eternity:
Glory for God and peace for men.

16

I Believe in God, Creator of Heaven
and Earth

Belief in God the creator is never an explanation, nor is it meant to be. This belief is good news, which says something about God and about man and the world in their relationship to one another. It is a message which people cannot perceive in the first place from one or another authority which is alien to their own experience; on the contrary, it is a voice which we can hear from the familiar world of our own experience, from nature and history. Nature and history are authorities in which and through which God discloses himself as creator, in and through our fundamental experiences of finitude. But belief in creation is liberating only if we understand creation neither in dualistic nor in emanationary terms. Within the Jewish-Christian tradition, a pure concept of creation has developed over a long history of experience. However, we have to note that in the course of history Christians, too, have often conceived of creation in an un-Christian way; the consequence of this has been that their theories have often brought them to a dead end, above all in the sphere of Christian action.

In this context *dualism* arose from the offence caused by the suffering, evil and injustice in our world. It therefore denies that God willed to create the world as it is and human beings as they are. Thus finitude is not seen as the normal condition of creation but is derived from some fault in it or from a mysterious primal sin. The created world having been interpreted in this way, salvation or being whole, that is, the true form of our humanity, is then set either in a previous lost paradise or in an apocalyptic new earth and a new humanity of the future which God will only bring into being as a second stage, on the ruins of this world, in an unexpected and sudden future which – given the ruined state in which we live – is near at hand. In this view the created world is a kind of compromise between God and some power of darkness. *Emanationism* is not essentially very different from dualism, but derives from a different sense of life, specifically from a concern to preserve God's transcendence. God is so great and so exalted that it is unworthy of him to concern himself directly with creation and to compromise himself. He entrusts creation to a representative, a lieutenant of a rather lower rank. In this view, the world and man are degradations of God – degraded deity, because this emanation of things from God is also seen as a necessary process.

In both cases – dualistic and emanationary views of creation – the salvation or well-being of man consists in his raising himself above his creaturely status, above his human condition and place in the world, and distilling from it that which makes him specifically human, so that in this way he can achieve a more-than-creaturely status. This is to mistake the good news of creation. The Genesis story in the Old Testament sees the so-called primal sin of mankind not in the fact that human beings simply want to be human beings in a world which is simply the world, but rather in the fact that they do not want to accept their finitude or contingency; they hanker after that which is not finitude, after immortality and omniscience, so that they can be like God.

In deliberate oppposition to such views of creation, Jewish and Christian creation faith says that God is God, the sun is the sun, the moon is the moon, and human beings are human beings.

The basic mistake of many misconceptions about creation lies in the fact that finitude is felt to be a flaw, a hurt which as such should not really have been one of the features of this world. Consequently people look for a separate cause for this finitude and find it in some dark power of evil or in some primal sin. In other words, finitude is thought to be improper, an ailment, even sinfulness or apostasy, a flaw in the existence of mankind and the world. There is a feeling that coming and going, mortality, failure, mistakes and ignorance should not be part of the normal condition of our humanity, and from the beginning people should be endowed with all kinds of 'supernatural' gifts like omniscience and immortality, which they are then thought to have lost because of the primal fall. On a precise reading, it emerges that the Genesis story sets out to make a protest precisely against such conceptions, albeit in mythical terms. If God is creator, then he creates that which is not-divine, that which is completely other than himself, in other words finite things. Creatures are not replicas of God. The Jewish and Christian creation faith saw this very clearly, though we have to concede that the conceptions of creation in it have often become very distorted under alien influences, even by many Christians. I want to shed light on the authentic characteristic of this Christian belief in creation, above all in two respects:

1. First of all, this belief means that we do not need altogether to transcend our contingent or finite nature and to escape from it or regard it as a flaw. We may and must simply be human beings in a living world which is simply the world: fascinating, but also mortal, failing, suffering. To want to transcend finitude is megalomania or arrogance which alienates people from themselves, from the world and from nature. Humanity and the world are not the result of a fall, an apostasy from God, nor are they a failure, much less a testing ground in expectation of better times. If God is the creator, then the creation is of course not-God; it is other than God. In that case it may be different, bringing with it the burden of subjection and ignorance, of suffering and mortality, of coming and going, of failing and making mistakes. Finitude or contingency mean that people and the world are in and of themselves in a complete vacuum. There is nothing that can be introduced between the world and God to interpret their relationship. This is what people mean when they speak in symbolic language of 'creation out of nothing'.

2. But the other side of this belief in creation is that the oppression caused by being poised above absolute nothingness is at the same time balanced by the absolute presence of God in and with the finite. Finite beings are a mixture of solitude and presence, and therefore belief in God the creator does not remove the finitude nor does it distort it into sinfulness or fallenness. It has this finitude taken up into the presence of God, without relieving the world and man of their finitude or regarding these as hostile. In this respect Christian creation faith also distinguishes itself from pantheistic conceptions; for if God's presence were to mean that everything else outside God were in some way to be explained as an illusion or as part of the actual definition of God, then God would not seem to have sufficient active presence to have the power to bring autonomous, non-godly beings into existence. From a Christian perspective, the world and man are totally other than God, but within the presence of the creator God. Therefore this other-than-God can never emigrate from the divine act of creation; in other words, God remains in and with the contingent, the other-than-God – the world in its nature as world, and mankind in its autonomous but finite humanity.

These two characteristics imply that in contrast to the views of dualism and emanationism, salvation from God never consists in God saving us *from* our finitude and *from* everything that this finitude involves. For a creator God, it is precisely at this point that God's own impotence is to be found. In that case he also wills this impotence, with absolute freedom. However, that means that he wills to be our God in

and for our humanity, in and with our finitude. That means that we
may be human beings in our humanity, albeit mortal and suffering. In
itself this is a very oppressive burden, but at the same time it means
that God is with and in us, even in our failures, our suffering and our
death, just as much as he is in and with all our positive experiences and
experiences of meaning. It also means that he is present in forgiveness
for the sinner. The boundary between God and us is our boundary, not
God's. This has important consequences. In the recognition and
acceptance of our limitations and of those of nature and history we
recognize the divinity of God; and to recognize the finite condition of
man and the world is to recognize what gives man and the world their
specific nature, at the same time to recognize that they are not God
and therefore limited, and to act accordingly.

Because God is ineffable, and it is only possible for us to talk about
him as creator in an indirect way through the medium of the world, i.e.
our contingent nature and history, both nature and the world are
experienced as that which is not-God: they may not be absolutized or
divinized. Here, as in other respects, we find the critical force of
creation faith, which at the same time therefore represents salvation
for man and the world and a judgment upon them. To want to abolish
this limit, from us in a Godward direction, is what the Bible calls the
fundamental human sin, which has been constantly repeated over the
course of history. On the other hand, this creation faith sets us free for
our own task in the world. To enjoy and love what is worldly in the
world, what is human in man, is to enjoy and to love what makes God
God. God's glory lies in the happiness and the well-being of mankind in
the world: this seems to me to be the best definition of what creation
means. Furthermore, creation is not a chronological event, somewhere
at the beginning, but a lasting, dynamic event. For us that means that
God wills to be the origin, here and now, of the worldliness of the
world and the humanity of mankind – that he wants to be with us in
and with our finite involvement in this world.

If the Jewish-Christian creation faith does not give us any explanation of our world and our humanity, it does make us ask quite different
questions from those we would ask if we wrongly understood creation
as an explanation. If God were the *explanation* of why things and
events are what they are, then any attempt to change them would
indeed be blasphemous. In that case our sole duty would be to fit in
with the predetermined and preconceived universe. In that case, God
would become the guarantor of the established order – not *salvator,* as
the Christians began to call him, but *conservator,* as Roman and
Hellenistic religion had called him.

The consequence of this is that if anything goes wrong, the only
meaningful transformation of the world and society lies in a restoration

of things to their ideal order. Whether one puts this ideal order at the beginning of time, in an earthly paradise, in a distant future or at the end of time, as a good time to come, makes very little structural difference. In both cases the concept of creation is falsified so that it becomes a misplaced explanation instead of being good news for mankind, poised over a frightening absolute nothingness. Whether history is ·seen as apostasy from an original ideal state or as a progressive evolving development towards an ideal future state makes no difference if presented as a pattern of explanation: in both instances people misunderstand contingency as the essential characteristic of man and the world. In that case historicity is derived either from a genetic development of prefabricated planning or a chronological progress in accordance with the logic of development. Here the most essential aspect of all historicity is neglected, i.e. finitude: everything might just as well not have been or could have been other than it in fact is.

This applies to every phenomenon in this world, in nature and in history. Even institutions, specific historical forms like languages, cultures and civilizations, and even the forms of religions, are mortal: they come and go, so none of us need be surprised that the day comes when in fact they do go. Nothing about this is non-contingent. This also means that the material world, too, as an interplay of chance and necessity, is a particular result which need not have been or could have been otherwise. The contingency of any process of development is abolished by a conception of creation which understands itself as an explanation of the phenomena in nature and history. On the human level this also applies to people. If we are created, and that means if we are created in the image· of God, then people must be other than conservers, restorers and discoverers of what is already given. In that case people themselves are the principle of what they do and what they will make of the world and of society – and of what might not have been, yet is, thanks to contingent human free will. God creates man as the principle of his own human action, who thus himself has to develop the world and its future and bring them into being within contingent situations. For God can never be the absolute origin of man's humanity, in other words he cannot be a creator, if he makes man only the one who implements a blueprint predetermined by the divine architect. On the contrary, he creates man to develop in freedom his own human future, to realize it in contingent situations by virtue of his finite human free will which can choose between different alternatives, even between good and evil. This is a difference which does not precede freedom ; man makes it by his own free choice. Otherwise in a subtle way the contingency, that is, the worldliness, of the world and man's humanity is removed.

At the beginning of the nineteenth century, a pope condemned the practice of inoculation against smallpox, an illness which at that time was interpreted as a divine punishment, again because of a mistaken conception of creation as explanation. Even now, while the birth of a deformed baby is perhaps no longer seen as a divine punishment, it is nevertheless interpreted as a lesson from God. Here too we have an understanding of creation as explanation. Such blasphemous interpretations would not have been necessary had people reflected more deeply on Christian creation faith and thus on the implications of contingency for incalculable possibilities for which neither God nor creation are responsible, which leave neither man nor God indifferent, and which challenge them to action.

The transformation of the world, the development of a better and more tolerable human society and a new earth has been given over into the hands of contingent man; therefore he cannot expect God to relieve him of his problems. Precisely on the basis of a proper creation faith we cannot pass over to God what is our task in this world, given the impassable frontier (on our side) between the infinite and the finite, which puts God in his world and man in this one. Overcoming suffering and evil, wherever we may encounter them, with all possible means of science and technology, with the help of our fellow human beings, and if necessary by revolution if nothing else will avail, is our task and our burden, in a situation characterized by finitude and contingency. It is not a matter for God, except that this task is performed in his absolute presence and therefore is a human concern which also is close to his heart. Despite all the chances and causal connections, we can also explain why the world looks as it does on the basis of the historical and social, contingent will of mankind itself in its dialectical relationship with nature.

That means that in principle there is a possibility of a transcending negation as an element in man's anticipation or his plans for the future. Creation faith does not give us any information about the internal constitution of man, the world and society; to discover this is the task of scholars and scientists. However, belief itself is aware of the contingency of all its forms and of the peculiar character of the world and of man: a potentiality that he can realize in all good conscience within a situation of contingency. The world offers the possibility to realize human plans in freedom, though the future is never completely the product of human planning and implementation and, being contingent, human life calls for a good deal of acceptance and even resignation. For the sake of human freedom we also need to have a certain degree of scepticism about the history of human freedom. The future can never be interpreted purely teleologically, in terms of cause and effect, nor can it be interpreted purely technologically, in terms of development. The future, too, is contingent, and therefore never falls completely into the firm grasp of equally contingent people in a contingent world. On the basis of creation faith only God is the Lord of history. He has begun this adventure, and so it is his supreme concern: but that is his sphere, not ours.

Misunderstanding of creation in its deepest dimension of finitude can be clearly demonstrated by means of two current views of history and human society. They are:

1. The view of those who identify 'change' in society with evil. When the Roman empire collapsed, many people had not realized that human institutions are mortal like all created things, that they can come and go, and that a day would therefore dawn when they did disappear. Rather, having seen contingency as a flaw, people began to look for a scapegoat, and found it in the decadence of the Romans and the wickedness of the barbarians. The believer's view of contingency naturally does not prevent people from looking for specific causes (perhaps even guilt) for the disappearance of this empire. All men are mortal; that is their normal condition. But that does not mean that within our horizontal perspective it is impossible to discover specific reasons for a particular decline or death. To the same degree, institutions, like languages, cultures, economic and political systems, and so on, are contingent and mortal, though in the horizontal dimension one can find specific causes for their actual demise (that indicates the specific form of their finitude). The basic fault in the view that change as such is wrong goes back to a mistaken concept of creation which postulates as a norm for our history a good time in the past. Deviation from that norm is then by definition apostasy. Anything not commensurate with this is alienation.

2. The view of others who cherish an optimistic view of 'change' but are in fact making use of the same pattern of explanation. They think that the social, economic, political and other cultural features of our history at a particular period disappear, in a process of ups and downs, because life and history *per se* mean progress. Unaware of the un-Christian character of this belief in progress, at least some theological eschatologies (present and future) have taken over this spiritual Darwinism and its progressive and teleological conception of history. In this perspective, the disappearance of particular historical cultural forms is simply the other side of a progressive development. People again misunderstand contingency, especially the fact that historical forms, seen at the deepest level, disappear because they are mortal and contingent and not because they are the other side of an evolutionary course of history.

Of course this is not to deny that in the horizontal dimension (which is where contingency gets its specific nature), there are all kinds of secular causes for their actual disappearance which can be specifically demonstrated. What seems to me wrong and unfounded here is the attitude that in the end this disappearance is not the result of finitude, but has to be seen as the other side of an optimistic course of history, the intrinsic result of which is said to be immune. In this view, too, people work with a predetermined blueprint according to which (in this instance) everything ends up at a great omega point, the crowning glory of a spiritual and cultural evolution which develops of its own accord – and it does not make much difference whether this is interpreted in Teilhardian terms or in Marxist and communist terms. Here, albeit in a dynamic perspective, we have the same kind of view as the older demand for the 'best world' – a form of emanationism in which the created world is not in fact seen as contingent but as intrinsically necessary. However, neither nature nor history, with its web of cause and effect and chance happenings, is a necessary process: these could always have been otherwise. No single law in man and the world can tell us (from our perspective) that finally good and not evil will triumph in us and in our world. Contingency as contingency does not give us any well-founded expectation: that can be given us only through God as the absolute presence among all this finitude.

Religious belief in creation therefore has its own critical and productive force over against these pessimistic and optimistic, and ultimately unrealistic, views of history and society. Even changes for the good do not necessarily happen in accordance with the logic of development, any more than changes *per se* must be reduced to human apostasy and perversity. Both the tendency towards conservatism and that towards a progressive development are in effect unhistorical: they are ultimately a rejection of the contingency and mortality of social, political and economic (even ecclesiastical) forms of history. Here, theologically speaking, the proviso of the Creator God always applies, which is often wrongly narrowed to an eschatological proviso: on our side of the boundary, this means non-acceptance of the contingency of man, the world and history. This belief in God's proviso does not just amount to an extra stress on finitude: God's proviso and the finitude of man in the world are two sides of the same coin. Rather than being a kind of foul (which would be a sign of dualism or emanationism), this proviso means that any hopelessness provoked by the finitude of our existence is caught up, through God's absolute presence, in his finite world of creation. And this presence stimulates the continual renewal of hope. He, the Creator, is the creator of the whole of the saeculum, so that he does not leave any times, any centuries, or even any hours without his witness.

This also means that the beginning of the history of human freedom coincides with the beginning of creation. In this light, it is difficult to find a place in philosophy and theology for the 'substantializing' of the future, in which the pre-critical and pre-modern past is condemned as an irrational prehistory. Here too the Christian belief in creation has a critical function. In many religions the dualistic tendency which seems to be innate in mankind is resolved by making both good and evil equally find their principle in the one God; their God is then a God who equally and with equal right bestows both life and death. Even Job rebelled against this. According to the Christian concept of God, however, God is not a God of the dead but of the living (Matt.22.32). In other words, this concept of God assigns pure positivity only to God; i.e., by nature God promotes good and opposes evil, injustice and suffering. This view is presented mythologically in the creation psalms, in which God the creator joins the fight against the demonic beast of evil, Leviathan. Seen in this light, for the person who believes in God the inspiration and orientation for all actions lie in a call to promote all goodness and righteousness and to oppose evil, injustice and suffering in all its forms. God must always be thought of in such a way that he is never thought evil of. Talk about God always stands under the primacy of praxis. It is subject to the question, Where are we going? Well, I would say that within all contingency, one concern for humanity is: For what kind of humanity are we ultimately making a choice? Here we should consider how far people take account of their creaturely status, i.e. not only of their own humanity, but also, because of their involvement in nature, of nature's creaturely status and consequent limitations. In the meantime we have learnt, from irresponsible behaviour, the specific implications of this finitude of nature. We have become aware of the limits to our sphere of living. As a consequence of all this we have also learnt to recognize the limits of economic growth: development is not unlimited, as we have learnt to our shame and to our hurt.

Thus we have really seen that we were occupied in doing what dualism and emanationism did in the past, albeit in the conditions of the modern world : looking for salvation in life above our creaturely existence. In addition, as a result, in an egotistic way we have robbed coming generations of their possible future. All this summons us to what I would call the urgency of a collective asceticism on the basis of our status as creatures: we are simply to be human beings in a sphere which is simply the world.

The kingdom of God, which has its ultimate foundation in the divine act of creation, is certainly not the goal of politics and economics. However, one certainly cannot say that the kingdom of God is indifferent, for example, to the prices in world trade. Creation faith cannot tell us directly how we should organize world trade here and now. Specific solutions are not determined by the inspiration and orientation of Christian faith (which, to put it in parentheses, is realized in the historical figure of Jesus: within this short space I cannot make a separate study of this realization of creation faith). Specific solutions must be sought through a scientific analysis of our social structures and a hermeneutical interpretation of them. However, what emerges on the basis of creation faith is not so much what is 'socially possible' and 'politically attainable' (that is the concern of politicians, certainly in a democratic society) as a prophetic impetus. In the light of what is in fact the unrelieved state of suffering in nature and society, this is urgently needed, and we must make it specifically possible with all the strength at our disposal.

It emerges finally from all this that Christians can preserve their identity only in and through a practical identification. Faith in God the creator is not simply a question of another interpretation or another theory without any relevance for praxis. As I have said, God's glory is human happiness. But this happiness is not simply an individual concern. Of course, individual action is in no way socially neutral or politically innocent, above all in modern conditions (as J.B. Metz, among others, is accustomed to say). That means that the believer's concern for God's honour is also a struggle for more justice in the world, a commitment to a new earth and an environment in which human beings can live fuller lives. If Christian salvation is salvation of and for human beings – men and women with flesh and blood, who by their very nature are directed towards creating free society for free human beings, this means that Christian salvation is not simply the salvation of souls but the healing, making whole, wholeness, of the whole person, the individual and society, in a natural world which is not abused. Thus Christian salvation also comprises ecological, social and political aspects, though it is not exhausted by these. Christian salvation is more than that, but it is that too. (This is not the place to say more than this about Christian salvation – that falls outside my brief.)

What in former times seems only to have attracted the interest of religious people is now a concern of all kinds of human sciences, technologies and activities. All strive for the healing, making whole or 'salvation' of human beings and their society. It is impossible to miss the fact that the question what form of human life is sound and worthwhile, is, *in the form of a question,* more than ever a vital one for our world, and that in our time the answer to this question becomes all the more urgent, the more we note that on the one hand people fall short, fail and above all are abused, and on the other hand already experience fragments of human healing and self-liberation. The question of a worthwhile human life is always raised within specific conditions of alienation, disintegration and all kinds of human oppression. The question of salvation which earlier was only a religious theme has more than ever become the great stimulus throughout our present-day existence, even among those who are not religious. The question of salvation is not only religious and theological, but in our time is also quite explicitly and consciously the great driving force of our contemporary history.

The fact that what was formerly only the concern of the religions and of Christianity is now experienced by all human beings as a common duty in no way weakens the Christian view of faith. Quite the opposite. Since when has a particular view of reality become less true because it has ultimately been universalized, i.e. has also been shared by many other people? Does not this argue, rather, for its correctness? But should we now argue that, while the introduction of many ideal values, above all in the West, is also a result of the tradition of Christian experience, now that they have become common property, while thanking Christianity for certain services, we can bid it farewell? Such a suggestion would be welcomed from both the right and the left.

I think that if we adopt this course we underestimate the inexhaustible potential of the Christian faith for expectation and inspiration. As a total thesis, the so-called tendency towards secularization which I have just noted, understood as the gradual universalizing of originally religious inspiration, seems to me to be a pernicious short cut. That is for two basic reasons. The first reason is finitude itself. Finitude, which is really the definition of all secularity, can never be completely secularized, for in that case the modern world would have to find a means of doing away with the essential finitude of man and the world. The second reason lies in the self-understanding of the religions and above all of Christianity. At least in the Christian tradition of experience, cohumanity, the focal point of secular experience, is meant not only as an ethical but also as a theological standard (*virtus theologica,* as the tradition puts it). The Christian tradition thus sees cohumanity as a dimension with religious depth which has to do with the insight of faith that finitude is not left in isolation but is supported by the absolute presence of the Creator God. And this presence remains an inexhaustible source which can never be secularized.

Let me clarify this by an example. In our society old people from whom performance, productivity or success can no longer be expected are simply written off, leaving aside a tendency for even more radical solutions. Christian creation faith protests against this collective and individualistic dismissal. From a Christian perspective, God's absolute presence also continues among and for these finite people. Within the perspective of creation faith, performance, success, productivity, in other words results, are not the sole criterion. God's absolute presence applies even to failure (we find this above all in belief in the forgiveness of sins). Provided that it is truly experienced, creation faith in no way encourages a privatized view; on the other hand, it does not favour the promotion of the abstract idea of 'humanity' or 'the genre of man' . It sets forth God's direct relationship with every man as an irreducible 'personal subject' which is an end in itself and cannot be used as a means for whatever else – a subject that beyond doubt comes into its own in social, economic and political structures which make possible true subjectivity of all and for all (and not just for an upper crust).

I believe that it is precisely the critical and productive force of authentic creation faith (as realized in Jesus) which issues in a constantly universalizable (and in this sense secularizable) value, inspiration and orientation which is to the advantage of all people and so as it were evades the monopoly or the particularity of the religions, and Christianity can never go beyond the inexhaustible potential of expectation and inspiration of creation faith. For secularity means finitude. And although non-religious secularity sees only finitude here, religious and Christian secularity sees in this finitude God's presence, which is inexhaustible because it is absolute. On this basis, to the end of days finitude or secularity will continue to be directed towards the source and ground, inspiration and orientation, which transcends all secularity, which believers call the living God, and which cannot be comprehended within any secularization. Precisely for that reason creation faith is also the foundation of prayer and mysticism.

17

I Believe in the Man Jesus: the Christ, the Only Beloved Son, Our Lord

Belief in God is impossible without belief in mankind. Christians express this in their creed which, though old, constantly remains new, in the following way: 'I believe in God, creator of heaven and earth, and in Jesus, the Christ, his only Son, our Lord'. This twofold faith, on the one hand in the unconditional love of the Creator for all that he calls into life and on the other hand in this man Jesus of Nazareth, is so paradoxical that it is only possible in the power of the spirit of God which also dwelt in Jesus in fullness: 'I Believe in the Holy Spirit'. Within this tripartite structure which from earliest times has been called 'the Apostles' Creed', I want to bring some clarification to the second part, belief in Jesus Christ. Of the many names or honorific titles in the New Testament, only three have made their way into the creed: 'Christ, God's only Son, our Lord'. Here the believers of the time who had come under the spell of Jesus tried to put into words on the basis of their own originally Jewish experience what Jesus the Jew came to mean for them, not just - as we would say - subjectively, but also as a gift of God - objectively. The formulae used in this creed are not of primary importance as such, although they are by no means unimportant. The fundamental factor is the tentative attempt by Christians, i.e. by believers along with their leaders, to express their concrete experience of salvation in Jesus, from God, and to express it in comprehensible terms. Their experience of salvation comes first. Only after that came further ongoing reflection on the intrinsic richness of the experience of faith seen in the light of new experiences, new problems and questions. The original experience out of which this creed was born is that Jesus of Nazareth, the prophet of the final kingdom, *is* Christ, i.e. salvation from God for men: Jesus is anointed ('Christus') by God's spirit to redeem his people (Isa.61.1;52.7).

After a number of Christian generations, the ancient church intuitively put this article of faith in the context of belief in God as the creator of heaven and earth. Both articles of faith shed light on each other, just as already in the Old Testament the traditions of covenant and creation, which were originally independent, influenced and enriched, purified, corrected and strengthened each other.[1]

Christian creation faith implies that God loves us without limits or conditions: without any restrictions, although we do not deserve his love and are unworthy of it. Creation is an act in which God on the one hand places us unconditionally in our finite, non-divine state, destined for true humanity, and on the other hand at the same time gives himself in unselfish love as our God: our salvation and our happiness, the supreme content of true and good humanity. God freely creates men and women for their own salvation and happiness; but in the same action, in sovereign freedom, he wants to be the deepest meaning, the salvation and the happiness of human life. He is a God of human beings, our God: Creator. That is the Christian belief in creation. But how can it be?

How this can be must emerge from the history which human beings make, for better or for worse. Creation faith means that the nature of God manifests itself. That is, who God is, the particular way in which God is God, is not defined or conditioned in any way but is *manifested,* in and through the whole of our history. Christians call God the Lord of this world history. From God's perspective the venture of calling human beings creatively to life is a vote of confidence in mankind and its history, without requiring any preconditions or guarantees on man's side. Creation is a blank cheque for which God himself stands guarantor. It is a vote of confidence which gives the person who believes in the Creator God courage to believe, in word and action, that despite many experiences of disaster, the kingdom of God, i.e. human salvation and happiness, is in fact in the making for mankind, in the power of God's creation which summons human beings to its realization. It is brought in by God's fight against all chaotic and alienating powers. In their creation faith, Christians bear witness to their belief that God's ownmost being, in absolute freedom, is love of men which achieves their redemption: salvation, happiness, indeed even delight, for human beings and among them. It is delight in believing in God. Therefore the one who can be trusted, in all his freedom, is a constant surprise for mankind: 'He who is and was and is to come' (Rev.1.8;4.8). The immutable, i.e. uncreated, being of God is that which is permanently new, on the basis of his eternal and absolute freedom for finite man. This newness is nevertheless recognizable as the action of one who is always the same God: 'There he is again!' Because God's creative action is his eternal, absolutely free being, his absoluteness or non-relativity is at the same time relational,[2] i.e. it relates to his creation in absolute freedom which nothing determines: mankind in the world. In creating, God takes the side of all that is created and vulnerable. For anyone who follows Jews and Christians in believing in the living God, man's concern is the concern of God himself, though that does not mean that human beings have any less responsibility for their own history.

'Christology' – the second article of faith: salvation in Jesus from God – can therefore only be understood as the specific realization of creation faith, a more specific realization of our human history and the historical appearing of Jesus of Nazareth in it. In Christian terms creation faith then means that God's nature is liberating love in Jesus the Christ for whatever is not God, whatever is vulnerable. It is evidently difficult for people to believe in a divine being which determines in complete freedom what and who and how 'it', 'he', 'she' (here human terms are just not enough) really is. Nevertheless this is what creation faith is. We ourselves can only determine to a very limited degree, restricted by all kinds of conditions, who, what and how we want to be in accordance with our own particular plan or view of life. And even then, to a large extent we still fail. By contrast, God's nature is completely and precisely what God wants it to be, without remainder. As God, he freely determines what he wants to be for himself and for us, not by some sovereign whim, but in unconditional love. For people who are opposed to death, injustice and alienation, and venture to choose life, this Christian creation faith is the fundamental factor, the basic foundation. 'God is love. And the love that God is has revealed itself among us since he sent his only son into the world to bring us life'(I John 4.8-9). According to the New Testament, the Word, which even in the Old Testament had spoken primarily of love, became flesh, 'incarnate love', in Jesus of Nazareth.

Christology is therefore *intensified,* concentrated creation: belief in creation as God wants it. It is not a new plan made by God because creation has gone wrong, as some religions interpret certain human experiences, but the supreme expression of God's eternally new being which we can only understand partially on the basis of ongoing creation and its history. In the creed, in which creation faith is essentially bound up with faith in the man Jesus as God's definitive salvation of and for men, we bear witness that we are prepared to accept that we are loved 'for nothing', unconditionally and without our deserving it, by a God who takes the side of mankind: he upholds the humanity of men and women. This is expressed most strongly in what Paul says: 'He loved us while we were still sinners'(Rom.5.8), or in the Johannine, 'Herein is love, not that we loved God but that he loved us'(I John 4.10).

Only through Christ can we confidently suppose that God has more under way than we might imagine from other evidence. God, the creator, the one in whom we can trust, is love that liberates men and women in a way which fulfils all human, personal, social and political expectations and indeed transcends them.

We can, indeed we must, ask on what clear grounds people who call themselves Christians arrived at the conviction that it is God's nature to love mankind and that he is not – as was often said earlier, even in the older parts of the Old Testament – a God who directs the life and death of human beings by his sovereign whim. Christians have taught this out of their experience, on the basis of the life of Jesus: on the basis of his message and the life-style that went with it , the specific circumstances of his death, and finally the apostolic witness to his resurrection from the dead.

It is striking that in the creed there is no mention of the kingdom of God and the life-style of Jesus which are the basis of his death and his resurrection (see further below).

'Kingdom of God' is the expression used in the Bible and above all in the New Testament for the nature of God – unconditional and liberating sovereign love – in so far as this is realized and manifests itself in the life of those who do God's will. It is enough to choose just one text at random out of the rich store of New Testament stories about Jesus' message and life-style – say, Luke's account of the calling of Peter (Luke 5.1-11). In it we hear of two boats drawn up on the shore and some fishermen who are mending their nets after a less than successful, indeed a completely disastrous, night's fishing. 'By chance' Jesus comes by. He stops at one of the two unmanned boats and says to one of the fishermen: 'Come on, let's go out to sea.' Peter looks at this man, who is as yet a stranger to him. Without knowing precisely why, he has to respond to him: he gets into the boat with Jesus. The others follow. Jesus then begins to tell them about a mysterious kingdom which he nevertheless describes in vivid terms: 'the kingdom of God'. This is a kingdom for poor fishermen, joy for those who weep, fullness for those who are hungry. Suddenly he gives another twist to the conversation and says, 'Come on, let's go further out to sea and then we shall catch big fish'. And indeed after a while the nets threaten to break under the weight of fish. After everything that Peter had heard about God's coming kingdom, coming above all to the poor, to fishermen with empty nets, he felt the imminent nearness of God, and said fearfully, 'Depart from me, Lord, for I am a sinful man.' Encountering God in their everyday world seems to make people anxious, just as small birds take fright at the approach of a great eagle which is going to devour them. But Jesus says, Don't be afraid.' And the story goes on: 'They drew up their boat on the beach, left everything and followed him.' It continues, 'Don't be afraid, from now on you will catch men.' But for Peter at that time this last comment was in no way the heart of the story. At that time Jesus' decisive word to him and his decisive experience was not that one day he would be a great apostle, but the comforting words, 'Don't be afraid.' In God's presence one must never be afraid.

In fact, in their innermost depths people have the most grotesque expectations of their God. They expect that if you give yourself completely to God and seek only to be concerned with God's cause, there will be nothing but God, the great eagle which swallows up all the smaller birds, so that we must discount ourselves and the whole of God's created world. That man's concern is God's concern and vice versa, and that this is meant by what Jesus calls the kingdom of God, surpasses all our human expectations of God. People imagine God in quite a different way from the way in which God sees and imagines himself. 'Does not even the sparrow find its own home? Does not the swallow have its own nest?' In that case, will the small bird fall prey to the great eagle? For human beings, thinking about God in human terms can indeed lead to bizarre notions. In former times people offered sacrifices to honour their God. Are things different in our time? Do not all kinds of disaster and suffering happen in our world in the name of God? But Jesus says, 'Don't be afraid.' If you feel God approaching, don't be afraid. God is a God of human beings, a God who, as Leviticus says, 'abhors men's sacrifices' (Lev.18.21-30; 20.1-5). God is a fire, indeed, but a fire which does not touch the burning bush, but leaves it intact. God's honour lies in human happiness.

It goes beyond our human powers of expression to put into words what this salvation and human happiness – the kingdom of God – really means. We get a weak sense of it on the one hand through human experiences of goodness, meaning and love, and on the other hand as it is reflected by situations in which we feel the human in us, personally and in society, to be threatened, enslaved and disregarded, so that we come to oppose the threat. However, these experiences only really stand out against the background of Jesus' life and the way in which he went round Palestine 'doing good'. The New Testament has expressed this in one of its earliest remembrances, when it says that with Jesus the kingdom of God has come near to us (Mark 12.28; Luke 11.20; see Matt.32.2; 4.17; 10.7; Mark 1.15). The kingdom of God is a new relationship of man to God, and its tangible and visible side is a new kind of liberating relationship between human beings within a peaceful and reconciled society. The wolf and the goat lie down next to each other and the child plays by the snake's hole. To believe in that, i.e. to believe in Jesus as the Christ, means at its deepest to confess and thus to recognize that Jesus has a permanent and constitutive significance for the approach of the kingdom of God and thus for the all-embracing healing and making whole of men and women. Our Christian creed is essentially concerned with Jesus' own, unique attitude to God's coming kingdom as salvation for human beings. 'I tell you that everyone who confesses me before men, him will the Son of man confess, when he recognizes him with God's angels' (i.e. at the last judgment): that is the way in which the New Testament assesses Jesus' own understanding of himself (Luke 12.8-9 = Matt.10.32-33; see also Mark 3.28-29; Matt.12.32; Luke 12.10). For believers, the person of Jesus is of world-historical significance. That with the coming of Jesus 'God comes close to us' is a basic Christian conviction which therefore must be expressed in one way or another in the creed.

Here of course we must remember that (as a legacy of the Jewish Yahwistic tradition) Jesus did not so much bring a new teaching about God; rather, he had a particularly acute prophetic perception of the specific social functions of this concept of God which, in the society of his time, worked to the disadvantage of the 'small man'. Jesus uncovered a concept of God which enslaves people. He fought for a vision of God as a God who liberates mankind, a vision that he had to express in particular actions. Therefore in the Christian gospel, both 'God' and 'Jesus' take on their own critical and productive, liberating force. A religion which in fact has a dehumanizing effect, in whatever way, is either a false religion or a religion which understands itself wrongly. This criterion of humanizing proclaimed by Jesus, this concern for the humanity of mankind, for its soundness and wholeness, is not a reduction or evacuation of religion as Jesus' opponents feared – and still fear today. It is the first condition for its human potentiality and credibility. Furthermore it is the only consistent conclusion to be drawn from the Christian view of the nature of God, experienced as love. It is of this God, and no other, that Jesus Christ is the 'great symbol', 'the image of the invisible God' (Col.1.15; see II Cor.4.3-4). At the same time Jesus is here the image of what humanity really needs to be: true and good humanity. The creed expresses the fact that in Jesus believers know themselves to be confronted in a unique way with God himself through its confession, 'I believe in Jesus, God's only son.' For in Jesus we are not only *confronted* with God; in him we are also *addressed* by God: in Jesus God confronts us with his own being. Jesus is therefore 'the word of God', i.e. not only the interpreter of man, someone who in word and deed lives out what true humanity can really be, but at the same time the interpreter or exegete of God, someone who in word and deed shows us who and how God himself is. Christians learnt to express the content of what 'God' is and the content of what 'man' is, in a stammering way, through the life of Jesus. Within its own later and different framework of thought the Council of Chalcedon had the same intention as the Apostles' Creed when it said: 'One and the same, Jesus Christ, is truly man and truly God.' Salvation from God in Jesus. The spirit in which we confess the Apostles' Creed in prayer is not that of rigid orthodoxy but the spirit of the gospel: 'Lord I believe, help my unbelief' (Mark 9.23).

Death is an inevitable element in any life, even that of Jesus. But death takes on a special significance when it is premature and even more so when, as was the case with Jesus, it is an execution: not a spontaneous lynching party by a people oppressed beyond all measure, but an execution by the authorities, and in particular by an occupying power. This is not just a marginal coincidence in the life of Jesus, still less a pure historical misunderstanding, as the executions of champions of a fuller humanity are often said to be. Jesus' message of the kingdom of God was a prophetic attack on the class of Jewish religious leaders, a fatal condemnation, implicit but clear, of the Roman forces of occupation: 'Jesus said to them, "The kings of the Gentiles exercise lordship over them and their authorities have themselves called benefactors. It shall not be so with you." ' (Luke 22.25). Matthew puts it even more sharply: 'Jesus said, "You know that the rulers of the Gentiles rule with an iron fist and make great misuse of their power. This may not be so with you" ' (Matt.20.25-26). The 'message of the kingdom of God', of a God concerned for men and women, can indeed mobilize peoples to opposition, as we can see today, for example in Latin America. Crucifixion, the Roman form of execution not only for criminals but also for politically dangerous men (those who protested against injustice) is the great historical testimony that the message of Jesus in fact had its politically dangerous side, as it still has for religious and political authorities and for anyone who does not have a concern for the real salvation of all men. The kingdom of God is opposed to any kingdom which can only stand firm by enslaving men, keeping them poor or even torturing them. 'He was crucified under Pontius Pilate.' This last phrase is not there without reason; within the creed it is a historically dangerous recollection. In the light of Jesus' message and life-style people must go on to assess his death, and only after that see it in the light of his resurrection. Otherwise the confession 'He died for our sins' is no longer comprehensible to modern men; it is an incredible formula. Above all when people disregard the message and conduct of Jesus which led to his death, they obscure the saving significance of this death. Jesus' death is historically the intrinsic consequence of the radicalism both of his message and of his life-style, which showed that all master-servant relationships are irreconcilable with the kingdom of God. The death of Jesus is the historical expression of the unconditional character of his proclamation and life-style, in the light of which the importance of the fatal consequences for his own life faded completely into the background. Jesus' death was suffering through and for others as the unconditional force of a life-style of doing good and opposing evil and suffering. Thus the life and death of Jesus must be seen as a whole. Furthermore it was not God, 'who always abominates human sacrifices', who brought Jesus to the cross. That was done by people who removed him from the scene because they felt that he was a threat to their status. Although God always comes 'in power', divine power does not recognize the use of force, even against people who want to crucify his Christ. But the misuse of power by people does not checkmate God's purposes. The kingdom of God still comes, despite the misuse of power by human beings and their rejection of the kingdom of God.

Thus the death of Jesus may never be interpreted in such a way that the 'for nothing', the unconditional character of the love of God manifested in Jesus, is undone. Reconciliation cannot mean that God suddenly ignores his unconditional love and must first see 'the blood' of his Son flow before he accepts us in love. He already loved us while we were still sinners. We must therefore also recognize an element of fiasco in the death of Jesus (as the result of human misuse of power). We can still detect that from a human point of view this fiasco was a real aspect of the death of Jesus in the initial doubts of his followers. Can this suffering, humiliated man be 'the Christ'? Their growing insight into the essential link between 'Jesus' and 'Christ' was initially disturbed by Jesus' suffering and death. It follows from this that we cannot clarify the complete identity of Jesus exclusively on the basis of his message and life-style. Many things also *happen* to people, and these contribute to their identity, precisely through the way in which those concerned either integrate particular events or do not know what to make of them. Therefore the identity of Jesus, his revelation of both the divinity of God and of true humanity, is incomplete if we leave out of account his death and resurrection. Jesus maintains to the death his radical concern for both God and man, despite the fact that he is rejected by men. The strong love of God for men and of men for God can also evidently be manifested in earthly weakness, which perhaps as a result is still the most disarming means of reconciliation. At the same time it indicates that salvation from God never means that God calls to us out of our finitude; he is with us in anything that the conditions of our finitude can bring, both in positive experiences and in failure, suffering and death. The boundary between God and creation is always our boundary, and never that of God. Therefore the death of Jesus is not the last word about him.

Just as Jesus' death cannot be separated from his life, so too we cannot

separate his resurrection from his life and death. To begin with, we
even have to say that Christian belief in the resurrection is in fact a
first gospel evaluation of Jesus' life and crucifixion, and especially the
recognition of the intrinsic, irrevocable significance of his proclamation
and praxis of the kingdom of God, which nothing can undo. People
undermine belief in the resurrection if they leave out this aspect of it.
But this belief comprises even more. However, this 'even more' also has
an intrinsic connection with Jesus' life and death. In the first instance
the resurrection of Jesus is the breakthrough or manifestation of
something that was already present in his death and life, namely his
intimacy with God which death could not break in any way. This
intimacy bears within itself the kernel of the resurrection: *vita mutatur
non tollitur*. But in addition, the resurrection also has a corrective
aspect: it is not just the prolongation of Jesus' intimacy with God
beyond death but also the inauguration of the kingdom of God: the
exaltation and glorification of Jesus. 'I believe in Jesus: the Lord'. That
is, through God Jesus lives from henceforth among his own, in his
community. Therefore the resurrection, personally accomplished in
Jesus, is at the same time the gift of God's spirit for us. We cannot
separate one from the other because if we do we make Jesus'
resurrection disappear into areas that we cannot reach, about which
people cannot say anything meaningful. The reason why we can say
something meaningful about it is because of the eschatological gift of
the spirit, which is sent to us from God by the living Jesus. So the
kingdom of God combines two notions: life with God and the kingdom
of love and righteousness already beginning to become visible in our
history. Thus the resurrection cannot be interpreted meaningfully in
exclusive terms as the authentication by God of Jesus' message and of
its permanent value,. This is only one aspect of the resurrection.
Moreover, resurrection faith is essentially connected with belief in the
permanent and abiding significance of the person of Jesus in the coming
of the kingdom of God. God does not simply approve visions and ideals.
He is a God of human beings and therefore identifies himself with the
person of Jesus, just as Jesus identified himself with God: 'God is love'.

The creed lays all the stress on Jesus' death and resurrection and is
ultimately silent about his message and life-style. But we should not
forget that the creed is a kind of concentrated summary of Christian
faith: Jesus' death and resurrection are in fact a resumé of his message
and life-style. We only see why that is the case when we keep well in
mind this message and life-style of Jesus on the basis of the New
Testament. In their time the four Gospels were already a reaction
against tendencies to derive the whole of the Christian creed from the
death and resurrection of Jesus and to focus exclusively on them.
Anyone who does this runs the risk of themselves coming under the

criticism of the message of Jesus with its concern for human beings. Political dictatorships, led by so-called Christians, who on Sunday celebrate the death and resurrection of Jesus, should be unthinkable if these authorities were aware of the fact that the death and resurrection of Jesus find their foundation in the message and the life-style of Jesus, in his praxis of the kingdom of God as the kingdom of a God concerned for mankind. Otherwise 'orthodoxy' becomes a flouting of the gospel and of Christianity.

There is another element in the article of faith about Jesus' death and resurrection: 'He descended into hell', which logically should really have been mentioned before the resurrection. However, I am only discussing it now and in so doing am of course following the historical growth of the creed. Only in the fourth century was the clause 'he descended into hell' inserted between 'suffered under Pontius Pilate, crucified, dead and buried', and 'the third day he rose from the dead'.

For the Old Testament, 'descending to hell' (= *sheol*, the underworld, not *gehenna*, or hell) is a realistic expression for real death: the dead person descended into the realm of the dead, which was located in the underworld. So to descend into hell simply means to be really dead. In polemics current in Christian antiquity the rumour constantly went the rounds that Jesus had not died on the cross but had survived crucifixion because of his robust health. This was thought to have been called 'resurrection' by Christians. Others told how, since Jesus was God, his humanity and thus also his death were only apparent (docetism); they wanted therefore to spare Jesus the utterly negative fate of death. It was also as a reaction against such notions that 'he descended into hell' was inserted into the creed. Jesus, in solidarity with us human beings, also really shared in the negative aspect of our death, in death itself. 'In all things like us...'(Heb.4.15). The consequence of this is that Jesus is 'no longer there'. Like all dead people he has empirically disappeared from our history for good. The time of his visible presence among us has gone by for ever. We may not trivialize this aspect of the absence of Jesus. Christians are therefore defenceless against all those who say mockingly, 'Your Jesus is dead, just as all mortal men will be one day.' Precisely for this reason, for his faithful followers the death of Jesus meant the disappearance of their own hope: 'We had hoped' (Luke 24.13-35: the Emmaus story).

For a long time in the Old Testament being dead was also regarded as being excluded not only from all men but also from God and his salvation. Only in Sheol was God a stranger: death is death. In Jesus' day things were completely different. As a result of many experiences, Jewish spirituality had learned to understand that living community with God cannot be broken off even by death. God reaches down even into Sheol. 'Love is stronger than death.' There is therefore no basis whatsoever in the New Testament for connecting the descent into hell with being rejected by God. However, this does not remove the fact that death, above all the death of an outcast executed by his fellow men, was a tragic event for Jesus. In the last resort, the Gospel of John interprets the painful situation correctly when it makes Jesus say, ' The hour is coming, indeed is already here, when you will be scattered on all sides and will leave me alone. Yet I am not alone because the Father is with me' (John 16.32). Real hell is to lose not only all one's fellow men but also God. That was not the case with Jesus, even though God remained silent. For Jesus this silence on the part of God was also a revelation of God.

There is yet more to be said. In the New Testament we find at least one text, I Peter 3.18-22 and 4.6, where although the death of Jesus, seen as the descent into hell, is not described as a triumphal progress (as it was thought to be by some of the church fathers), it is nevertheless seen as a last chance of salvation for all those who had died, thanks to Jesus' 'presence in the kingdom of the dead' (although the New Testament here respects the mystery and says nothing about the way in which the dead react to this last chance of salvation).[3] In any case, the 'descent into hell' in the Christian creed seeks to indicate that Jesus' death has a universal significance, for both the living and the dead. Jesus is the hope not only of living generations and generations to come, but even of those who have been written off by our history: for those who have already died, people who no longer have a future in our earthly régime, those who are completely excluded – even for people who have never known Jesus. Seen in the light of the resurrection, belief in the 'descent into hell' is the expression of the Christian belief (however primitive the way in which it is formulated) that in Jesus God gives a future even to those who no longer see a future. This is the extreme consequence of Jesus' message of the unconditional love of a God who is concerned for the future of all men: 'the kingdom of God'. This part of our faith also stresses God's predilection for the lowly and the outcast . Quite apart from the way in which it is expressed, the 'descent into hell' is not folklore or a myth which needs to be demythologized, but one of the most sensitive points in the whole of the Christian creed: God wills the salvation of all men.

Resurrection is therefore not only a foundation for the future but also reconciliation with the past. It applies not only to the future but also to the broken past. No earthly ideology imitates Christianity here. For God, no human being is disposable. (What our modern times call 'human rights' is a weak, albeit real, secular version of this Christian view.)

We can sum up belief in Jesus as the Christ, God's only Son, our Lord, as follows. The question of Christian identity is essentially concerned with the question of human integrity, soundness and wholeness. This belief therefore includes: 1. primarily a confession in faith of God's actions in connection with Jesus of Nazareth. God shows his solidarity with Jesus, the prophet of the kingdom of God, who was rejected and cast out by men because of his message. There is salvation in Jesus from God. God endorses in a definitive way not only the message and the life-style which goes with it, but also the very person of Jesus, in a definitive way. He is a God of human beings. That is what is meant by resurrection. 2. It also consists in a life-style consistent with this belief, a praxis which accords with the kingdom of God, especially, (a) in the sense that anyone who believes in Jesus Christ must dare, following Jesus, to stand up in an utterly unselfish way for the oppressed and humiliated, for his or her fellow men; (b) on the one hand knowing that, like Jesus, he or she also runs the risk of being oppressed and done away with by this world: 'the disciple is not better than the master'; (c) and on the other hand convinced in faith that he or she too, likewise following Jesus, is irrevocably accepted by God. 'For as we share in his suffering, so too we shall share in his glorification' (Rom.8.17b). This is the New Testament faith which, despite all worldly appearances and often despite the appearance of the church, 'overcomes the world' (I John 5.4).

To sum up: I am quite clear that to take the part of those in trouble means to follow God himself, God as he has shown his deepest sympathy with human beings in Jesus, ' He loved us when we were still in wretchedness'.

God's concern for man becomes the criterion, that is the standard and at the same time the boundless measure, of our concern for those who are oppressed and in need. This boundless sensitivity to human needs only develops to the full from an experience of God's gracious Yes to all men. God says to us, 'Yes, you may live, you may live', as an expression of his nature, 'God is love', which is expressed by theologians as 'justification by grace alone' – a scholarly term for God's love for mankind. Precisely this divine boundlessness is not so obvious to us human beings. It goes beyond what we usually call cohumanity. Of course it is obvious to all those who have themselves experienced God's mercy, in other words to all believers, to Christians; it is also the test of the authenticity of our prayer, of our liturgy and eucharist, which rightly lauds and praises Jesus as the Lord. But one of the Gospels also says that it is not enough to cry 'Lord, Lord'. The important thing is whether our life-style in fact shows that we believe in Jesus as the Lord.

According to Vondel and all kinds of apocrypha (non-biblical Christian writings from antiquity), even angels are jealous of God's predilection for mankind. In the last resort Jesus, too, whom we may name his only beloved Son, is a human being like you and me, except that he is more human.

18

He is the King of the Universe
(The Feast of 'Christ the King')

'He is the king of the universe. May all in heaven and earth acclaim your glory, and never cease to praise you' (Prayer for the Feast of Christ the King). In itself this is a very biblical notion! But in very specific social and historical circumstances, on 11 December 1925 in his encyclical *Quas Primas* Pope Pius IX gave an explanation of this new liturgical feast of Christ the King. Of course for centuries, especially on Easter Day, Christians had celebrated Jesus as the glorious Risen One, the Lord and King. However, the quite specific historical conditions in which the feast was inaugurated play a considerable role in the modern festival of 'Christ the King'. This is already evident from the encyclical, in which a political view is given of the threefold powers of authority: the legislative, the executive and the judicial power. The feast that people are to celebrate is not directly understandable on the basis of the gospel, whatever the biblical foundation for the title 'king' may be; it derives from a particular new political situation of the church, specifically within a society which could no longer be called 'Christendom' as before, and which had escaped from the grasp of the church's authority. Confronted with this situation of isolation, the church sought solace in a critical recollection of the gospel datum that Christ nevertheless rules over this world: he is and remains the king. That is not to be doubted; it is an authentic biblical datum. But the encyclical clearly wants to lay stress on the rights of Christ over society at a time when this society wants to live without Christ. Again, that is a very accurate diagnosis. The encyclical and the new festival unmistakably presented themselves as a criticism of society and above all as a criticism of authority in reaction to a very widespread conception that religion is a private matter. The question is, of course, how far this Christian reaction to the historical situation respects the deepest stimuli of the Christian gospel. Both the encyclical and the feast of Christ the King inspired by it were a form of political theology, albeit in the old style, with a barely concealed nostalgia for the old ideology: society as Christendom. Catholic Action, which arose at that time in the same climate, had the same perspective on the re-Christianizing of society. In this sense, in origin the feast of Christ the King undeniably emerged from a reactionary church movement, the opposite of what present-day political theology, with its Christian impulse towards an ethics of change, seeks to be. Furthermore, in this encyclical there is almost unconsciously an obvious but suspicious transition from confessing 'Christ the King' to the historically 'fortuitous' old idea of the authority of the church over the world which was thought to be have been wrongly weakened. (This authority was evidently indentified with the church's hierarchy.) In fact this encyclical also sought to re-establish the church's age-old position of power. It is a historical document from church history.

However, the liturgical instinct of this same church was more purely oriented on the gospel than was its ideology. First of all we must note that a sure instinct of faith put the feast of Christ the King on the last Sunday of the church's year, just before the new beginning with 'The Advent of the Lord'. Here Jesus' kingship functions as an eschatological, final, religious vision of the future. And there is more. In the liturgical festival, above all as it appears in the threefold order of service in the new missal, we find nothing of the background mentality which produced the Christ the King encyclical. So for Year A the kingship of Christ stands under the token of 'the Good Shepherd' (Ex.34.11-12,15-17). Year B puts Jesus the King in the context of the 'Danielic Son of Man' (Dan.7.13-14) and in the perspective of God as the alpha and the omega of all reality (Rev.1.5-8). Finally, only Year C puts the kingship of Jesus in the context of Jewish 'Davidic messiahship'(II Sam.5.1-3; Ps.122; Luke 23.35-43) – an idea which to some degree can give support to the ideology of 'Christ the King' but which historically, in terms of criticism of the Gospels, can only be based on a very narrow foundation.

This flexibility accepted in the liturgy indicates that from a biblical perspective it is possible for there to be different models through which Jesus can be confessed as Lord and King by Christians. This opens up the possibility of giving Jesus, experienced and confessed as decisive salvation, new names on the basis of new situations, detached from the old categories of king and even of sovereign power, above all if we remember that God's omnipotence showed itself in Jesus in the form of a love which took upon itself the helplessness of death on the cross. This seems to have little to do with the threefold power of the sovereignty of the realm. Therefore in its sincere homage to God in Jesus Christ, the feast inaugurated in 1925 becomes a criticism of any ideology of power, whether in the world or in the church. 'You know that the rulers of the nations rule with their iron fist and that the powerful misuse their power over them . This shall not be so with you' (Matt.20.25-28). The eucharistic thanksgiving of the feast of the kingship of Jesus speaks consistently of 'a kingdom of truth and life, holiness and grace, justice, love and peace'. 'Despite' the specific relationship to the historic present (in itself a Christian interest which is to be welcomed), the liturgical feast of Christ the King is inspired by the gospel remembrance of Jesus confessed as the Christ.

The basic meaning of the Hebrew root *mlk (melek,* king) remains uncertain; scholars hesitate between the concept of property – a king is someone who has 'possession' of his kingdom, land and people – and the concept of judge – someone who leads and judges the people, makes a distinction between good and evil and thus 'pronounces judgment' – in fact the kings of Israel succeed 'the judges' and the charismatic gifts of the latter are ascribed to them: these 'uphold Yahweh's justice' (II Kings 17.26; Jer.5.4; 8.7). Kings in Israel therefore had to be Jews who were 'men of the Spirit' (Hos.9.7; Isa.48.16; Ezek.2.2), 'led by God's spirit'; 'the Lord is with them' and they 'are with the Lord' (Judg.6.16; 3.10; 6.34; 11.29 etc.; I Sam.11.6; 16.13). 'Christ' or 'anointed king' thus came to mean ' God with us' and 'man with God'. The heart of the anointed is 'undivided with God' (I Kings 11.4), he walks 'before God in purity and uprightness of heart' (I Kings 9.4). Finally, 'Christ' or the anointed is the one filled with God's spirit (Zech.7.12; Neh.9.30). Although the connection which Micah 5.3 makes between 'king' and the 'good shepherd' is not borrowed from the Eastern concept of kingship as such (and is even alien to it), it is an extremely sensitive interpretation of the Yahwistic conception which pious Jews cherished in faith about 'Israel's king' which must be reflected in 'King YHWH'(the Lord), 'the kingdom of God'.

For Jesus himself the 'kingly rule of God' was the key word in his preaching. That is, God is a God who is concerned for humanity. For Jesus, God's kingly rule is his divinity. Our recognition of this brings about humanity, salvation and peace among men. The Letter to Titus rightly says: 'The goodness and loving-kindness of our God has appeared' (Titus 3.4). Jesus talks of God as salvation for man. His God is a God who is concerned for man. It is here at the same time that we have the power of the reality of God to criticize men and women, culture, church and society. God's rule manifests itself in peace and communication without any discrimination. That this kingdom is coming is manifest in Jesus' arrival: where he appears, the sick are cured, the demons yield, and communication is achieved. Jesus did not give any definition of the kingly rule of God: in his 'praxis of the kingdom of God', the coming of the kingdom of God is visible for those who believe (Luke 11.20; 17.20-21). For those who believe! For people must take the initiative if they are to enter the kingdom of God (Matt.19.23; Mark 10.15; Matt.10.29-30). Jesus' whole life was a celebration of this kingdom of God, and at the same time orthopraxis, that is, praxis in accordance with it. The message of the approaching kingly rule of God of which Jesus' life is itself an eloquent parable therefore essentially means salvation in Jesus from God, manifest in a new human life-style pioneered by Jesus himself. The lowly humanity in which Jesus lived out his being-from-the-Father in his existence for others, his fellow human beings, does not really conceal his kingship but manifests it to the eyes of faith.

The link with a Deuteronomistic tradition which has found a place in the book of Exodus has been of essential significance for the ultimate Christian identification of the 'kingdom of God' with 'Jesus Christ', albeit under the pressure of the historical force of what Jesus of Nazareth really was. 'Behold, I send my messenger before you, to guard you on the way and to bring you to the place which I have prepared. Give heed to him and hearken to his voice, do not rebel against him, for he will not pardon your transgression; for my name is present in him. But if you hearken attentively to his word and do all that I say, then I will be an enemy to your enemies and an adversary to your adversaries. My messenger will go before you' (Ex.23.20-23). As eschatological messenger from God, Jesus is called 'Lord' and 'King' in God's own name: in a prophetic association of identification, Jesus is called Lord and king. In the synoptic gospels it is said (along the lines of this old messenger tradition), 'Anyone who confesses me before men, him also shall I confess as mine before my Father in heaven' (Matt.10.32-33; Luke 12.8-9; see John 12.48). Therefore: 'Blessed is he who takes no offence at me' (Matt.11.6; Luke 7.23). Here the prophetic identification of Jesus with God's concern – the salvation of humanity – is clear. Attitudes towards this 'messenger from God' have an eschatological relevance: they are a definitive decision for or against God. 'Therefore God has highly exalted him and given him the name which is above every name, that at the name of Jesus every knee shall bow in heaven and on earth and among the spirits, and every tongue confess that Jesus Christ is the Lord to the glory of God the Father' (Phil.2.9-11). In the biblical stories about the fascination of this Christ the King it becomes clear that his career does not take the course of human or political success but that of misfortune. Historically, messianism is alien to the nature of Christianity. The Risen One continues to bear the stigmata of the cross. The one who is rejected but vindicated by God is Messiah or Christ.

The confession 'Jesus is King' or 'Lord' puts into words his significance for others. Here we also confess that we may experience definitive and decisive salvation 'from God' in Jesus.

This belief in Jesus as the Christ founds the church. Jesus himself is 'the foundation' of this community (I Cor.3.11). The church is erected on this foundation as 'God's building' (I Cor.3.9); that is, the churches are always in scaffolding. To be church is therefore an event: believers are at the same time those who are sent; the church is mission. Christ is king where God's will is done in listening to Jesus' word and acting accordingly. At that moment we are brothers of Jesus (see Luke 8.21). Furthermore, the church community, in its ministry and its members, is governed by the norm and the criterion of the kingdom of God as it takes concrete form in Christ. It is not the kingdom of God, but serves it and mediates it in the world and its history, through which the kingdom of God in Christ is communicated in a particular way. The course of the church, following Jesus, is not a course of success and triumph, but one of failure, transcended by the saving omnipotence of God who has 'exalted' and given power to the Jesus who historically was a failure. The church must therefore be the sphere where, following Jesus, the praxis of the kingdom of God becomes visible, so that it is clear to everyone through this praxis that despite everything there is ground for hope: 'so that you do not mourn like others who have no hope' (I Thess.4.13). The message which Christians present must therefore become eloquent praxis within the community; this may be called good news precisely because it brings about communication — that is, in so far as it is specific. Being the church is ministering to the hope for the world: we confess this when we pray on the feast of Christ the King in the words of Matt.25.31-46: 'I tell you solemnly, in so far as you did this for one of the least of these brothers of mine, you did it for me.' For the church it must therefore be the case that, 'There are set the thrones of judgment' (Ps.122; year C). The liturgical feast of Christ the King therefore prompts us to critical self-examination, to reorientation or (to put it in the 'old' words, which are critical and practical) *metanoia*. It is not just a matter of confessing in words that Jesus is King, but living it out in the concrete sphere of our historical humanity. Where love reigns and the lowly receive their rights, Christ the King begins to rule; there the kingdom of God approaches and salvation is realized for human beings.

Indeed 'He makes the world a new creation' (Preface for Christ the King). Rather than being a reactionary celebration which provides legitimation and confirmation, 'Christ the King' is thus a feast of change and renewal in the world and the church. In a non-monarchical society like ours, 'Christ the King' thus becomes the symbol of unrest in an established order, the symbol of justice and peace for those who experience injustice and have no peace, with the prospect that he 'will wipe away all tears from their eyes, for the former things are past' (Rev.21.1-5). The feast of Christ the King therefore serves to criticize society and the church in a way in which the original Sitz im Leben of this feast was not directly aware. It is not the church but 'Jesus the King' who is the Lord of history.

19

Liberation from Panic
(Easter Faith)

Naive success and confidence can have their disturbing side, and fiascos are not without hope. The first disciples of Jesus had to learn this the painful way, after a lot of disillusionment. It cost them a good deal to believe in what we now call, perhaps too nonchalantly, the Christ of the church. In a 'first naivety' they had innocently put their trust in Jesus of Nazareth, who had spoken to them about the completely new element that would change their world. But as a result of Jesus' ignominious arrest and death, disillusionment overtook them. 'We had hoped' (Luke 24.21). They had to wrestle with panic, doubt and suspicion before they arrived at a 'second innocence' and a tried faith, a faith in which they experienced that Jesus can indeed be trusted: though in a different way from before, he still remained really present in their midst. His life with them was not a deception, nor had he himself lived with an illusion.

They experienced this second innocence as the fruit of a divine grace which liberated them from the panic caused by a lack of faith, as conversion, and *thus* as the actual work of the risen Jesus. Jesus brought them back to one another from their panic-stricken dispersal; his resurrection gathered them together for new life, 'the community of Christ', a clumsy but sincere beginning to a society of peace.

The Easter experience, the resurrection of Jesus to the Father, the formation of a new community of liberated men brought together by Jesus from their dispersal, is a great saving event which has two facets. In it both the truth about Jesus and the truth about these first Christians breaks through with a divine certainty which penetrates the consciousness of the newly assembled disciples. Therefore it is right for people to speak of the church's Christ, that is, Jesus of Nazareth, who, through his resurrection, forms for himself a community in our history and brings people together.

However paradoxical it may be, this Christian Easter faith, which has perhaps become problematical for many people, is a message which is written on the heart of our time.

Christianity seems to be suffering from panic and the phenomenon of weariness. It also bears the marks of almost two thousand years of history!

Furthermore, whereas it once had a monopoly in Western culture, it is now confronted with many rival world-views which similarly present perspectives, prospects of new life, and which even have scientific credentials. The 'first naivety' has disappeared from our culture, a culture in which Western Christians also live. Christians experience painfully how many of their friends and acquaintances are bidding farewell to the Christianity which they have shared in joy, and also supported and championed in suffering. If they themselves remain within the church they are often disillusioned by everything that goes on in it, burdened as it is with the remnants of a long and turbulent history, furrowed by suffering borne and undergone: a church which itself sometimes reacts in a panic-stricken and faithless way to its own growing isolation.

And there is more. Since the eighteenth and nineteenth centuries the West has lived in a suspicious culture which is mistrustful of everything that is called religion, in our case specifically Christianity. This suspicion becomes part of our historical society, and also backfires on the hearts of believers, as a result conjuring up a degree of inner doubt. Of course a look at the history of the church and of Christians shows us that in human hands any religion can also become extremely dangerous: hampering and noxious to the individual, and stultifying and restrictive for society. As a result of this modern suspicion, many people now relegate what for the first Christians became a 'second innocence', tested by doubt and disillusionment, namely their Easter faith, to the primitive sphere of uncritical superstition.

In the meantime, it had seemed that believers could breathe again. They noted with relief that after the experience of disenchantment with an enthusiastic belief in progress and too facile a belief that things hardened by history could be changed, modern man was beginning to experience limitations to his knowledge and achievements, so that many people again began to look beyond these boundaries. In all kinds of ways, and in a great proliferation, a religious revival began. The radical theory of secularization was obviously contradicted, and many believers welcomed the new phenomenon with enlightened satisfaction. But quite apart from the fact that these revivalist movements are above all to be found outside the walls of the traditional churches, and it has been virtually impossible to light the flame within them, in the meantime on the basis of their critical attitude many people inside and outside Christianity have already indicated the many ambivalent elements in this religious revival. In fact we cannot avoid doing so: for a Westerner at least, a return to the 'first innocence' is quite impossible and indeed unjustified. Only through criticism of a really suspicious culture and thus through the pain of renewed reflection is it possible to arrive at a 'second innocence' in which perhaps a new attachment to the Christian Easter experience can grow.

In our time Christians are rightly looking for a living connection between belief in God and human experience. Christian belief is indeed empty, powerless and irrelevant if it has no relationship to our experience as human beings. But however much we must therefore criticize historical conceptions of Christian belief as alien to our new experiences (though in their day these conceptions did relate to real earlier experiences), we must also consider whether we ourselves have not been alienated from real human truth, entangled and impoverished by the one-sided Western view of what 'experience' is possible within this society. In that case it may perhaps appear that our society is so impoverished and our sphere of experience so narrow that it is no longer possible to have any innocent experience of what is announced in the Christian proclamation. The Christian Easter experience could then perhaps contain a criticism of the anaemia afflicting the possibilities of real experience which have survived in our culture. The phenomena of paralysis could be those of Western men and their culture, in which Christians, too, allow themselves to be uncritically immersed, so that they can no longer understand their own belief, much less experience it.

At present we seem to be living in a time in which we have had to lay aside our first innocence but are still in the tunnel of the crucial 'critical' period, without any prospect of a true 'second innocence'. We live, as once did the first disciples, in the period between Good Friday, the day on which the ideal of the revered prophet was shattered, and the time when their eyes were opened in a new innocence, the Christian Easter experience. We live in the intermediate period of panic and disillusionment, of doubt and suspicion.

Again, this is not as bad as all that: God is after all concerned for our truth, and in that case he is never served by lies. But... in addition he wants *his* truth to dawn on us.

The urgent question before us is therefore, 'Are we on the road to Emmaus?' In other words, are we experiencing an increasing apathy and indifference because what we are doing now is not the road to Emmaus? Does some warmth burn in our hearts despite doubt, suspicion and inability (see Luke 24.52)? Is that just because we are 'going together', are together on the way to Emmaus? In this case there is a second innocence in the offing, an innocence through which on our 'journey together', in a real experience of solidarity with all men ('He judged the cause of the poor and needy. Is not this to know me, says the Lord?', Jer.22.16), we experience suddenly or in gradual growth (despite the whispered 'we had hoped' that we sometimes hear), that where two or three are gathered together in his name in fact he is also in our midst. For that is the Easter experience, something like a source experience, or the overwhelming discovery of a new dimension, so convincing - even emotionally – that the first Christians could only express it with the cry, 'We have seen him! He showed himself to us!'

Given the nature of people in this ancient culture, it seems to me unnecessary to deny any visual element *per se* in this experience of the first disciples. Their whole hearts were filled; the effect this would have had on such people seems to me to be obvious. But we are not concerned with the secondary phenomena; these are at most an emotive sign of what was really an overwhelming experience. And this experience is our concern: the experience of these disciples in sure faith, coming from God, that when they gathered together again they found renewed community, a new common life as the 'community of God', the personal presence of the living Jesus. There seems to be something of this kind which as experience is faith and as faith is experience – that is, for those who are not just rationalists.

To put it in a metaphorical way: this re-forming of the Jesus Movement into the Christ Movement is as it were a spark on earth from the fiery event of Jesus' being clothed with the Holy Spirit through and with the Father. Only this historical spark (their reunion) made the disciples realize what had really happened to Jesus: Jesus comes into their midst, in person, as the living one. This overwhelming experience was so convincing that in less than five years the 'community of Christ' was already widespread in the Near East: the basic outlines of a world religion became clear after these few years and were above all put into practice, albeit often in broken human form. Human daydreams can do a great deal, but they cannot explain the creation of so attractive a hoax in so short a time. From a historical point of view this is unparalleled. No critical person can explain it away.

Of course no secular argument can ever prove the validity of Christian belief. Without a profoundly human experience of communication such as that which the disciples had, it is impossible to start. But the very secularity of the argument prompts us to a critical second reflection, as a possible way of finding conversion to a 'second innocence'. Perhaps this will be a well-tried guilelessness on the part of many people who in new self-surrender (having undergone the effects of painful criticism), purified and liberated from panic which is disruptive and always divisive, are reunited and establish human community in the awareness that the spirit of Jesus is at work in it.

Such a mysterious force does not emanate from a *dead man* who was once a prophet of freedom and liberation; and although this might once have been the case, it will have been so only for a short while. In the long run these recollections fade, and in following generations they melt into the distance where colours blur – until finally they are only a subject for the investigation of some learned historians. Human memory is short-lived, infinitely shorter than God's recollection which, in 'recollection' of Jesus, recalls all others who were murdered for the sake of the truth – the whole of mankind, above all those who suffered innocently.

The question therefore is: must not something have happened to Jesus, something quite special, so that precisely for that reason something important can also happen to us? Just as it happened to his first disciples who have handed down the account of their conversion in the Gospels? A new form of existence, which precisely in its very newness fulfils the promises which were to be found in their concrete humanity? Jesus asked for *metanoia,* conversion, i.e. turning round. In that case it should be possible to enter into the kingdom of God with a critically tested new innocence, like children (Mark 1.15; Matt. 18.3; 19.14). Belief in the resurrection, only possible in a 'second innocence', is therefore not just belief in the risen Jesus but because of the second reflection – necessary in our culture for a critical adult innocence – at the same time belief in the *possibility* of religious belief, even within a culture of despair and suspicion.

Those who believe in Jesus' experience, the Easter experience, and have come up against modern criticism, therefore talk not only about the risen Jesus but at the same time about our truth, our humanity, our life. Human beings are not just critically, grimly and helplessly projects for the future. Belief in the resurrection gives a basis for our plans for a better world which stands under a positive promise; that is, if people do not just 'project' but also know how to listen to what makes their plans possible and gives them a basis. In that case the Easter experience is still always accessible to us today through truly human experience which has been broadened by criticism.

From what I have just said it is evident that testimony to the resurrection of Jesus can only be given in a story of our own religious experience: 'What we have seen with our own eyes ..., of that we bear witness', the First Letter of John (1.4) says enthusiastically. The author did not know the historical Jesus, nor (as we usually understand the case) had he had 'resurrection appearances'. Nevertheless, these Christians had had experience of the Risen One: 'Anyone who does not love his brother whom he has seen,' the letter says later on, 'cannot love God whom he has not seen' (I John 4.20). These Christians remembered Jeremiah's remark about God: 'He supported the poor and the needy; that is what I call knowing me.' Therefore he also taught them how to see Jesus. For Christian believers, seeing and hearing evidently have a deeper significance than Western, stunted experiences seem to believe to be possible – that is the reason why we often no longer understand the biblical 'seeing Jesus'.

Becoming a Christian (who *is* a Christian?) means having one's own life story inscribed in the family story of the Christian community so that as a result one's own life story takes on a new, 'converted', orientation and at the same time continues the thread of the Christian story in its own way.In so far as it is truly Christian, action of this kind makes our own life part of a living gospel, a 'fifth' gospel. In the story of the Christian community Christians themselves can therefore find a place to belong. So the Christian is not deprived of critical remembrances; he or she can find their own place in the present and do not remain without hope of expectation for the future - above all. And on the basis of this hope, a Christian's solidarity, his commitment to man and society, becomes understandable and obvious. A 'second innocence' is never naive. That is modern, critical Easter faith.

20

I Believe in the Resurrection of the Body

Round about the year 1700 a murderer was condemned to be broken on the wheel in the most excruciating way possible. He was then offered a pardon on condition that he joined in a celebration of the Witches' Sabbath on Walpurgisnacht. The condemned man rejected the offered pardon out of hand: better to be broken on the wheel than to be deprived of eternal life hereafter in the form of bodily resurrection (see E.Bloch, *Atheismus im Christentum,* Frankfurt 1968, pp.338f.).

The power of this belief, if not the belief itself, once the soul of our entire culture, is now visibly fading, even among Christians. The better world hereafter – belief which made the humanly impossible still possible and the most grievous absurdity tolerable – is giving place to the vision of a better 'earthly' future in our history, a belief through which millions come to oppose meaninglessness and injustice, and show practical commitment to a world on earth more fit for men and women to live in, and in which a good life must be possible for all.

As a reaction to one-sided belief in the hereafter, which wipes away all the tears of those below but does not trouble to try to remove what caused these tears on earth, the present-day Christian can and may go a long way with those who live on the basis of these new earthly utopias and dream of a better world. While they are alive, men and women cannot do enough to remove all forms of premature, violent and inhuman dying, because those who are dying are helpless to offer any resistance.

Statistics show that in many modern countries, only about forty per cent of people still believe in an eternal life and moreover that this belief has no actual force or real significance for the daily life or social actions of many of this forty per cent: it is simply part and parcel of their cultural views, just as they know that the earth is shaped like a sphere or a lemon, without this having any more influence on the way in which they live. Of course, statistics do not decide what is true. But they do make us aware that there are universal social and cultural factors which make things much more difficult, if not impossible for many people still to believe in a physical resurrection. Usually it is not a question of vigorous radicalism, much less of ill will; for many people in fact it is an existential matter which could not be otherwise. Consequently insisting on the belief in an even more authoritarian way, as a reaction, does not resolve the difficulty; moreover it is improper, if we remember that in essence belief is, and needs to be, a freely accepted, deep conviction of life. It is therefore important to recognize the factors which seem to make this belief in the resurrection superfluous for many people. But although belief is in fact free surrender to the transcendent which appears gently and almost hesitantly in our life, and therefore cannot ever be rationalized completely, on the other hand we do not believe in the hocus pocus of a body conjured up alive from the grave. Such a notion has nothing to do with religion. To understand to some degree what Christians mean when they confess, 'I believe in the resurrection of the body', and only later add, 'and in eternal life', is therefore a necessary condition of proclaiming faith in a way which people can believe, make sense of and live out, above all in our time. For the Jews who became Christians, belief in the resurrection of Jesus had some preparation in Jewish expectations; at all events, at least in Jesus' day, the conviction of a general resurrection of all men was part of the world view which most people took for granted and which belonged to their culture. For the pagan Greeks things were completely different: they did not have this human expectation. Indeed, it was completely alien and undesirable to them. Only if they could believe in the resurrection at least of Jesus of Nazareth could they finally also have meaningful hope for their own physical resurrection. (In the Bible the writings of Luke, in particular, bear witness to this veneer of Jewish Christianity on the Gentile-Christian view.) We modern men and women are in the same situation as these Gentiles: the general resurrection and indeed even the Greek idea of the immortality of the soul is no longer part of the general world view that we take for granted; it is actually alien to it. And, I think, rightly so. Therefore only the life and death of Jesus of Nazareth can show us the way to make belief in eternal life, in the form of physical resurrection, possible and even meaningful for men and women. Perhaps despite all the difficulties presented to our way of thinking, we are even in a better position to understand the uniqueness of the Christian message, as distinct from an idea of resurrection which is part of a particular, albeit religious, view of the world. In the last resort Christianity, as belief in a very specific historical person, Jesus of Nazareth, is not a world view. It is a matter of coming under the spell, in faith, of a person in whom the appearance of transcendence, gentle and hesitant, and therefore always capable of misunderstanding, can and may be experienced as gracious towards all men.

Sisters and brothers, I want to confess that I have seldom found any sermon as difficult to write as this one, about the resurrection of the body. Not because I myself have doubts about it: for me it is an evidence of Christian faith, without which any expression of the heart of Christianity would be utopian - albeit in an important way. But I feel almost painfully helpless in trying to communicate this evidence of faith in any sense, trying to make it understandable as the incomprehensible, unmerited, free consequence of God's utter trustworthiness. It is risky for us human beings to talk in this way about the consequence of divine trustworthiness. If we do, we are acting as though we can know what may be a consequence for God. Of ourselves we cannot in fact say anything meaningful, and perhaps we shall talk a lot of nonsense. Human logic is by no means divine logic; as Isaiah says of God, 'My ways are not your ways.' Furthermore, belief in the resurrection is not a matter of human egoism or human rights; it is not even as if in the last resort we could not think meaningfully about our human existence without belief in the resurrection. Evidently many people can do precisely this, and why should our thought be more logical and more consistent than theirs? So something completely different is at stake in belief in the resurrection: belief in God. Paul connects God's demand and desire to be all in all with our resurrection (I Cor.15.28). Thus the resurrection is first of all a question of God, of God who takes his identity seriously. Only in this way, and not otherwise, is the resurrection also a question of the identity of our humanity and its ultimate meaning – although of course we see it first of all from our side. In that case it may appear that God's true identity can only be recognized in and through our identification of the man Jesus of Nazareth as the Christ. Although they are not identical, the grace of Christian identity and our human integrity which has been attained or is still to be attained, come very close to each other.

If we are in search of factors which make belief in the resurrection difficult in our time, then we can see clearly that our modern society has argued death away and manipulated it away from public awareness. Modern man is almost compelled by the very nature of our society to differ from his forebears in thinking about death. We no longer think about death metaphysically but functionally; it becomes an object which can be handled by psychology and sociology, by medical care and welfare provisions, and finally by funeral customs and burial. And it is good that this should be the case. This demythologizing or secularizing of death has made room for a critical analysis of the biological, psychological and socio-political crisis-points which are the cause of premature, painful, inhuman and violent death. Many people are involved in changing and improving things. For modern man, thinking about death no longer raises directly, and almost compulsively, the question of what happens to the dead, as it used to, but rather makes people ask how we should treat those who survive, and how we can rid death of its painful aspects.

But at this point the question arises whether the gain represented by this functional thinking is not in fact accompanied by a loss in the question of meaning.

At all events, Christian belief in the resurrection gives us something to think about: this is a resurrection of *dead* people. Death is presupposed by belief in the resurrection. This may seem a trivial observation, but it has far-reaching implications. Belief in the resurrection does not argue away the fact of death; it allows death to be death, a radical and definitive ending to the particular historical existence of a human being, for good. The dead never return to our history; that is and remains definitively past time. In that case we must consider the following: the one universal democratic fact *par excellence* is that we all die, the rich as well as the poor, the pope as well as the emperor, the married and the single, the skilled and the ignorant, the good and the evil. All are ultimately compelled to lay down the official garb of their social or anti-social role. In a way which is hardly out of date and represented a scarcely veiled criticism of society, the pope and the emperor, with a degree of black humour, though in all seriousness, the bas-reliefs in mediaeval cathedrals have portrayed in their *dances macabres* the way in which death has the democratic effect of making all men equal. This was the only social criticism available at that time. In the face of death we are all helpless; it removes us completely and inexorably from our own selves and from the bonds of love and friendship we had with those who are left behind. No one escapes it. Precisely because that is the case, people invent all kinds of jokes or humorous figures, using skeletons or death with his sickle.This gallows humour is an attempt to relieve the tension caused by the unassimilated fact of the radically democratizing tendency of death. This week, I read with approval in a newspaper, 'Anyone who has been in a group under great pressure knows that it produces a biting kind of humour, black humour'. Caricatures of various types show that the whole of mankind feels the pressure of death. People are well aware of this inexorable levelling effect of death, but do not understand it. The death of a beloved child who dies from leukemia is not the same thing as the peaceful passing away of a wife or husband after a full and rich life, 'old and full of days'. The hangman's death is not the same as the deaths of those who were gassed, for example, at Auschwitz, or the millions of refugees who were killed in Asia and elsewhere. Were that the case, cynicism would be the heart of reality; the levelling effect of death would mean that its guillotine made everyone's head equally grey. Were that so, we would indeed live in an ultimately cynical world. However, the difficulty is that while the brute fact of inescapable death can be assuaged and to some degree humanized, the drear fact that it comes to all equally cannot be removed, not even by crying or cursing. Resisting it can only be a Sisyphus-like attempt which ultimately proves to be a farce. The mediaeval criticism of society and history is an extremely radical one: no one escapes it.

I think that the death of one of us, the historical Jesus of Nazareth, can offer us a perspective on this particular dilemma; light comes, however, not from Jesus himself but from the one whom he called 'God and Father'.

There was something special about the death of this man who nevertheless died a death like so many others: a violent, inhuman death, the execution of an innocent person. Of course, here too we can mention Jesus' resurrection too soon, so that it becomes a kind of *deus ex machina*. But anyone who looks more closely can see that here there is no desperate expedient, no solution at all, but a deep belief in God. It only makes sense to speak about Jesus of Nazareth in the language of faith, that is, in christological terms, especially as the one who though dead is yet risen, if we first listen to the content of his life, to what he proclaimed about God in word and deed. Had people known before Jesus' death that he was the Son of God, then his death would not have been a problem and the resurrection would have been the solution to it. But on the contrary, death and resurrection were the only ground on which belief in Jesus as the Son of God could flourish, not elsewhere. Only on the basis of belief in 'the God of Jesus' can we say anything in christological terms about the 'Jesus of God'.

This man spoke almost exclusively about the coming kingdom of God in terms of an approaching, indeed imminent rule of a God who was concerned for men. His actions, life and words were a parable of God; that is, in the life of Jesus it became manifest that his God was a God who is concerned for human beings. In his concern for men and women, above all for those who were outcasts from the rest of human society, Jesus wanted to illustrate the rule of a God concerned for mankind as in a large-scale parable. Here he proclaimed not himself, but God's concern: the trustworthiness of God whom he called his father (in Aramaic even *Abba,* a term of tender familiarity), and who was coming to bring people salvation.

But when this great parable of God, Jesus, was crucified, alongside and with two resistance fighters, he did not receive any kind of favoured help or treatment from the God in whom he trusted so much. The God whom he proclaimed, the rule of God concerned for humankind, did not lift a finger to help him – or the two so-called thieves. God does not intervene on behalf of those who trust in him, just as he did not intervene even in Dachau or Auschwitz. Jesus' death therefore seemed to go against the whole of his life and the proclamation of God's utter trustworthiness, to declare it invalid and prove it wrong. One of the few historically certain facts about Jesus' death is that when he hung on the cross he *cried out* – though we cannot reconstruct with any certainty the content of this historical cry. In any event the death of Jesus was not the self-assured, heroic, humanistic death of Socrates, of whom Plato says in his *Phaedo* that the bystanders did not know whether they were to laugh or weep.

As a result of the life which preceded it, the death of Jesus of Nazareth confronts us with a very fundamental question about God and only two alternatives. Either we must say that God, that is, the God of the kingdom of God proclaimed by Jesus, was an illusion on the part of Jesus which disillusioned his followers; or, this death compels us to revise radically our understanding of God, our own conceptions of God and give them up as invalid, discovering the real nature of God only in the life and death of this Jesus. In that case only the God of the kingdom of God as proclaimed by Jesus is the revelation of the true nature of God. In other words, the God of whose complete trustworthiness Jesus spoke is either a tragic farce or we have to acknowledge the God of Jesus as he revealed himself in Jesus, silent until his death and so apparently contradicting Jesus' own message. Nevertheless to believe in this God is not just a confession of God but at the same time also a confession of Christ.

It is striking that only when Jesus was removed from human sight by his death were the eyes of his followers opened and faith in Jesus became equally faith in God. At all events the New Testament bears witness to this. Through his death the cause which Jesus proclaimed and which was his life's concern – the rule of a God concerned for humanity – became one with the person of Jesus himself. His life and his death show that God's faithfulness cannot be calculated on the basis of human experiences, not even those of Jesus. This God retains his freedom, even over against the man Jesus and his expectations about the specific form and manner of the coming of the kingdom of God.

Jesus' death compels us to raise the question of God precisely because of the life which preceded it. On the cross, revelation, reconciliation and faith come together, unless with Jesus we also reject his God.

This only brings us to the significance of the physical resurrection of Jesus. For without this resurrection Jesus of Nazareth is one of the many utopias in which mankind abounds and which in fact can supply the strength by which we can take hold of life despite everything, and work for others with more commitment and more courage – at least as long as this commitment is not overwhelmed by actual death. The fact of death then makes what is definitively good a utopia. It is different with the resurrection, which is something radically other than the projection of a utopian daydream. First of all, Jesus' resurrection is not a return to life as in the story of Lazarus. Nor is it simply to be identified with the origin of Christian belief; it is certainly not a miracle of intervention in natural laws to raise a corpse to heavenly life. Of course the creed does not say, 'I believe in the resurrection of a dead body or a corpse' but, 'I believe in the resurrection of the body, eternal life.' In that case, what is the resurrection? Scripture says: 'God raised up Jesus.' God did it and his action was specifically concerned with Jesus and not, for example, with the two others who were crucified with him: on that day there were eventually three dead bodies on Golgotha. Despite the way in which death makes all men equal, God, at least, does not look on the death of everyone in the same way, but sees it in the light of the life preceding that death. If he is not a God who is concerned for mankind, the death of each person indeed has the last word and that fate cynically awaits everyone without exception. If he is a living God, then God's divinity in supreme freedom is the last word over each and every human history. This does not imply that resurrection necessarily follows of itself. But it shows how resurrection must be understood as a free gift of God.

According to scripture, the resurrection is an event which is indissolubly bound up with this Jesus, whose death was an apparent farce, seen as the historical end-result of his life of trust in God. This trust does not seem to have been justified. But belief in the resurrection of Jesus then says that while the whole of Jesus' life may seem a fiasco, it nevertheless bears God's seal of approval. The reason why in the view of scripture this is no *deus ex machina* is that God does not just become faithful to himself, to this Jesus and to all creation after Jesus' death; he already *was* faithful, albeit tacitly, in Jesus' life and death. Through the resurrection God simply confirms his trust and trustworthiness in which Jesus continued to believe - even when perhaps he could not understand how this could be possible when his mission was broken off prematurely by the cross and he uttered a loud cry. The resurrection is the divine confirmation of the validity and the rightness of Jesus' life and message. The resurrection confirms that God always was with Jesus right through his life, even in the desolation of his crucifixion. The resurrection is not a comforting rescue afterwards. It is the free consequence of God's trust. Moreover, if it were only a matter of Jesus' own relationship with God, this resurrection could in the last resort remain secret, a confidential event between the God of Jesus and the Jesus of this God. But we may not forget that Jesus was concerned with the God of the kingdom of God, with the rule of God who is concerned for humanity, which he proclaimed and which he had promised to his followers. Therefore the resurrection of Jesus is at the same time the confirmation of God's commitment to and endorsement of those who believe this Jesus and are willing to follow him. 'He is the firstfruits of the resurrection', says scripture. Here is the promise of our resurrection for those who, like Jesus, put their trust in this God, despite his silence in our history. People talk about the *word* of God as revelation, but through Jesus I am taught that God has revealed himself through *silence*! To believe in a universal resurrection is possible now only for those who have faith in Jesus' resurrection as belief in the free consequence of the trustworthiness of his God: I cannot see any other possibility. Therefore belief in the resurrection does not really add anything new to unconditional faith in the God of Jesus of Nazareth. But this implies the insight of faith, namely that the kingdom of God cannot be realized from below, through us human beings, even through Jesus before his death. The kingdom of God is God's identification even with the dead Jesus; it begins with the resurrection of Jesus and God's promise in that to us all. Resurrection says that reality is ultimately well-disposed towards us and that precisely because of that it is possible and meaningful to make our world a better home in which good will come to all. In that case our improvement of the world does not become grim and brusque, but takes the form of grateful trust in the God of the resurrection, the God 'who calls into being that which does not exist'(Rom.4.7).

Thus belief in the physical resurrection is openness to an *event,* an event which is not identical with dying itself, but is rather the free event of God's own divinity which overcomes even death. This happened to Jesus as a promise for us (II Cor.4.15). The physical resurrection is the eternally new event of God himself who identifies himself with the dead Jesus. I might put it like this: the death of Jesus concerns us all because he was personally concerned with God. Thus the person who believes in God is reconciled by Jesus' death with death, with life, and with history, because he is reconciled with a God who himself suffers in Jesus' death and nevertheless will not intervene in history. Given this incomprehensible fact, there are only two meaningful alternatives. Either one cannot believe in such a God and in Jesus' message, or one surrenders oneself in faith to this God of Jesus and this Jesus of God. That is belief in the resurrection of Jesus. We human beings who cannot believe in a God who intervenes are at the same time the first to blame him for not intervening when thousands or millions are tortured to death. In fact we cannot justify God's action. But in identifying God with this dead Jesus, in the traces of human sinfulness which can be perceived in God himself, we may know ourselves to be reconciled with our history in incomprehending surrender, which does not paralyse but rather stimulates commitment to a better world. In rational terms, this incomprehending surrender at least has the advantage that, objectively, any other solution takes a cynical and merciless view of man and his history precisely because there is so much cynicism and mercilessness in our history and we can see no historical reason why we human beings should ever be able to change it radically.

Understanding and trusting God on the basis of Jesus' life and death, that is, looking through Jesus to God, means coming to terms with our own incompleteness, with the character of our existence which is not justified and not reconciled. A Christian who believes in the resurrection is therefore freed from the pressure to justify himself and from the demand that God should publicly take under his protection and ratify all those who believe in him. He is a God who makes the rain fall and the sun shine on good and evil alike. Like Jesus, the Christian dares to entrust himself and the justification for his life to God; he is prepared to receive this justification only where Jesus did: beyond death. Therefore because he is reconciled with the way of God's action, he is also reconciled with himself, with others and with history; he can forego utopias, violence and cruelty and devote himself completely to improving this world as far as is possible, and making it a juster and happier world for everyone, for a happy and peaceful world is in fact God's deepest intention which he confirms for eternity in the resurrection. Thus the Christian, believing in the resurrection, lives unprotected and unguarded, defenceless and vulnerable, like Jesus on the cross between two others (who make the fact that Jesus, too, hung on the cross historically ambiguous), between two condemned men, apparently without being any different from them – except that he was dead to self-righteousness, to false securities, even to human conceptions of how in particular the one God whom he continues to trust shows his trustworthiness. He, I imagine, did not know how this would come about any more than we do.

Resurrection is not the action of a Superman who suddenly comes down from the clouds as in the TV series, to raise Jesus from the tomb, to the dumb amazement of the many people standing before an empty grave. Even in the scriptures, perhaps in self-defence, some of the first Christians already allowed themselves to be led astray in the direction of such imagery in scripture; Paul seems to be combatting this when he speaks of a brand new body which comes from heaven. However, Jesus' corporeality is not something like an alien, borrowed garment, but is the authentic corporeal, unbroken expression of what Jesus personally is. In the wider context of salvation in which resurrection is set, the question 'What really happened when Jesus rose?' is almost misplaced, as misplaced as the question of just how in particular the creation of everything from nothing in fact 'took place', or the world will end. As a believer, I just do not know. We can only talk about it in parables and visions – dialectically, like Paul. It is true corporeality, he says, but not earthly, not as you would immediately understand it; it is heavenly, but not something alien which is not really yourself; it is rather like the identity between the seed and the ripe fruit. It is corporeal and yet completely different. On the basis of the earthly prelude of corporeal, deeply human experiences and convictions of joy from what - all things considered - is still a quite primitive instrument of our earthly corporeality, how can we put into words the corporeal resonance which the symphony of heavenly experience will produce in those who are saved? Just compare in your mind the physical difference between the dumb look of an animal and the smile of an attractive girl. The difference in the same corporeality comes from a personal presence. There are bodies and bodies, says Paul, and their *doxa* differs (I Cor.15.40-4l); the expression makes the difference. In the example I have given we have material for comparison and we can see the difference. But the physical expression of someone who finds complete personal fulfilment in God, in whom God himself has become completely transcendent in the hallowed human figure, transcends all our earthly capacities for imagination. Glorified corporeality is pure expression without physical alienation. I do not know how it will work out. But that is no reason for not believing in it, when we reflect that we ourselves cannot even now begin to put into words our own deepest, most authentic and most joyful experiences. The earthly, the creation in which God remains definitively faithful in perfect freedom, gives us reason for composing the most exalted images and visions, as is witnessed by the Book of Revelation. These apocalyptic images, above all of the new heaven and the new earth and the heavenly Jerusalem, show us that what has already been achieved and what is still to be achieved in our history is to be identified with the final consummation that is the gift of God, the divine confirmation of all that is good, beautiful and holy in history. At the same time, they give us a set of models through which the Christian community sees the character of the approaching God who upholds us in conversion or *metanoia* and in responsible life in our history. Those are pictures of liberation which rejects the idolatry of the present and holds open the future. At the same time salvation is promised to the whole of man and not just to his soul. It has always struck me that the Greeks have criticized Christianity for being a *genos philosomaton,* i.e. a kind of people who attach too much importance to corporeality. The first fierce reactions of Christians against a misunderstanding of Jesus was directed against docetism, i.e. the view of those who thought that since Jesus was God's Son, it was impossible for him really to have been a corporeal human being like you or me. Here man prescribes for God what is thought to be compatible with God's majesty and in the end fails to understand himself. For what can human consummation ultimately mean for human beings if it leaves out the corporeality which is so familiar to us? In that case I am no longer 'I', and this 'I' has not achieved definitive salvation. But we cannot express such expectations in appropriate categories.

With the resurrection we are like the child who wants a train from Santa Claus. Before Christmas he dreams of the train; he can already imagine it; he pictures all its details, its colour and its form, its streamlining and how heavy or how light it will be. When the day finally dawns and he sees the train that he has really been given, it is quite different from anything that he had dreamed of, but so marvellously attractive and overwhelming that he has already forgotten all his earlier dreams and fantasies.

21

I Believe in Eternal Life

If the security of our physical, biological survival here on earth seems to be threatened, these days belief in eternal life beyond death also seems to be becoming incredible. As an experience, this is new in our history. In former days, the impossibility of living here and now sometimes led people to a belief in the hereafter. Since Hiroshima, this has changed. Historians of the human psyche have established that in Hiroshima people were not in a state to find a correct interpretation, within the context of the Buddhist, Shinto or in some case Christian belief in which they had grown up, of their subjection to atomic bombing, which came upon them as an eschatological event. 'Where the present does not blossom, trust in the future does not bear fruit'. This experience is important. For in contrast to former times it implies that eternal life must be based on earthly, temporal presuppositions and beginnings if it is going to be experienced meaningfully and be capable of being discussed in human terms. We cannot really trust God over our hereafter if we cannot build on him here and now on earth for the immediate future.

'I believe in eternal life.' Nowhere in the creed is the unity of faith and hope so clearly expressed as here: I believe in the future, even for the dead. Here faith is not concerned with what has already happened, an event about which historians can already tell us a great deal. Here faith is concerned with the unfathomable future of a history which is itself fundamentally ambiguous. Our history may well come to grief. Yet in Jesus as the Christ we are promised a good future, even for those who in and of themselves have no prospect of a future, those who are written off, chewed up in and through our history, even to the point of death.

Of course there are people whom we write off, extremely glad that we can finally forget them. Others, by contrast, die but continue to be remembered in our grateful remembrance. But even this remembrance is *in* history and dies within history. Ultimately everyone without exception is written off by our history. But over against this real experience the Christian message nevertheless says: God gives future precisely to those who have been written off through our history. History does not have the last word.

That is a belief which is only possible through hope. Hope always involves a risk: the result of it also depends on factors which are not under our control. It depends upon others, upon God. And that is the vital question: whether we can trust God more than we trust ourselves. Are we more sure of God than we are of ourselves? In Christian hope I live simply on the basis of a promise. And usually this promise is radically contradicted by everything that I experience in history. Hoping, I in fact live only on the basis of the unmerited, free consequence of God's utter trustworthiness, which nevertheless I can neither understand nor 'place'. For I cannot really find a place for Dachau, Auschwitz and so many other things.

The only question is whether life on the basis of faith in the unconditional trustworthiness of God does not already encourage the growth of something in our hearts which intrinsically is ultimately stronger than death, more durable than the limited temporal span which is allotted to us as finite beings between birth and death. The primal stories of our human history show that people strive to acquire invulnerablility and divine immortality by bringing bring fire from heaven or by eating some efficacious fruit, by acquiring a special pearl or taking a miraculous bath, like Siegfried. They seem to live on the longing and conviction that this must somehow be possible. But they always look for it in magic, in the bizarre: they try to filch eternal life, and these attempts fail, time and again.

One person, we claim, did succeed: Jesus of Nazareth. But he looked in the most obvious and simplest place in the world. He did not actually *look* for anything: he simply allowed himself to be loved by the eternal God. It does not occur to a child in its mother's loving care to ask whether the mother will still continue to care the next day. The child lets itself be loved, and leaves the rest to look after itself; it does not worry about that.

So eternal life does not seem to be a question of filching or trying to gain something that does not belong to mankind. Eternity certainly does not belong to mankind, but people cannot get away from the idea of it. Rather, eternal life is rather like love-play both in its playful element and its deadly seriousness. However, we must remember that letting oneself be loved by God – who is love, albeit not in human fashion – is revealed and realized within our history only in the form of love and concern for our fellow human beings: I cannot see any other possibility. This is put very sensitively into words in the creed. First we confess, 'I believe in the resurrection of the body', and only after that does there follow, 'and in eternal life'. Only after that. There is a deep intuition here. The body is the outward appearance of the human being, his or her public face, and we always present it to others and not to ourselves. Has any of you ever seen your own face? In a mirror, yes, but not as it really is: 'Friendliness which looks at itself in a mirror turns to stone.' In reality we always see only other people's faces, other people who look at us, make demands on us, pose questions or answer our questions about life. Human corporeality, concentrated in eyes and face, is essentially there for others. Human corporeality makes it clear that to the depths of our soul we are there for others, for our fellow human beings - and not for ourselves, though we experience this 'being there for others' in our own corporeality.

Physical resurrection, as God's second gift, is therefore God's definitive amen or affirmation of our openness for each other, of the human love which – albeit to a limited extent – has filled our earthly life. Risen, glorified corporeality, eternal life, is the fulfilled and successful form of our being there for the other, as a form of letting ourselves be loved by God.

Eternal life, dear people, is concerned with the loving quality of our earthly life here and now. The difference lies in the fact that in that case we no longer just *believe* that God is present wherever love forgets itself and is transcendent towards the other. The mystery of love then becomes transparent: we then see and experience God in the face of our fellow men, face to face, as Paul says. Eternal life is and remains human life, but human life experienced to its core, to its very source. It is a source experience, as when on his journey a primitive man suddenly discovers a spring. Here, unasked for and unmerited despite all the thirst, is living water burrowing up from a mysterious underground depth, even generously given. In that case life itself is rediscovered in a new way. We remain the same; we shall meet those who were dear to us; nothing of what was good, beautiful and holy in earthly life, nothing of that will escape us. We shall then forget all our sinfulness and mutual brokenness: that will be of no interest: then we shall experience what beforehand was formerly just faith in the unexperienceable. Only then will it become clear how fine earthly life could have been. *Si scires donum Dei!* If only we had known!

Jesus of Nazareth has disclosed earthly life to us by filling our temporality with such love that time broke on it: it burst apart. His death was therefore a conquest of death. Eternal life cannot be seized: only responsible love in the temporal here and now of our human history can give human and temporal form to God's eternal love. In that case there is something of God in and with us in our history wherever love declares itself to be forfeit to others. The historical temporalized breath of eternity is tough yet tender love; it alone is stronger than death and through God is extended into eternity. If God is love, then he allows himself to be outwitted only by love, not by the fruits of paradise, miraculous baths and cheques on eternity, much less by science and technology.

Belief in eternal life is therefore openness to an event, a happening, an event which is exclusively concerned with the nature and quality of our earthly human life and nevertheless with the nature and quality of our acceptance of death. However, it is not identical even with that.

Eternal life is the free event of God's divinity itself, which overcomes death and has happened in Jesus as a promise to us (II Cor.4.15). Resurrection of the body or eternal life is the eternally new event of God who identifies himself with the dead Jesus, the relic of the gift of love in a loveless world. In the resurrection we experience the year in which the wine still matured under a doubtful sun. 'We know,' says one of John's letters, 'that we have passed from death to life, because we love the brethren'(John 3.14).

Eternal life is future which has already begun. If it has not already begun in our love and care for our fellow men, then eternal life is an ideology and an illusion, a phantom; furthermore, it is disillusionment for those who believe in it in orthodox fashion, but without orthopraxy or deeds of love which can be demonstrated in a concrete way. In that case there is nothing in our life on which God can build on which can therefore be extended by him. The Gospel of John puts it in a splendidly human way: 'He who loves me will be loved by my Father and I shall love him and show myself to him' (John 14.21): eternal life is the appearance of the beloved which is celebrated in faith only when we serve our fellow human beings on earth. Only love for our fellow men, above all giving a glass of water to the needy who ask for it, and perhaps ask for our money as well, keeps God within our history and makes our human history salvation history. God's light burns in our world with the oil of our life. Therefore there is future within our history and beyond. Eternal life is God's complete assent to our own love-filled temporality. So at death such temporality cannot be completely past time: in that case it becomes a history of God's own life of love, a story with an eternal content. Here are crooked lines with God's fair hand on them. We need not worry about this eternity now. We shall enjoy its content for ever. The only thing that concerns us now is our responsibility here and now, wherever need, distress and a crying human face confront us.

Eternal life is at the same time both a gift and an obligation. We are like children. When we were small we got money from mother to buy something for her on her birthday. Then we came along with a little present which we had bought with our mother's money, and which in the meantime had become battered and dented. Of course it was a present that mother couldn't do anything with. But she was really pleased with our dreadful offering. It is just the same with us grown-up people who call themselves Christians. In rather exalted language Paul says: 'The love of God is stored up in our hearts through the spirit which is given us' (Rom.5.5). Finally we return this gift in and through Christ : *De tuis donis et datis* says the old eucharistic canon. But as soon as this gift comes into human hands it gets battered and dented. What we have to do is honestly, however lamely, to take our fellow man on our shoulders or go with him, if necessary through the flood of the Red Sea, and get him safely to the other side. And on the other side we shall then fall into God's hands: eternal life!

22

Belief in 'a New Heaven and a New Earth' (Rev.21.1-5)

'Then I saw a new heaven and new earth; for the first heaven and the first earth had passed away, and the sea was no more. And I saw the holy city, new Jerusalem, coming down out of heaven from God, prepared as a bride adorned for her husband; and I heard a great voice from the throne saying, "Behold, the dwelling of God is with men. He will dwell with them and they shall be his people, and God himself shall be with them; he will wipe away every tear from their eyes, and death shall be no more, neither shall there be mourning nor crying nor pain any more, for the former things have passed away."

And he who sat upon the throne said, "Behold, I make all things new." Also he said, "Write this, for these words are trustworthy and true" ' (Rev.21.1-5).

If human reason still has anything to say after putting all its reflections and analyses into words, something that it cannot go on to express in rational terms, it takes refuge in parables or visions. 'I have a dream.' There is no better way of expressing the deepest mysteries of life. So when Jesus too wanted to put anything into words over and alongside what was conveyed by his life, he spoke in parables – because he had things to say which touch on the heart of our existence. The vision of the new heaven and the new earth where God himself will wipe away the tears from our eyes, where there will be no more mourning, no crying, no pain, is such a parable. It is put in purely negative terms: it is nothing concrete, nothing that we know and possess, nothing tangible; it is not realized anywhere before our eyes: *shalom* as reconciliation with ourselves, with one another, with the world, with God is a reality which we simply do not experience in the normal course of our human history. And although we may already begin to realize this in smaller or larger communities, in the end we are brutally confronted with our utter defencelessness against one final event: the sheerly inescapable fact that we shall die and that death is an attack on all our dreams of universal reconciliation and universal peace: death is the opposite to life as life for and with others. Death is the great impasse of life: it is the break with all that we love, a break which overwhelms us, which is imposed on us.

Fortunately we modern men and women have begun to think about death less in individualistic terms. We know that life goes on after we have died; the world continues with what the dead person has given and contributed to it. And we have all repeatedly experienced how people who die have shared themselves out completely to those who survive. They have given themselves up for the benefit of those coming after them. This thought gives us strength. It shows us life as the limited space given to us by God in which we can devote ourselves utterly to others, passing on when we have shared everything, so that when we are no more, world history has nevertheless become a bit richer, rather more transparent and rather more reconciled with itself – a bit better. In that case eternity is experienced within the limited space of a bit of temporal history in which righteousness and love are attained. This bit of history is a person's measure. In that case, having to die should be a challenge to us to be ready to relativize our own contribution to human history, to put it in its proper perspective: we leave the future open to others. In that case having to die itself becomes a summons to a fundamental concern for a good future for all. Those who are to die no longer have control of their own destiny and are therefore challenged to surrender all self-righteousness. In this sense death is indeed the relativizing of what humanity has already been achieved and brought into existence for the benefit of a humanity to come. This demythologizing of death at the same time contains a challenge to make a critical analysis of social trouble spots which are also the cause of distress, misery and even death. This puts medical service not only in the context of therapy but also in that of the search for a better world, a world in which tears have already been wiped away now.

These thoughts are inspiring and exciting. But they are not enough; in the end they threaten to trivialize death. They leave questions open, the answer to which can perhaps only be given in the form of a parable as a protest against any attempt to make death understandable. For if death is a matter of surrendering oneself, it is also a matter of surrendering oneself in uttermost human love; for what is the self if not the power to love? And with death, loved ones are left behind: we say our last farewells to them. Death is terrifying, not so much because of what it means for our own life but because of the way in which it affects social and human relationships. Not only will I be unable to finish my own work and tasks – in that respect I am not irreplaceable – but I shall no longer be able to transcend myself for others. Henceforward, from a human point of view, my own promised being, which becomes itself through giving to others and was also a gift to me, will be utterly finished. The promise suffers a definitive defeat.

The believer feels the absurdity of this even more deeply. The saints of the Old Testament felt the absurdity of death above all in the ending of their love of God by death. Here death is clearly seen as the contradiction of all life, life not only with and for our fellow men, but above all with and for the living God. This was the incomprehensible impasse in the death of the saints of Israel. Death is a problem in both human and religious terms. At the moment, of course, we talk about death but in so doing forget the fact that death itself cannot be 'discussed' directly: death is a boundary which no one ever crosses *alive,* and the one who has died cannot tell us whether anything else has happened to him or her. The sciences have demythologized death, taught us to see it as a natural phenomenon of all biological life. 'Having to die' is thus removed from its mythological framework and made a natural biological law. Death is analysed as a secular event which to some degree can be manipulated. And it is good that this should be so. But to conclude from that that 'having to die' is not an alien event in our existence is to miss the specifically human element in this event. Without doubt, instructed by the sciences, we shall no longer have to connect this 'having to die' with an original human primal fall which is thought to have brought death upon us as a punishment. But on the other hand we misunderstand the significance of death if we reduce having to die to a characteristic of the living being that we call man. This having to die is simple facticity, that is, pure event, and has the inescapability of the brute fact. The incomprehensibility of death lies in the fact that it shows that men and women are beings who in the end cannot by themselves realize their own nature, promised and in the future. (Christians can already see here a pre-understanding of their conviction that the nature and future of men and women can only come to them as unmerited grace.) There is therefore no one meaningful way of grasping the fact of death. Death is unthinkable; it remains an alien element in our life. It is impossible for me to incorporate death in the programme of my life, to make it something that I can as it were manipulate. I therefore experience death as something which in the most complete way remains alien to my life. I cannot see it as the end or the pleasant crown of a life which will achieve its consummation in death. In this sense there is no changing death as a brute fact, not even by our Christian faith, nor even by our expectation of the resurrection. Faith does not *explain* death.

In death we are confronted with a fact which remains alien to the notion that existing is a right in itself. Death has in common with life the fact that it comes upon us, is given to us, or is inflicted on us. But what comes upon us in death is the absurdity of an event which cannot be rationalized: being taken away from oneself and from others. Therefore we cannot just see death as an end and a limit to life. This boundary puts in question the very meaning of earthly life. Death shows that despite their increasing capacity for control, human beings cannot take in hand their life and their whole existence, and that therefore all that they are and do does not belong solely to them. Thus death casts a shadow forward over life itself; we cannot trivialize people and see them only in the succession of generations as a temporal link in the chain of history.

Is the absurdity of death the final end of human life? In its vision of the new heaven and the new earth, inspired by the resurrection of Jesus, the good news of the gospel says, 'No, there is indeed a future even for those who are dead. This is no certainty on which we can bank and which we can programme into a manipulable human life; it is a believing hope which is based on the prayerful confession expressed in the *cri de coeur,* 'My God, my all'. Anyone who lives by faith in the living God can also entrust himself to God in the absurdity of death. The absurdity of death remains, but so too does the security of being in God's hands. In their Psalms, the Old Testament saints were still suspended between these two certainties. God, who was love but also righteousness, and therefore poured out wrath as well as mercy upon his people, had not yet revealed himself finally and definitively. The balance had not yet been struck between the *verbum irae* and the *verbum misericordiae.* In Christ we know that God's final judgment upon the world is a word of mercy, forgiveness and free reconciliation: an unmerited surplus of meaning over against our surplus of meaninglessness. The believer now knows that God's living presence is stronger and penetrates further than the absurdity of death. Despite that, he believes in his God. In that Jesus has gone before us, he makes that confidence possible for us. Our belief in the resurrection and the expectation of our resurrection does not comprise more than that. But this is an inconceivable surplus. It is openness towards an event which is not identical with the absurd event of death: it is the event of God's own divinity, which happens even for the dead and which happened to Jesus as a promise to us. Our openness to this final event is therefore based on what has already happened in Jesus Christ. We can interpret it on the basis of different models. But they are all secondary: the overcoming of death is basically the eternally new event of God himself, internalized in the surrender of man to his God despite the absurdity of death, a surrender which in death amounts to a radical self-surrender in which God becomes all in all. But incomprehensibly this 'all in all' on the part of God does not compete with the ultimate consummation of the humanity that we surrendered. How we ourselves reach our highest development in community with others in the *shalom* of the perfection of the human world is God's secret, which as a mystery will be an eternal surprise for us.

23

Belief in Jesus as Salvation for the Outcast

No poet, no philosopher, no theologian, nor anyone else can explain the reality of injustice and suffering in the way in which they disrupt and distort mankind. People curse God or try to justify him; they blame Adam or the devil, or refuse to accept any responsibility for it themselves. Any explanation of suffering trivializes this painful experience or asks too much of human responsibility; it looks for an excuse for this incomprehensible occurrence or finally makes God a torturer intent on teaching a divine lesson. No one will deny that there is suffering which enriches the human temperament by providing meaning and through love; people themselves can come to maturity through an utterly good personality which compels wonderment and respect and which reduces to silence those who experience it, even enriches them through the experience of such a human life, brought to gentle wisdom. A robot human world in which there is no room for passion and some suffering is felt rather to be inhuman, an inessential world.

However, there is an *excess* of suffering, injustice and human oppression. There is a barbarous excess which resists all explanation and interpretation. There is too much innocent and senseless suffering for us to be able to place this history of human suffering within any honest system of explanation or to overcome it through purely rational action.

So here we are, gathered round the great outcast of this earth, Jesus of Nazareth. Why, dear people? Why? What does Jesus mean for us, someone who a long way off in space and time, about two thousand years ago, led a remarkably brief life, of some thirty years, and spent one or at the most two years as a prophet, finally being executed while he was still a young man? This was evidently because he had spoken about the kingdom of a God who was concerned for humanity, who took mercy on the lowly and the oppressed who needed a glass of water and clothing: the poor, the mourners and those who weep, who are mentioned in the Sermon on the Mount. About twenty-five years later the Roman emperor Nero was to have the Stoic Seneca, who at that time was his adviser, killed because Seneca continually pointed out to this inhuman and monstrous emperor that imperial rule had to be concerned with humanity: *humanitas* and *clementia*. But we are not gathered here in the name of Seneca. This confronts us fairly and squarely with the question, Why are we followers of this Jesus? Why do we come here, all together, in his name? This fact is clearly before us: here we are, a number of us, at this spot, gathered together as a community of Jesus, brothers and sisters with a single focal point – Jesus. Yet we are not gathered here to celebrate a dead man or the funeral of the most exalted prophetic ideal among us, or to recall our memories of a beloved person already long dead and buried. Still, we are here, and this meeting stands under the sign of the person of Jesus. In that case there must be more than reminiscences of an old tale of suffering in which we recognize our own misfortune and suffering, whether narcissistically or grimly, more than a stylization of old memories in which we are the active partners, and the Jesus of the past is some passive object of the interplay of our memories. Such mysterious forces do not emanate from a dead man; and though this may once have been the case, it was so only for a short while. In the long run these memories wear thin, and in later generations they fade into that area where colours blur, so that ultimately they are only the object for the investigations of learned historians.

With Jesus, in whose name we are assembled here, something else must therefore be involved. Did something happen with him which for that very reason can also happen especially to us? We are here together in his name. But the story goes further, because, 'Where two or three are gathered together in his name Jesus is there in their midst.' Here the lowly are raised up, here the outcasts are accepted. Here we celebrate the conquest of our history of suffering and listen to our mission to identify ourselves with the oppressed and to free them from their constricting fetters. Here we know that Jesus is involved in person precisely in this 'concern of Jesus', which we represent and carry on. We can talk about Jesus only in the human language of grace, the language of our relationship with God. Here we remember above all that God has raised up this rejected one. Therefore it is he, the one who has been raised up and exalted, who now recalls our history of suffering. He brings us together here because here he give us reason for expectation. What happens here can only be understood if Jesus appears to us against the deeper background of a God concerned for humanity, who joins the fight against our history of suffering. This gathering does not make much sense unless it is supported by a faith (perhaps unspoken, possibly full of doubts – and yet full of longing), a living conviction that in Jesus the power of God liberates us for abiding love for one another, a love which is concerned to overcome the suffering of others, knowing that they may entrust their own suffering – not understanding, but from the heart – to God. Because of that, we call Jesus the living one, the risen and crucified one, the weak one who becomes strong, appointed with power to support and strengthen our weakness and to help us to gain the victory . Here among us, travellers toiling along the way to Emmaus, he keeps the lamp alight: 'Did not our hearts burn within us while he spoke to us on the way and expounded the scriptures' (Luke 24.52). Through and in Jesus we are aware that we are human beings for whom God is concerned. This establishes communication, breaks open that which is held fast, softens that which seems hard.

It is only possible for us to believe in the story of this living one, to confess Jesus as the Christ, because previously we have begun to stand under the cross of this executed man and have arrived at the conviction that God the Creator identifies himself with those who are oppressed by their fellow men, outcast and rejected, written off and defenceless. He identifies himself with innocent victims of crucifixion. These are therefore in God's hand in a special way. So, too, they are also entrusted to us in a special way, to our active hands. What was achieved through Jesus on the cross had of course previously been the content of his message: the good news for the poor, for those who mourn and weep, that from now on the God who is concerned for man has begun to rule. All oppression, all torment and tears must disappear; God himself will become the servant of us all: he wills a future for those who in human terms cannot see any future. He wants a world in which God's smile on his beloved creation appears on the face of every man so that we may bring grace and liberation and happiness to one another against the background of a world ablaze with beauty whose splendour we can enjoy. That is the meaning of *shalom* in the Old Testament and in Judaism. For Jesus that is also the kingdom of God, the rule of God which he proclaims in a prophetic way. Nor did he just proclaim it; his liberating and joyous dealings with men and women were the living illustration, the concrete realization of his good news. He seeks out tax collectors and sinners, with whom it was tabu to share a table; and where he appears, sickness, blindness and deafness disappear. All that hinders communication between people vanishes. Through his prophetic and critical message and a life-style to match, he seeks to change injustice, our history of human suffering, which someone once called 'the great oecumene of suffering', and to recreate the oecumene or great community of *shalom,* of peace and love, justice and communication, bringing the unspeakable joy that we can and may all be 'one another's happiness'. As Jesus has gone before, this is not a utopia or a pious dream, but something that can and must be realized by each of us, personally and in society. If it is not to be a pious ideology, our being Christian must make us aware of those areas where the poor and the oppressed are rejected as outcasts by people who may believe a lot but who at the same time deprive people of their humanity, the enormous gift of allowing human beings to be human beings. But if we really do want to follow Jesus as Christians, Jesus whom we celebrate here and express in word and sacrament, simply as a celebration, we can and may say to each other, 'Yes, you may live. Believe me, you may live.' Is not this the beginning of the great raising up of the outcasts?'

III

Spirituality and Life-style

24

Christian Identity and Human Integrity

Much of what is adorned with the specific title of 'humanism' barely conceals its ideological character. This is evident from slogans that one can find in literature. On the one hand one can read, 'What is Christian is human and what is human is Christian.' On the other hand, I read somewhere, 'What is communist is human and what is human is communist.' One could find more examples of the same kind of statement. However, ideological misuse should not distract our attention from the real question of the relationship between 'humanity', and what is proposed by religion and philosophy as the deepest convictions about life: it is a warning against premature syntheses and identifications.

Whatever other wealth it may contain, Christian faith is certainly concerned with 'humanity'. There are people who believe in God, but no one has a monopoly of true humanity: that is something for everyone. In any case, 'humanity' is an abstraction. It exists only in very diverse cultural forms, though this may be on the basis of a fundamentally identical biogenetic substratum.The hegemony of a particular culture is therefore pernicious; it is marked by 'regionalism' and imperialism.

If there is anywhere in theology where we have an accumulation of pseudo-problems it is in the case of 'twin concepts' like humanity and Christianity, human freedom and grace, evolution and creation, and even self-liberation and justification by grace alone. Often, such opposed concepts, which in fact have some support in reality, are projected *as such* on to reality, where they then become two opposing realities which have to be dialectically reconciled! That is, of course, a hopeless task, as is evident from the dispute over grace which has taken place in the Roman Catholic church.In such cases we find ourselves up a blind alley.

At the level of concepts and their expression in words, 'humanity' and 'Christianity' (or the approach of the kingdom of God) are in fact set alongside and in succession to each other.They are then often put together or included in the same proposition as though they were two realities – e.g. grace and freedom. But the question is whether they *can* be added together. A good human action, performed freely, is grace in the concrete which at the same time nevertheless transcends freedom. In this way a Christian can rightly experience a case of acquired 'humanity' as 'Christian'.

In such statements, the language of faith and analytical language point to one and the same reality, but in both language games we must respect the pertinence and formal perspective of each and not play them off against each other. Otherwise we are acting like a chess player who suddenly puts the knave of hearts on the board – a meaningless and absurd gesture (the image comes from Wittgenstein). The theologian who only studies the causes, the legalities and the intrinsic structures of 'human action' is not yet formally occupied with theology: he is reconnoitring the approaches to the area about which he is going to say something in 'Christian' terms. The reconnaissance of the ground is a theological task for him in that without this reconnaissance his real theological work becomes completely meaningless and remains in a vacuum (though as a theologian he is also dependent on other sciences). It is therefore important that he should not forget that the first reconnaissance involves other than purely theological competence. If he is concerned with this reconnaissance of the sphere in which salvation and disaster are fought over, a theologian will first listen carefully to human experiences, especially to negative experiences of contrast, and see what other human sciences may be able to tell him. As Thomas Aquinas pointed out, *multa praecognoscere (theologus) oportet*[1]: before the theologian acts as a theologian he has a good deal of reconnoitring to do. At that level it is very important to listen for the way in which men and women want to realize their humanity. Interdisciplinary study is essential. However, the theologian is only on formally and distinctively theological ground in which his own competence comes into play when he includes the ground that he has already reconnoitred in a different language game, asks different questions and looks at it from a different perspective: specifically, he brings it within the language of faith which speaks of salvation from God in Jesus the Christ. This is not a matter of speaking of a different reality, but of speaking of the same reality which has already been reconnoitred in a 'human' way. Here interdisciplinary collaboration ceases to be of help and indeed is out of place. If we brought it into play we should be looking with a squint at what appears on the one hand as 'human' and on the other hand as 'Christian'. Two divergent language games are involved, because the reality itself has many dimensions which cannot all be expressed at the same time in one language game. The material that has first been analysed by reason is then decoded or deciphered by a theologian in the light of faith. That material is as it were a text which the theologian has to interpret in accordance with the grammar of Christian hope, of belief in God, who is the source of universal, all-embracing and definitive salvation. The question for the theologian is therefore whether a coming, and approach (not *the* coming) of the kingdom of God can be seen in this particular human action.

Speaking about God as the one who brings men salvation and freedom is thus done in a second 'language game'. It is speaking about something that has already been discussed, in a 'first discourse'. What is first seen as 'human reality' is then discussed by Christians in the light of its 'Christian content' or the opposite, in terms of salvation or its absence. It does not, however, in any way follow from the character of faith as 'second discourse' that faith and theology always come too late. This coming too late is not a feature of faith and theology as such; it happens because believers and theologians often arrive too late at the phenomena which have to be discussed theologically in a second discourse. Christians may have the searchlight of faith, but they often do not realize that a new object is presenting itself in our human experiences and that this new object is in special need of theological interpretation. Anyone who arrives at the phenomena too late is also of course too late to throw Christian light on them with a view to a better Christian praxis.

Theology is a matter of speaking about the absolute which appears within the relative, that is, in historical human praxis, and which is often a matter of life and death. Theology expresses the ultimate and transcendent commitment of men in historical praxis, since for a believer specific human activity, including political activity, is always related to the coming of the kingdom of God – positively or negatively, but never neutrally. Although this kingdom must be realized in and through this or that particular human action, it cannot be reduced to this or that praxis. That does not mean that the absolute and total character of the commitment of faith cannot be expressed in a very specific human praxis, sometimes in very definite contexts. We are ultimately judged on whether we have given a glass of water to the thirsty (Matt.25.40)!

Christianity is thus essentially concerned with human integrity: with being whole or 'salvation'. That does not mean a reduction of 'Christianity' simply to 'humanity', but it does constitute the historical conditions within which alone Christianity can be given form. The absolute character of Christian faith is thus necessarily revealed in a particular, historical and relative way: in historical humanity, although humanity and Christianity are not the same thing. Anyone who wants to experience the absolute purely and simply, as it were unwrapped, will never be confronted with it, except... as idolatry. We can only arrive at 'God's word' within the horizon of our cultural and material possibilities, within the horizon of our historical life. The absolute manifests itself only in the everyday things of human life, small or great. There it will emerge how God's concern can also be man's concern in the context of our human life and society, whether that is on a smaller or a larger scale. That is what the theologian wants to decipher: that is what he is a theologian for.

To end these first considerations, then, we can establish that the transcendence of Christian salvation and faith in God can never be used as a pretext for a neutral attitude to the promotion of the humanum, still less for political neutrality. Whatever its content may be, that which is Christian and 'universally human' can only be realized within very definite human particularity.The absolute humanity of the Enlightenment has taught us sufficiently how ideological the bourgeois idea of the 'universally human' actually was.

The Christian is certainly concerned with a relationship between God and man in which, however, the world and human history are as it were inserted between him and us as a translation of his inner discourse, and moreover as a medium in and through which man's attention is explicitly drawn to this inner speaking, in the end as the sphere in which a person can respond with his or her life to this invitation.

Christians rightly interpret certain actions, including social and political actions, as Christian, that is, soteriological, even if humanists call this same praxis humanist (i.e. non-Christian). After all, specific social and political actions cannot be regarded as exempt from their own particular rationality, substance and specific aims; in this sense there is no action in the world which the Christian can claim entirely for himself or herself. The dream, the vision, indeed the promise of a better society, a fuller life for humanity, a society 'with a human face', is, however, of the essence of the Christian gospel, which is the message of the God who is concerned for humanity and wants people to be similarly concerned. Thus Christian faith is bound up with an ethics of humanity. The criteria for social and political action cannot of course be derived directly from the 'utopia' of the kingdom of God, but a believer takes up this ethical action, which has to be judged according to its own criteria, into the theologal virtues of faith, hope and love. Thus, for Christians, even a political praxis which is oriented on a more human society is itself at the same time the social and political content of the Christian hope in terms of a historical praxis. For the believer, the 'social and political' dimension cannot be reduced simply to its social and political components: there is more at stake than that. And it is with this 'more' that the theologian is concerned.

Ideas of liberation, salvation and human happiness are always developed from particular experiences and reflection on the reality of disaster, misery and alienation. They are the result of an accumulation of negative experiences in a centuries-long history of suffering shot through with flashes of promising meaning and happiness, partial experiences of salvation and meaning in a history, lasting over many generations, of unfulfilled expectations, guilt and evil. In the long run this gives rise to a vision (characterized though it is by cultural and even geographical diversity) of what is regarded as necessary for a true, good and happy state for individuals and for society. The constant human longing for happiness, salvation and justice, subjected as it is to constant criticism by the facts, but ultimately flying in the face of them, therefore inevitably takes on in different forms the loaded connotation of 'salvation from', 'liberation from' meaninglessness, suffering and alienation, and at the same time of 'entering into a completely new world'.

What is striking in this human process of the experience of the absence of salvation or the presence of partial salvation among human beings is that a particular people's own conceptions of salvation are an attempt not only to fathom the deep and boundless extent of suffering, but also to interpret the causes, the origin and the consequences of it. Because this experience of the absence of salvation cannot ever be completely fathomed in theory or completely eliminated in practice, it always has a religious dimension, not only in the ancient world, but also as the spontaneous experience of all peoples, In the spontaneous insight of men and women, the absence of salvation and alienation cannot be measured in human terms, whether theoretically or in practice. Consequently experiences of salvation acquire a religious name. Humanity has come to expect salvation from beyond itself, 'from God'. Despite all experiences to the contrary it has come to learn to expect gentleness and mercy at the deepest heart of reality.

But what do we see in our so-called secular society?

What in the past seemed almost exclusively the concern of religious people has now become a concern of all kinds of human sciences, technologies and activities: everyone is looking for healing , for human salvation and liberation from enslaving societies. It is hardly possible to deny that – apart from the difference between faith and reason – the question of a sound and worthwhile humanity, as a question, is more alive than ever before throughout mankind. In our time the answer to it has become all the more urgent, the more we note on the one hand that people are inadequate, fail and above all are wronged, and on the other hand that we may already experience fragments of human healing and self-liberation. Of course the question of salvation and liberation, of a human life that is really worth living, has always been raised within actual conditions of disintegration, alienation and all kinds of human oppression. The question of salvation and liberation, the basic theme of all religions, has now more than ever become the great stimulus throughout present-day human existence, and what is more it is asked outside the religious sphere. Religions no longer provide an explicit thematization of human salvation; the question of salvation – redemption and liberation – is not just a religious and theological theme but is now above all the great driving force of our present-day, so-called 'secular' history. More than ever it becomes clear that human history is the place where decisions, conscious decisions, are made about man's healing and liberation.

We may therefore draw a second conclusion in the course of this story. Anyone who now wants to speak meaningfully about God, about human Christian redemption, must do this within the contextual situation of the contemporary theme of salvation and liberation. It is ultimately a question whether we can show that in the liberation and emancipation of men and women in search of a more worthwhile humanity something absolute is at stake – the absolute itself; thus whether we can show that man's concern can also be God's concern. Only in this way can it emerge how God himself can become a human concern. And if this is the case, this religious dimension of our human life also requires an expression, an articulation, and a liturgical celebration of thanksgiving. Ultimately it also requires a tangible human translation of this mystery, to be given, in various circumstances, in terms of a praxis of the kingdom of God which everyone can recognize.

Christian belief in creation has a critical and productive force with regard to pessimistic and optimistic (and ultimately unrealistic) views of human salvation that could be realized in history and society. I said earlier that what was once only the concern of religions now seems to have become the shared task of all men, even those who are not religious. The conclusion that has been sometimes drawn is this. Granted that we owe the introduction of many human values to the Christian tradition of experience, they have now become common property so that now, while thanking Christianity for past services, we can say farewell to Christian belief. However, I believe that this would be a very minimal way of thinking about the inexhaustible potential for expectation and inspiration in Christian creation faith and the activity of the spirit of God. It can be demonstrated from history that what were originally religious inspirations gradually become 'universalized' in humanity, i.e. they are introduced into the saeculum, secularized. However, as an argument and a demand for totality this is a dangerous conclusion to jump to, above all because of our finitude or contingency, which may really be seen as the definition of 'secularity', the absence of religion. For the believer this finitude can never be separated from the absolute creative saving presence of God, and therefore it can never be 'secularized': never cease to exist. This creative saving presence of God is an inexhaustible source of expectation and future hope which clearly transcends any finite potential for action.

People seem to find it difficult to believe in a divine being which fully determines what and who and how 'It', 'He', 'She' (here human words seem to fall short) – God – really is. Nevertheless this is belief in God. We ourselves can only determine in a very limited way, restricted by all kinds of conditions, who, what and how we want to be in accordance with our own plan or view of life. Even there, we still largely fail. By contrast, God's being is precisely as God wills it to be, without any elusive or independent remainder. He determines freely what he wants to be as God, for himself and for us: not arbitrarily, but in unconditional love. That is the Christian confession of faith.

This divine nature is revealed to us in Jesus. God, the creator, the one in whom we can trust, is love which sets people free, in a way which fulfils and transcends all human, personal, social and political expectations. God's being is promise for men and women.

That is why our human history can never replace the inexhaustible potential of expectation and inspiration in belief in creation faith. It releases reserves of hope and energy for believers which cannot simply be reduced to purely human expectations and wishes. In this sense a person can realize the promise of their own being only as grace. As Ignatius of Antioch rightly said: *'Ekei paragenomenos anthropos esomai':* 'When I arrive there I shall be a man.'[2] Ultimately humanity is an eschatological gift of the Spirit, the fruit of God's liberating love in Jesus Christ, a fruit which God allows to ripen in and through the historical praxis of human beings, while he always transcends this in a sovereign manner.

The indefinable character of definitive salvation and eschatological freedom, that is, of the humanum which is sought and found only fragmentarily, and moreover is always threatened, can therefore only be expressed in the symbolic language of metaphorical speech, which goes further than all conceptuality. We find three great 'metaphors' in the New Testament, which suggest the complete humanum. First is the definitive salvation or radical liberation of all men and women for a sisterly and brotherly community or society which is no longer dominated by master-servant relationships: this is called the kingdom of God. Secondly, there is the complete salvation and happiness of the individual person (whom the New Testament names *sarx* or flesh) within this perfected society, which Christian tradition calls the resurrection of the flesh, that is, of the human person including his corporeality. Thirdly, there is the perfection of the 'ecological environment' which is necessary for human life; that is suggested by the biblical idea of 'the new heaven and the new earth'.

These three metaphorical visions orientate the action of Christians in this world in a direction which is not undefined but very definite (indicated by the dynamic character of these symbols), though they can never provide a direct blueprint for personal, social and political action here and now without being mediated in a human context.

From what I have already said, we can understand that any religious and Christian talk about God is at the same time productive and critical talk about man, while religious or Christian talk about man is at the same time talk about God. Precisely because God's being is 'love for man', these two facets can never be separated. This inevitably means that what is specifically religious and Christian is essentially concerned with what is specifically human. Christianity is not Christianity if it does not take 'the human' seriously – humanity is the very place where God is sought and encountered. Creation and christology as the realities of Christian experience (which only become 'theological themes' in the second instance) give us this insight in faith. Our temporality as present, past and future – trust, remembrance and expectation – is given its shape by this 'hermeneutical circle' of protology and eschatology, of remembrance and expectation of the future.

When Ignatius of Antioch wrote down his well-known saying, 'When I arrive there I shall be a man', it was the eve of his martyrdom and he was under its shadow. However, true humanity is also concerned with the way of suffering through others and for others, the basic theme above all of the Gospel of Mark, I Peter and the Epistle to the Hebrews. It is really the theme of the whole of the New Testament. In this respect, too, 'the Christian' takes on the form of 'the human' in its heights and depths; however, this is a 'human' which can trust in God's absolute saving presence in suffering and helplessness, in prosperity and adversity. Active search for the incomprehensible mystery of the ultimate Humanum, which always takes place within a particular cultural, social and even geographical context, in fact merges into the mystery of the 'suffering righteous man' which has been presented and entrusted to us through the eschatological 'suffering prophet', Jesus, 'the Holy and Righteous One'(Acts 3.14), rightly called Son of God. It is here that the power (the biblical *dynamis*) of defenceless and disarming love is revealed. In the appearance of Jesus the suffering of the other person is experienced as a task. Jesus' death is the result of the irresistible power of goodness. Men and women can either be won over by it or they can oppose it, but in the latter case only by torturing and disposing of someone, in an act which bears witness, indirectly but in a very real way, to their own impotence. This is the heart of the testimony of Judaism and Christianity which is already evident in the Old Testament and confirmed in the New: suffering through and for others as an expression of the unconditional validity of a praxis of doing good and opposing evil and innocent suffering. Anyone who does not limit their own concern for the suffering of others will sooner or later pay for this with their death – even today. Jesus 'reconciled himself' to precisely that. He remained consistent to his dedication to man as God's concern. Given the nature of 'this world', standing up for 'man's concern' indeed meant suffering for the good cause. 'Self-realization of humanism' which does not take this seriously is neither realistic nor in the end 'humanist'.

God's choice for humanism would appear to be directed towards a 'humanism of the rejected'. 'Blessed are the poor, the hungry, those who weep' (Matt. 5.4-12), for they are not the oppressors. They do not reject anyone; they are the ones who are rejected!

'He loved us when we were still sinners'(Rom.5.8).

25

Introverted or Turned towards the World?

I want to begin this introduction to tonight's talk with a quotation and with two things which happened last week in Holland.

First the quotation. 'Ours is a time of religious decay; the permanent vitality of religion has been lost, the mass of the people have become either superstitious or credulous or indifferent to religion; the elite of society are agnostic or sceptical; the political leaders are hypocrites; the youth are in open conflict with established society and with the authority of the past; people are experimenting with eastern religions and techniques of meditation. The majority of mankind is affected by the decay of the times.' That's it. Evidently a recent, very modern piece. Nevertheless it comes from the Annals of Tacitus (VI, 7) and was written about two thousand years ago. History repeats itself.

Now the second point: two events which happened last week in Holland, specifically in Amsterdam. A few days ago, almost all over Holland and especially here in Amsterdam, a festival was held in honour of the Latin American bishop Oscar Romero. This week Amsterdam is celebrating a Festival of India. At first sight perhaps you could not see a greater contrast between two fundamentally different choices of life. Here we come right up against the heart of the question which concerns us today: the liberation of the human world either through interiorization and renunciation of the world and self or through the sometimes fatal selfless battle against the powers of this world which can result in the martyrdom of those who fight for freedom. Nevertheless, on both sides people are seeking liberating salvation for humanity.

Before I say anything substantial about the encounter between East and West, let me first ask you to consider for a moment the spirit in which our conversation must take place.

At all events, encounter between East and West must mean that both these perspectives have something to say to each other and that they should remind one another above all of each other's weak points. Once we see that, it will also be possible to talk about the contribution of their strengths. For my starting point is that none of us thinks that she or he has a monopoly of the truth. Truth is never a fixed possession and it is certainly not a piece of private property. We are sick of all dogmatism, as we are of all scepticism. Furthermore, my starting point is that the perfect state is not Greek unity, of which all plurality and differentiation is then simply a pale shadow, fragmentation and decay; the plurality of experiences always has more truth to it than can be found in a particular cultural experience or a religion. We should never think of our own identity in such a way that the identity of others is judged purely negatively. Of course that is typically Asiatic: reality can be approached from different sides. But this implies than each cultural tradition has a very distinct main perspective, a paradigm of its own within which people experience and interpret all their specific experiences. At the same time there is a difference that we cannot reduce for the sake of convenience to a basic unity. The differences are real.That means that in the relationship between human beings and the absolute or the divine (or however else one may imagine it), aspects of experience are present which are not thematized or experienced in and through the particular religious tradition within which people stand; indeed perhaps they cannot be experienced at all, usually because we do not have the right screen for them or the right code with which to read them.

It is therefore part of the true identity of any particular religious tradition that the possible relations of people to the absolute must be seen as an abundant richness and not as a negation of one's own position in reality. That is one thing. It may seem strange to us , but it is nevertheless positive. These perhaps irreducible differences are the means by which the unique, the divine, must be conceived. The unique and ultimate is one in such a way that it can only be discussed in multicoloured experiences and never in grey uniformity.

Now let us first consider a few facts. Today many people have a problem of identity; they experience what is called an identity crisis. They are in search of integrity and salvation, wholeness, in short, identity. Now the search for identity does not mean that those who are looking for it do not have any identity; rather, they live discordant and disrupted lives with an identity which is forced on them and given to them by society, upbringing or tradition. For that reason they no longer feel happy. In opposition to a forced and imposed identity, they are in search of a new identity. This is always to some degree a painful process, in which the old premature identity is discarded and a new one is built up.

Thus in our time the question of identity and the search for it no longer tend to take the form of an identification with a particular cultural group or class. Modern men and women have experienced more than ever that, however important social structures may be, they themselves are nevertheless greater than the social roles which others want to impose upon them. Precisely this demand for more is connected with the human experience that we do not consist exclusively of, and thus may not be swamped by, our social relationships, far less by our own small egos. Complete identification with social relationships or with his or her own ego alienates a person from his or her self, from others and from the deeper mystery of life.

Earlier, this need was felt more through the great religions of the world, specifically through those of the particular cultural tradition in which a person lived. However, where this need can no longer derive any specific content from a great religious tradition, it is left in a vacuum. In that case people begin to fill up the empty space in their own way. That seems to be the case at present.The fact that in our Western culture, in order to fulfil this need for more, many people are beginning to look outside their own great tradition and towards Eastern traditions indicates that their own religious tradition, i.e. the traditional churches, is no longer in a position to fulfil their need for something more meaningful and recognizable. This already brings us to a first conclusion: the present revival of Eastern religions in the West is itself a symptom of the shortcomings of our own Western religious tradition, a sign that it has hardened and become rigid. For many people it no longer seems to be a possible searchlight, but rather a fire extinguisher.

To some extent, and let me make this quite clear, to *some extent,* this phenomenon of emigration from a culture is reciprocal. Both in the East and in the West there are people who can no longer accept their own cultural heritage. Above all in America, there are many Hindus and Buddhists who want to make the acquaintance of the Jewish-Christian tradition, while from the West many people want to know more about the religious traditions of Asia. This has often happened in history. It shows that at a certain point great religious cultures seem to show some degree of satiation : for many people their inventive power of renewal is as it were exhausted. People then seek inspiration and orientation elsewhere.

This development is connected not so much with the authentic religious sources of a particular tradition as with the fact that in their specific experience of a tradition many people feel alienated from its living sources. This is clear in the case of the West. Since the seventeenth and eighteenth centuries, with the rise of trade capitalism and later with industrial and monopolistic capitalism, our society has been dominated by the profit motive and consumerism; it is a harsh society characterized by competition, prestige and rivalry, concerned with freedom if necessary at the cost of someone else's freedom, It is a society in which you almost have to nudge the structures with your elbow in order to survive. It is a society in which the state seems to have the task of harmonizing the egotisms of the many by legislation so that life is to some degree livable. This modern bourgeois atmosphere is not only to be found in the structures but has also made its way inwards: it is also alive in our own hearts. As a result, whole areas of human existential possibility have been impoverished and come to lie fallow. At the same time our capacity for experience is impoverished by the fact that we have only nurtured the 'active' capacity of our human spiritual life. We usually fail to see some things which are in fact there to be seen; we are incapable of that because we have learnt to see everything from the standpoint of utility, potentiality and usefulness. In one way or another this will take its toll in the long run. Our capacity for vision has been narrowed by our technocratic culture. A story may make this clear. When a Western European landed with his aircraft in a throng of African natives, who looked up in amazement at this strange great bird, he proudly said: ' In one day I have covered the distance for which I formerly needed thirty days.' Thereupon the wise black chieftain came forward and asked, ' Sir, what do you do with the other twenty-nine?' Here we have a clear expression of a two-fold human potentiality: on the one hand technical rationality; on the other, the question of the meaning of human action and human life. Legitimate though it is, this Western scientific society and technocracy has attacked the present form of the old Jewish-Christian, religious tradition, above all because it serves a capitalistic means of production. Private ownership of the means of production by the few has called to life this movement towards unbridled progress.

From ancient times, Asiatic means of production had a completely different character. It has been in modern times, not through internal factors but through the importation of Western means of production, that the ancient Asiatic conditions of production have been completely changed. Both in India and in ancient China, as well as in some Moslem countries, Asian productivity was characterized by the fact that private ownership of land and of the means of production was unknown there. Geographical and climatic conditions required a large-scale irrigation system which only a central authority could provide. Here we come up against the special role of despotic states on which the economy was dependent. Trade rarely developed: cities were neither centres of trade nor centres of industry and there was virtually no middle class. The traditional villages survived in social and technical stagnation for centuries. Thus there arose an East Asian culture which had no expectation of constant progress, a culture which sought contact with the depth of life in the present, with the ever-present Absolute. Here the Absolute is not bound up with a better future in this world, as it is in the West, but with the capacity in the present to dwell on the sources of all reality, in the depth of the universe and the depth of one's own inwardness. Peace, tranquillity, detachment and abandonment of the world lie at the heart of this culture, a cultural life which has been made impossible in the West by our modern drive towards unlimited production, which always keeps people busy, active and selfish.

And so we come to a second conclusion. At least implicitly, the search of Western men and women for Eastern spirituality is a sharp criticism of our Western, egocentric, miserly and often loveless society in which people give the impression of having nothing better to do than to compete with one another to the death. So the search for Eastern spirituality represents a certain sharp criticism of society, though we must not forget that this criticism leaves this society as it is and looks for salvation in inwardness. After the revolts of young people in the 1960s it was realized that the social structures which were challenged are tougher than youthful over-enthusiasm had been led to believe. This caused some of them apathetically to accept integration into the system. At all events one could increasingly perceive a strong feeling of impotence to change this world for the better. Others had a desire to begin with themselves, a desire for a change in their own hearts in the form of a renewal of their own inwardness by immersing themselves, through meditation, in the depths of their own egos. This ego was an obscuring factor, but through the obscurity there was access to a sphere of infinity, an unknown, utterly different world which was yet very near. There all things were reconciled with everyone and everything and the oppositions experienced so painfully in everyday life were already removed. Thus through self-abandonment it would finally be possible, surprisingly, to find salvation.

I must now sketch out the typical characteristics of authentic Eastern and authentic Western spirituality. First of all, I want to point out that both spiritualities were born and developed in the same continent, i.e. Asia, so that we must really speak on the one hand of East Asian types of religion and on the other hand of West Asian types of religion, namely Judaism, Christianity and Islam. In other words, all the great living world religions are of Asian origin. Without analysing this further, and because (since we only have this evening) I cannot say anything about, for example, African religion, there can be no question of an absolute contrast. I shall simply describe the main atmosphere and the distinctive paradigms of these two great religious types.

The East Asian religions (Hinduism, Jainism, Buddhism and Taoism) are primarily religions of inwardness – though this need in no way exclude an extremely complex external ritual. The dichotomy or break between inwardness and outwardness is more an appearance, an impression, than reality. In these religions (in contrast to the other type) there is no confrontation, as it were, in the sense of a clash between the human and the divine. The divine is found in a gift, so to speak as a new world which opens up – the ground of the deepest self and of the cosmos, in which the many has become one. In that case the divine is not at all personal, or rather it is meta-personal: a kind of mystery of compassion which pervades all things, transcending all attributes. In the light of the divine, men and the world fade: here the human personality is not accentuated, as it is in Judaism, Christianity and Islam. Furthermore, history and commitment to an improvement of the world are relativized as a result. The prototypical form of these religions is embodied in the Yogin sitting in a lotus position, silent, turned away from the world, passive, introverted: one with the all-reconciling force.

In contrast to these East Asian types of religion there are the West Asian types: Judaism, Christianity and Islam. The typical feature of these three monotheistic religions is not so much monotheism as such, however important that may be (but think of the Christian Trinity, with which Islam and Judaism have so many difficulties, and fundamental ones at that! In other words, the unity of God can still be experienced here in different ways). The characteristic of this group of religions seems to me rather to be the experience of a God as a personal God who addresses, continually talks with, and challenges human beings: a confrontational God. God here confronts man as an active agent man and he does so through prophets: these are essentially prophetic religions (Zoroaster, the prophets of YHWH, Jesus, the eschatological prophet, and Mohammed, Allah's prophet). Here a God of human history is honoured and celebrated, a God who makes human beings, in the role of his vizier or image on earth, responsible for our history, a responsiblity for which we shall be asked to give account. The conception of God as personal here is not anthropomorphic, as has so often been said. On the contrary, this heightened concept of human personality only arose in Judaism and Christianity in the encounter and even the opposition to this God (think of Jacob's struggle with the angel of God as a result of which he received his name or his identity, 'Israel'). This concept of person did not exist beforehand, but developed in and through the historical confrontation of the people with this God. This kind of belief in God stands at the very origin of the so-called

Western concept of person. In encounter with the living God man receives his profile as a person, as will, as a being who can speak and use words, a being who can express himself and who sometimes even provides criticism of traditional images of God (like Job). Thus in its social and historical forms history itself becomes the sphere of the action of man with God and of God with man. These three religions are thus personalized (I am not saying, privatized), historical and at the same time oriented on ethical action, that is, on the founding of the kingdom of God as the kingdom of justice among human beings. Nevertheless, the inspiration of these world-directed religions is a very central mystical experience. For the Jews, Moses, the political leader who brought his people liberation, was the mystic 'who spoke to God face to face', 'as someone speaks with a close friend'. For Islam, Mohammed had nocturnal encounters with angels of Allah who communicated the Qu'ran to him straight from heaven. For Jesus, the mystical experience of God as Abba or Father was the heart of his whole mission on behalf of the poor and the oppressed.

Put very schematically, those are the basic outlines of Eastern and so-called Western spirituality. Although we find fundamentally the same themes in all the great world religions, we must nevertheless say that there are very characteristic differences between the West Asian and the East Asian types which cannot be reconciled by the wave of a hand, though the two basic types are rooted in mystical experiences. Religion without mysticism is an intrinsic contradiction. Religions are not distinguished from one another by the absence or the presence of mysticism, but by the way in which this mysticism functions. Furthermore, it is very striking that for example a key figure in Western Christian mysticism, Meister Eckhardt (in whose spirituality those who know India and those who know Eckhardt see fundamental and sometimes literal similarities to Indian mysticism), does not ultimately present the contemplative Mary but the busy, serving Martha as the pattern for Christian mysticism. It is also said that shortly before his last ascent into unity with the Ultimate Buddha had preferred to return to the unliberated world, to help his brothers who had not yet attained to the final kingdom. As long as there are still unredeemed, unliberated people, true mystics in both East and West refuse to take possession of full happiness for themselves. So despite fundamental oppositions, there are amazing similarities and convergences.

Not only are the two great types of world religions, all of which saw the light in Asia – *ex oriente lux* – connected with each other through Iran and its own dualistic religion, which for a long time was the vehicle for the reciprocal influence of these two types on each other, but in addition we see that within the particular historical tradition of each of these two types of religion a certain anti-history has also arisen.

By this I mean a kind of critical counter-movement to the main accent of a particular religion. All three prophetic religions, Judaism, Christianity and Islam, have their own mystical trend which counters the one-sidedness of prophetism. In India, too, there are Indian cross-currents which criticize the one-sidedness of mysticism and couple this criticism with a spirituality directed towards the world. However, the fact that on both sides the critical cross-current is condemned by the religion which is officially dominant (Judaism, Christianity and Islam have often condemned their greatest mystics, and something of this kind also happened in the East with mysticism directed towards the world) indicates that the official religion wants to safeguard its own type of religion, whether prophetic or mystical, against possible deterioriation. From this we can see precisely what the main accent in these religions is. One can often best learn the basic tendencies of a particular religion through the history of its 'heresies'.

A third conclusion may emerge: there are in fact common foundations for a dialogue between Western and Eastern spirituality; but the dialogue is still at a very early stage and is more difficult than people perhaps suppose. For the time being there can be no question of a higher synthesis between, for example, Christianity and Eastern religion, although there are Buddhist Christians and even already typical Indian christologies. My question is whether these are faithful to both Eastern spirituality and to the nature of Christianity. It is not so easy to arrive at a higher synthesis between two cultures. The Hellenization of late Judaism and early Christianity took centuries to achieve.

So what is the position? In the East, spiritual methods and the East Asian cultural tradition come together automatically. The methods themselves are supported by a whole spirituality. We Westerners, on the other hand, have not participated in the Eastern cultural tradition from within: we can often only appropriate its external shell, take over the method as such, whereas it is the whole of the religious setting which gives a soul to the use of the methods. This seems to me to be particularly important. However, I must concede that these methods as such can contribute towards making people whole and helping them towards psychological health, if only by teaching them to breathe (which Westerners often seem to have no time to do, so that we are always breathless and never seem to be able to do ordinary things as peaceful and balanced people). That of itself is gain.

If we consider the phenomenon of the Western search for Eastern spirituality in a wider historical perspective, this move Eastwards does not seem so much a departure towards the authentic sources of Jewish Christian religion as a reaction against the modern bourgeois colouration of this Christian tradition since the Enlightenment and the nineteenth century. This is a reaction to the liberal belief in progress in which the Christian tradition is diminished and robbed of its prophetic element and its mystic nucleus. Thus authentic Christianity can recognize something of its own authenticity in this revival of Eastern religion. Truly human culture always has mystical sources.

However, our attitude needs to remain critical. There is a danger, less from the inner Eastern experiences of Westerners than from the misuse that Western society and its controlling forces could make of this mystical revival. I do not mean a kind of commercialization which in fact tries to control everything, even this revival. I mean something deeper. In America, many meditation centres receive outside financial support, not so much because people want to subsidize a praiseworthy cultural phenomenon but often on the basis of the cool calculation that the more young people drop out of society as contemplatives, the less revolutionary potential will remain to offer fierce criticism of the social structures and react violently with calls for change. The very thing that many contemplatives challenge, our society bent on success and achieved through vicious competition, is confirmed and safeguarded by their own marginalization. This society does not look for better things; if it did, it would not be disturbed by critical elements.

I fully concede that mysticism has intrinsic value, not just as a result of its social and political consequences (though I do think that true mysticism always has such consequences). So mystical experience, as the experience of a vision of the universal reconciliation of everything with all people and all things – and this can take many forms – cannot therefore accept or be reconciled to unfair competition in our social life: in and through its search for universal liberation and all-embracing reconciliation it offers radical opposition to the intrinsic contradictions which also exist in our society. Furthermore, mysticism can take two directions: either that of flight into inwardness without consequences for society or the prophetic direction in which mysticism and propheticism are intrinsically connected together. Precisely in this respect the encounter between East and West can become fruitful for the salvation of the whole world.

On the other hand, in its tradition of monks and religious the Christian religious tradition (for example) has always accepted that there can also be some specialization within a tradition, i.e of propheticism on the one hand and mysticism on the other. 'Contemplatives' devote themselves above all to mysticism, while 'active' religious represent the critical prophetic function. Without specialists – doctors, for example – a group cannot have a serious concern for healthy people. Specialists are needed as a constant reminder to everyone. So there must be centres of prophecy and centres of mysticism, so that as time goes on the mystics become more prophetic and the prophets become more mystical. That was the case with Moses, with Buddha and with Jesus of Nazareth and Mohammed. Where there is ultimately a complete break between the two elements, a religious cultural tradition threatens to become stagnant and satiated so that in the long run it does not challenge and speak to anyone. I therefore believe that the great event of the future could in fact be a certain synthesis (without eclecticism) between the Eastern and Western traditions of religious experience, even if we are still some way from it.

Finally, I want to point not so much to a danger as to a historical combination of circumstances which seems to me to be important and which is not as much of a coincidence as it might seem.

The beginning of the Western trend towards Eastern spirituality coincided almost exactly with the rise, above all in American Christian theology, of the so-called 'death-of-God' theology. There is a connection between our Western secularized world, for which God or the divine has become a fable, something no longer worth our attention, and the death-of-God theology and this trend towards Eastern spirituality. Like the secularization of the West, the death-of-God theology has something in common with certain types of Hindu religion which are sometimes called atheistic. However, secularized Western man seems to need a kind of transcendence, something infinite, an 'ultimate concern'. Many people, originally Christians, had lost their God long since, certainly on the practical side of their life; they were secularized to the bone and marrow before they became aware of the fact. But they came to discover how grey and lonely life becomes, a kind of fate, a lottery, a cynical game, if it lacks any element of the transcendent, of discovery that something like a mystery of mercy has its source in the deepest impulses of the universe and the human soul, a mystery on the basis of which people (who are in fact our ultimate concern) do not have the last word, and that we are grasped by an inexpressible something not of ourselves which may almost have no name. I would say that there is an authentic experience which for many people has also proved to be a liberation. Here is a touch of liberating grace in life. Humanity must begin to discover its divine origin, just as at the beginning of human history people also very gradually, and through many false turns, mistakes and conjectures, began to come to God. Ex-Christians sometimes rediscover Jesus of Nazareth in both his mystical and his prophetic power by way of India (is that really a detour?).

This whole religious phenomenon of Eastern techniques of meditation in the West – which perhaps is not always religious – seems to me to be a confirmation that the future of all religions will be found less in the great, 'official' religious institutions than in the smaller, vital basic communities, living centres in which both mysticism and prophecy can be heard and seen. These are perhaps the great future sources from which people will be able to draw nourishment.

Perhaps it is a dream for the future that one day a Latin American Festival could coincide with a Festival of India without producing any jarring notes.

Be this as it may, what we need, as also in the struggle for a better world, is spirituality which on the one hand does not camouflage and conceal the struggle, and on the other hand does not grimly secularize it, but takes it up into loving commitment to the poor and the enslaved on the basis of a concern for the universality of love for all and an eye to universal liberation and reconciliation. This would be a mysticism that was aware that the absolute and the divine can even be involved in the political liberation of men and women and that man's concern is at the same time God's concern, just as God's concern also needs to be man's concern.

Perhaps 'Moses and Aaron' might represent an anticipatory dream of this, settled in a sometimes silent, sometimes noisy but whatever else, open abode. The mystical political leader Moses and the priestly prophet Aaron: signs of hope. Although neither of them could enter into the promised land, they remain monuments of hope.

26

The 'Gospel of the Poor' for Prosperous People   (Luke 6.17,20-26)

Jesus does not call any virtuous people happy, nor does he say that poverty and misery are a good thing. He calls poor people happy: poor people who cry out aloud for hunger. He calls them happy because with him the kingdom of God has come among men. God is concerned for humanity, and in particular is in search of people in distress, the weak, the lonely, the insignificant members of our society, people who have dropped out, or have even been thrown out, of the normal processes of communication. These poor marginal people usually seek comfort from one another. They come together like the clochards in Paris, gathering together under a bridge somewhere to find whatever scant warmth they can from one another, bosom companions in shared misery.

It was the same in Palestine. As Jesus was coming down from a mountain with the twelve, at the half-way stage he came across a crowd of people. In Israel at that time a meeting with such a person always aroused the vague expectation that God would bring about some great miracle. There was a dulled certainty that there is also a future for the poor, a future in which the powerful and the prominent no longer oppress the poor, the weak and the insignificant among us. For that was the old message: it lived on in Israel only among the poor, searching and looking out for a better life. They had already heard of a man from Nazareth who talked of a mysterious new future: it was called the kingdom of God. This was a new, happy life, a kingdom for poor fishermen, joy for those who weep, fullness for those who are hungry. And here was this Jesus, suddenly large as life before them, surrounded by his fishermen who had left everything to follow him.

Then something happened that always happens in a crowd of people who suddenly begin to move. The whole crowd tried to touch him, for a power went out from him which healed them all. There were the impotent gestures of close-packed people who are looking for contact, begging: 'Just speak one word and salvation, communication, will be restored.' Jesus sees this crowd and the crowd knows it all: in Jesus, God is concerned for them. Then the great saying suddenly rings out over the plain. Jesus says, 'Happy are you poor who weep for hunger. Congratulations, you lucky people, because the kingdom of God has come to you, and everyone will be so satisfied that they laugh for joy.' On hearing that, these poor people must have had a vision of a laden table with pots of meat, fine bread made of meal and oil, everything that goes to make up a festive meal, in which communication is established and laughter becomes infectious.

A first reaction to Jesus' message is still very ambiguous. Hungry people are listening to Jesus; you could hardly object to that. They have not yet understood that Jesus does not want to be the fulfiller of unfulfilled daydreams. Yet Jesus outlines a new future for the poor by means of the image of the rich who laugh and are satisfied round a laden table. 'Is this misleading the people?', you might ask, for Jesus calls people happy who do not feel happy by human standards and indeed are not happy. In many respects this Gospel of Luke is an irritating text for us; of course it is inspiring, but in addition it is rather irritating. We do not know what to make of it, whether we are rich or poor. Either way we are stuck after hearing the gospel for today.

It was just the same for the three evangelists, Mark, Matthew and Luke, who wanted to bring their community new and topical inspiration by this old recollection of Jesus' gospel for the poor. Sometimes it becomes rather different, but sometimes it reflects Jesus' own original purpose. For us now these differences are also a challenge, an incentive not to treat this text romantically, but to let it speak to us here and now. This text is concerned to give a direction to our action. So let us look rather more closely at what Luke means by it.

When Luke wrote his Gospel, he was thinking of a very particular Christian community, somewhere in a great city of the Roman Empire outside Palestine. And it emerges from this Gospel that this Christian community consisted of a prosperous middle class with all kinds of major or minor social conflicts between the prosperous and the less important members of the community. It was on the basis of these social conflicts, and with an eye to them, that he wrote his Gospel. In it he described the new conditions which Jesus had promised earlier. First, Luke makes Jesus pray all through the night. Then Jesus chooses from his many disciples just those twelve of whom Luke says that they had left everything or had sold all their possessions to serve the kingdom of God. In between, Luke also tells us about a failed calling.

There was a deeply religious, rich young man, who could not, however, bring himself to give everything to the poor in order to follow Jesus. Surrounded by the twelve, who have actually accepted the call to voluntary poverty, Jesus comes down from the mountain and appoints his twelve poor fishermen, his poor fellow-workers, to serve the crowd. In Luke, the crowd was already his own Christian 'middle-class church'. Jesus then praises these apostles, in the presence of the Christian church, for having willingly given up all their possessions in the service of God's concern for the poor.

Luke's Christian community found this hard. His Gospel begins to fill in the details. Following the example of Jesus' apostles who left everything, Luke gives a guideline to the rich people in his church. Like Zacchaeus, you must give half your possessions for the poor in your church: fifty per cent. At the moment we haggle whether we should give two or four per cent of our own income for the Third World. Luke says fifty per cent. The whole of his Gospel and the Acts of the Apostles suggest that Luke is building up a very specific utopian society, at least for the Christian community. Here at least it is possible to realize what at that time was impossible in the bourgeois world. In the Christian community there is to be no difference between rich and poor, between the powerful, the important and the unimportant. This Christian, Luke, has understood Jesus' message very well. To take the part of those in need is to follow God himself, God as he has shown his deepest concern for people in Jesus with his twelve poor men who went round doing good in Palestine. God's concern for the unimportant becomes the criterion, the standard and at the same time the boundless measure, of our concern for the needy and the oppressed. This boundless sensitivity to human need only develops fully from a personal experience of God's own gracious Yes to all men. Yes, you may live: you here in church and you there looking at the television screen. You may live. This divine boundlessness in particular is not so obvious to us human beings. Of course it is obvious to all those who themselves have experienced God's mercy, in other words to religious believers. God is more human than any human being. I believe that we human beings find it difficult to understand the love of God for all men, who because they are human, fall short, fail and above all are oppressed. And according to Vondel and all kinds of apocryphal writings even angels argued over this predilection of God for human beings, for the humble, the wretched and the lonely, man or woman.

Finally, Jesus too, whom we may confess as the one beloved Son, was a human being like you and me, but more human. This gospel from Luke teaches us today that human love is a religious, Christian event. Luke does not leave this vague. Within the church he is clearly concerned that possessions should be shared, so that there will not be poor Christians alongside rich Christians. For Luke the beatitudes of Jesus are praise of the rich who give half their possessions to the poor in the community. From a social perspective, that, and only that, is life according to the gospel. It is not the whole of Christian life, but it is also Christian life. Furthermore, it is striking that Luke deliberately but consistently changes the familiar liturgical words at the celebration of the eucharist in his community, ' Drink you all of this', into, ' Share this cup with one another'. Everything is to be shared with one another. Luke translates Jesus' gospel for the poor into a gospel for the rich, since in his day the original church of the poor and the underdogs had become a community of both poor and rich. And Luke wants to exploit this new situation. In almost every chapter of his Gospel his demand for the social solidarity of rich Christians with poor Christians has a prominent place.

Translated for today's world, above all in its beatitudes, the Gospel of Luke is a direct indictment of our bourgeois existence, our bourgeois behaviour and our bourgeois society. This bourgeois character has also attacked the hearts of Christians and of the church itself. Of course we cannot derive any suitable social programme for our time from the Gospel. But the plan that Luke sketches of a truly Christian community in accordance with the gospel – half of what you possess for the unimportant among us – remains a challenge which can make us lie awake at nights worrying whether we are taking Christ's gospel seriously. At all events this message of Luke does not let present-day Christians get off scot-free.

In terms of the modern world, what Luke says to us describes precisely the scandal in which the present church is involved, How is it possible for defenders of oppressive systems and those they oppress, all of us and the Third World, to celebrate the one eucharist together as Christians? We drink from our full cups but do not share the one cup among one another. The great scandal among us is not intercommunion among Christians of different communions: that is a sign of hope. The scandal is the intercommunion of rich Christians who remain rich and poor Christians who remain poor while celebrating the same eucharist, taking no notice of the Christian model of sharing possessions: the sharing of the one cup of salvation among one another. For this salvation also has social and economic consequences. Everyone, not just an elite group, has to be full enough to be able to laugh because salvation has happened to him or her. Jesus said, 'Today salvation has come to the house of Zacchaeus', because Zacchaeus gave away to the poor half of what he possessed.

Is not all this more urgent than our petty problems within the church, however real they may be at the time? God does not want human suffering, he wants life, and life in abundance. And he wants it for all and not simply for one third of the world's population.

What about our abundance? That is Luke's critical question, a concrete challenge to all of us, here and now.

27

How Shall We Sing the Lord's Song
in a Strange Land?   (Ps.137.4)

He also told this parable to some who trusted in themselves that they were righteous and despised others: 'Two men went up into the temple to pray, one a Pharisee and the other a tax collector. The Pharisee stood and prayed thus with himself, "God, I thank you that I am not like other men, extortioners, unjust, adulterers or even like this tax collector. I fast twice a week, I give tithes of all that I get." But the tax collector, standing far off, would not even lift up his eyes to heaven, but beat his breast, saying, "God, be merciful to me a sinner." I tell you, this man went down to his house justified rather than the other' (Luke 18.9-14a).

This is a very popular parable which appeals to us all, particularly because we spontaneously identify ourselves with the attitude of the tax collector. However, Jesus had in mind hearers who spontaneously identified themselves with the Pharisee. That was why this parable was so shocking to them. We do not feel the element of shock in it because within the Christian tradition we tend rather to identify with the publican, and thus we by-pass the shock effect that is also meant for us. So have we understood the point of New Testament spirituality as it is meant for us here and now? I don't believe so. This parable is certainly not meant to be praise and approval of the average twentieth-century Christian who does not take God's will very seriously, like the tax collector of that time.

   Where we modern readers identify ourselves spontaneously with the publican, the audience in Jesus' time identified themselves with the pious Pharisee. He tried to fulfil God's Torah, his will as manifested in the Law, with a good deal of effort and pious devotion. Yet salvation was promised to the tax collector, while it by-passed the Pharisee. That makes us think. The parable is not really about those who are good (the Pharisee) or bad (the tax collector) according to the Law. The miserly tax collector, who moreover in Jesus' time collaborated with the Roman forces of occupation, is at the same time fundamentally wrong. The parable does not disguise this in any way. But Jesus transcends the human classifications of being good and being bad from a third quite different perspective, namely the nucleus of his message, which Paul would later formulate in an acute way: ' God loved us while we were still sinners' (Rom.5.8). The kingdom of God becomes visible among us in the real course of Jesus' life. And that kingdom of God means a God who is concerned for communication among people, who therefore does not exclude anyone from the community, does not 'excommunicate' anyone, but wants to establish communication among everyone, good and bad. Because all have been called by God to communicate with one another, Jesus prefers those who have been cast out of the community of Israel, the publicans and the sinners. From Jesus' perspective, the Pharisee was in no way at fault in his spirituality or piety. But from the New Testament perspective he was a particular type of Pharisee: one who is indeed pious but who has impaired his own spirituality by rejecting all those who do not live as he does. This pious man refrains from all communication with the sinner who has been cast out of his community. The sinner was marginalized and as a result thrust still deeper in to the misery of complete alienation from his own fellows. The story is certainly not about the pious Pharisee who does God's will in everything , even with a degree of radicalism: it is about those Pharisees who think on the quiet ('he prayed to himself'): 'I'm not like other people.' These Pharisees (though 'Pharisee' is already becoming a New Testament cliché for all Pharisees) do not want to have dealings with sinful people; they are the ones who cause the rejection of their 'sinful' fellow human beings. This is what provokes radical opposition in Jesus, the witness to God's action. On the basis of this opposition, Jesus seeks contact with tax-collectors and sinners, and eats and drinks with them to establish communication with the outcast and those who have been marginalized. This is also the point of the parable.

But how does the tax collector fare in this story? In twofold humiliation he completely accepts the role and identity which is assigned to him through public opinion. Furthermore he feels himself to be outcast: ' I am only a sinner.' Under the pressure of his rejection by others he dare not even lift up his eyes to God. He is the outcast; he knows it and feels it. In his life and in his body he feels the rejection which other people accord him and inflict on him. Furthermore, the tax collector also thinks that unlike the Pharisee he will not go away justified: he just confesses his sinfulness to God and again leaves the temple as an outcast.

The tax collector does not think or say anything about the salvation that comes upon him. It is Jesus himself, like God, concerned for communication among all men, who announces, 'He has received God's salvation; the other, the Pharisee, has excluded himself from all salvation by his rejection of the sinner.'

To us modern readers, the parable thus has a different message (though it is still the same) from the one it had for the listeners of the time. It must also have a shock effect on us, if it is to convey to us Jesus' meaning and thus lead us, Christians, to penitence and conversion. This parable is aimed at anyone who reads it now. Then we read in it that the temple (in which the whole scene takes place) can prove to be a structure of alienation, which can estrange both the Pharisee and the tax collector from themselves: both are its victims. However, Jesus is not concerned with these role-expectations which are conveyed by the temple, whether that of the Pharisee or that of the publican. He resolutely adopts the standpoint of the God who is concerned for the outcast, who seeks to establish true communication where this is lacking. This, of course, is the whole pattern of Jesus' life.[1] It is striking that where he is compelled by others to pass judgment on whether specific people are good or evil, he never gives a direct answer. Sometimes he appeals to the third possibility, God's possibility, which is evidently not ours. This becomes particularly evident when someone calls himself good. Jesus himself reacts promptly with the words, 'No one is good save God alone' (Luke 18.19; Matt.19.17; Mark 10.18). He himself does not want to judge in terms of good and evil. Nor, however, does he emerge as a kind old grandparent who through the experiential wisdom that he has gained relativizes everything, providing the miserly tax collector, the collaborator, with cheap and easy grace. These divisive categories are alien to Jesus. He has something deeper in mind: God loved us while we were still sinners. God seeks out the humble and the outcast. The restoration of communication for those whom others have rejected is at the heart of Jesus' message, of all his parables and miraculous signs, and finally also of his own execution; because of his message which establishes communication Jesus is himself excluded from the human community by his fellow men. For the outcast, rejection here even becomes a way of salvation.

If we middle-class twentieth-century Christians look in this light on the parable which Jesus himself embodies, it is not to the Jewish Pharisee of his time that it strikes home fatally, but to us. In our spontaneous identification with the publican we are really acting the Pharisee. For we often exclude others through our progressive or conservatively inclined spirituality. It follows from all that I have said so far that in any view of spirituality, 'morality' is not to be given pride of place, because here we come to grips with the heart of the Christian gospel, which must activate all Christian spirituality: establishing community.

Because God raised Jesus from the dead, this message, this life-style, this death of the outcast Jesus is endorsed by him for all time: that is the right way of living for men and women. And that is what is involved here, for spirituality is a way of life, a particular way of being human.

When people are aware of an identity which is forced on them by others, an identity with which they are at variance, one talks of an identity crisis. A crisis of one's own identity is always really opposition to an identity or role which is imposed on us by society. Therefore many believers are in search of true, freely chosen identity, their own way of life, their spirituality.

Spirituality, then, is the attraction of that which is not enforced, even within a tradition of religious experience with an eagerly accepted identity or identification which then takes shape in everything – both major and minor matters – and is also recognizable to others: in prayer, in work, in social and political action and so on. Spirituality is in no sense being what was once called a person, women or man, 'all of a piece'. That can be disturbing, one-sidedly crude and almost dictatorial. Nor does spirituality mean that Christians should need to live 'only for God', while in the meantime nature, our fellow men and our history can go to the dogs around us. The history of Christian spirituality teaches us that a Christian is made up of many pieces, with pores open to all the facets of what is meant by human life, in opposition and responsibility, in wonderment and agreement, in suffering and patient tolerance. But all this always has a Christian profile. Spirituality is not the permanent nucleus which exists abstractly and generally as inwardness behind the phenomena of changing history. However, that merely adds urgency to this question. What makes representatives of such different worlds as those of Jesus, Paul and Augustine, of the desert monks, of Popes Leo and Gregory, of Bonaventure and Thomas, of Master Eckhardt, John of the Cross, Thérèse of Lisieux and present-day martyrs from Latin America, true Christians, bearers of authentic spirituality? As Christian spirituality is essentially concerned also with human integrity and identity, the Christian continuity in all these divergent, contextually connected and even intrinsically irreconcilable pictures of the world, man and God is grounded on one and the same deeper vision of God and mankind in its history. Nevertheless, it happens again and again, in the sense that these different historical, even geographical and regional, social and psychological, class contexts and boundaries, these boundaries are in each case transcended in a very Christian way. Transcendence is only visible in immanence or contextuality. Following Jesus, discipleship, can therefore never be a material repetition of some earlier Christian spirituality, of whatever kind. This discipleship is Christian creativity in a historical context, which however at the same time sometimes breaks down and transcends its own context and boundaries, and precisely in so doing shares in the surprising new element that has appeared with Jesus. Time and again, therefore, spirituality is a new adventure of which Abraham, 'the Father of faith', is a model: 'Abraham set out going on a journey – not knowing where he was going' (see Heb.11.8).

What does the particular context in which we now live require of our Christian spirituality? What is the aspect of our spirituality for us here and now, today and tomorrow? The answer to this question is really: 'Look at what is happening around us; see how Christians today test and experiment.' Here I simply want to point to some features which come to the fore. I can see two indissoluble elements in our Christian faith: one can call them the aspects of 'interiority' and 'exteriority', and they belong together in such a way that both the 'interiority' and the 'exteriority' threaten to become false if in one way or another this unbreakable unity is either divided or broken.

Given the modern situation in which the world and society are experienced without 'Christian references' (both in Western middle-class society and in Communist state capitalism), that is, given the fact that we live in a world in which the gospel as such does not function as a motivation and orientation for all kinds of public social, political and economic decisions, there is an enormous danger that spirituality will be reduced to the sphere which is not occupied by public society, specifically the sphere of 'inwardness', the inner life and a private circle of friends. If that happens, however, people will be grotesquely deceived into thinking that inwardness should be a free, open and unoccupied sphere where (quite apart from what is happening in society), by individual choice, either personal redemption or personal enslavement can take place (however this may be interpreted, whether 'naturally' or 'supernaturally'). Here people forget that willy-nilly, the so-called 'open' society is also assimilated inwardly, so that our own inwardness itself bears all the marks of our middle-class society. Anyone who forces spirituality back into 'the inner life' reduces the 'Christian concern for interiority' simply to a reflection of this society. Further-more, the important thing about the latter is that consequently religions with their spirituality retreat within the bounds of interiority, of 'I' and 'We' experience, without paying attention to the so-called external social and economic sub-structures of these experiences. In this case people above all deprive Christian spirituality of its historical force. In that case, under a distorting mask, it becomes the slavish subject of social and political powers and becomes spirituality 'without a context'. Under the slogan of the 'primacy of the spiritual', spirituality is then in fact kept under the thumb by the primacy of materialistic and harsh laws of rivalry and competition which it furthers precisely by its flight into inwardness.

In Christian terms, inwardness or spirituality is therefore decidedly concerned with 'materiality', that is, with the whole reality of the socio-economic and political context in which human life takes its course. Christian spirituality is therefore impossible without a sensitive nose for 'the signs of the time'. It is a matter of human concern for man's humanity, believing at the same time in the God who is concerned for human beings. The heart of Christian spirituality is really nothing other than what Pauline theology calls 'imitating God'(Eph.5.1): imitating God who does not leave himself without a witness at any time. Concern for the living God (the kingdom of God) manifests itself in a contextual praxis in accordance with the kingdom of 'God, who descends to liberate men' (Exodus 3.7-8), here and now.

Christian spirituality, therefore, has quite a different aspect from purely mystical inwardness; it is also quite different from purely political and social involvement; it is not a copy and repetition of what non-Christians are already doing and often doing well. Contemporary Christian spirituality arrives at the insight that only in and through the critically active participation of Christians in the dynamics of our concrete history will authentic mystical forces be set free for more humanity and greater justice for all. The struggle over breathing-space for all men and women can only take place in the sphere of struggle, and the sphere of commitment (praxis in accordance with the kingdom of God) is at the same time the sphere in which prayer and mysticism find their concrete context. Precisely in that respect, spirituality which is nevertheless contextual breaks and transcends its own bounds.

Something of this kind was already expressed in the initial doubt of the Jewish people which they nevertheless overcame: 'How can we sing the Lord's song in a strange land?' (Ps.137.4). This was the question asked by the people living in captivity in Babylon, who to begin with had doubts: must we not free ourselves first and only later, once we are free, sing and celebrate our liberation? We have the same initial doubts: are there not many people – poor, oppressed, lowly, we ourselves – who are living in the captivity of their middle-class welfare states? But with the prophets in exile in Babylon, and also with present-day Latin American communities of believers and liberation theologians, we can overcome the doubt on the basis of the very specific experience that joy, prayer and singing are subversive within a world of oppressive societies. This kind of praying and singing makes the oppressive authorities tremble in their boots. Oppressors look for anxiety and obeisance, bowing and scraping, to perpetuate their rule, not a happy song of hope and love. The unexpected surprise – the supreme criticism of what people and their structures make of fellow human beings and their society – is expressed most strongly in the singing of songs of hope in captivity.

Confidence in the Christian source of spirituality is not a mere archaeological reconnaissance of old sources. The 'rechannelling' of Christian spirituality is only possible by our making new fountains spring up here and now, as disciples of Jesus, in which the same living water of the gospel is channelled down to our time. A spring, that is the hopeful vision of the kingdom of God and the new heaven and earth, a kingdom which only approaches in praxis commensurate with this kingdom of God: 'the works of the kingdom of God.' Rechannelling: that is, performing the works which are necessary here and now for establishing the kingdom of God in the light of this vision which we share of the kingdom of the God who is still concerned for men and women in our twentieth-century context. This Christian hope always has a cross-grained character: it goes against the world and society in so far as these do not act according to norms which are commensurate with that kingdom. It is also contrary to the human heart which deals in too bourgeois a way with the norms of the kingdom of God. To say that everything depends on prayer sounds pious, and it is in fact false; it is contrary to Jesus' demand for the salvation or wholeness of all men: 'Seek first the kingdom of God and his righteousness'(Matt.6.33), i.e. bring peace and justice among men. For the sin from which Jesus has redeemed us extends over the whole of mankind, including our economic, social and political conditions. The salvation that is given to us in Jesus is to be realized in all these dimensions. But on the other hand the grim impatient attitude that prayer and mysticism must wait until people have finished with their own process of liberation is a misunderstanding of 'what brings men and women salvation' in the full sense of the word – wholeness.

The interiority and experiential wisdom that we in fact need amount to a Christian wisdom which is aware that on the one hand no technology and strategy of salvation can liberate the world at its deepest level, but that on the other hand this is impossible without socio-economic policies, strategies and political plans. Otherwise spirituality abandons technology and politics to themselves, and they would like nothing better than for the wise men and the mystics to be confined to their own historically inefficient, harmless inwardness. This false inwardness gives free play to 'the powers of this world'. In that case, the enslaving power (whether the tyrant or the liberator) becomes or remains a new catastrophe for most people, above all for those who are not in power. Only contextual spirituality can overcome this dilemma.

What I have put into words in fleeting reflections simply expresses what we hear in the reports of new Christian experiments of many groups of believers in Belgium and Holland. In the new forms of spirituality which are already being practised, perhaps by trial and error, we can also see a critical reaction against an impoverished spirituality which is only of the spirit, and against a secular involvement without true inwardness and brotherly solidarity. These experiments also have a dynamic effect on many people. If as time goes on more believers identify themselves with the 'new' spirituality, in the long run they may become the model for the contextual spirituality of Christians which we need for our time, because they will acquire normative significance as the contemporary *sensus fidei* or intuition of faith held by believing communities.

The only adaptation, the only *aggiornamento* that Christians know is the constant adaptation of ourselves and the Christian community of faith to the praxis of the kingdom of God. But this adaptation, which is not a 'conforming to this world', corresponds contextually to a certain accent in contemporary Christian spirituality. A distinctive feature of our time and life in it is the paradoxical situation that within the churches spirituality is still often proclaimed and practised in an unrealistic and unmaterialistic sense (as purely vertical, unmediated prayer and contemplation), while on the other hand within the world social and political involvement is proclaimed as the only effective technology for salvation, without reflection, wisdom, retreat and prayer. Our time therefore imposes on us the task of stressing two things at the same time, both of which we need to realize an authentic two-in-oneness. Precisely in Jesus Christ this unmistakable two-in-oneness becomes manifest in one indivisible personality. On the one hand Jesus identifies himself with God's concern; essentially this spirituality is concerned with God. On the other hand he identifies himself with man's concern; essentially spirituality is concerned with human beings and the life that they live; spirituality serves man's humanity. Finally, in Jesus these two concerns seem to be simply one concern: man's concern is God's concern and God's concern is also man's concern. Precisely in expressing this through the central idea of Jesus' message, the kingdom of God among men, present-day Christian contextual spirituality can be recognized.

28

A Religious House worth Living In
(The Gospel of John)

A constant theme of the Gospel of John is indicated by the word *eskenosen,* 'He dwelt among us'(John 1.14). Monks and nuns, religious, and many others are in search of 'a religious house which is worth living in'. In a rather deeper sense of the word this is ultimately a matter of a pressing need for a dwelling: a need for somewhere to live together as human beings which is nevertheless religious, in which we can feel welling up within us the thought, 'It is good to live here.' What does our living together mean for us as religious – for ourselves and for many others outside? This is our basic question.

From the Johannine communities, which in all probability were chiefly made up of a large number of house communities in a great city, we have received a rather mysterious Gospel by which nevertheless these house communities lived out an authentic existence. It is a Gospel in which the problem of the human need for a spiritual dwelling plays a central role.

This problem is already indicated in the prologue. 'The Word became flesh and dwelt among us.' Johannine theology is essentially concerned with men and women living together with the man Jesus, the Son of man who came to dwell among us in the name of God. This Gospel seeks gradually to convey to its readers, using the literary tactic of suggesting a good deal of misunderstanding, what this living together really involves.

After a first extremely mysterious illustration of Jesus' living among us in the story of John the Baptist (1.19-34), in this Gospel Jesus proceeds directly to the choice of some disciples. In this Gospel they do not completely coincide with the so-called Twelve chosen in the

Synoptic Gospels: these communities have their own bearers of tradition who are different from the other Christian communities; they also have a different view of Jesus. It is also striking that in contrast to the Synoptics, the first question which the first two to be called put to Jesus sounds surprising: 'Rabbi, where do you live?' (1.38b). Jesus replies, 'Come and see.' To be able to follow Jesus and to want to follow him, to be able to set off with him, you must first know where and how he lives. Living together is the inspiration for all the rest. The Gospel says, 'So the disciples went with him and saw where he lived', and, 'On that day they stayed with him' (1.39): it was evidently good to live there. We hear this, but we do not discover from the story where and how Jesus lives. Mysteriously, the Gospel still keeps this secret. The so-called Messianic secret of the first three Gospels becomes in John the secret of Jesus' dwelling.

Philip, one of the first two disciples who already knew where Jesus lived, also says to Jesus' third follower, Nathanael, who had first said that nothing good could come out of Nazareth, 'Come and see' (1.46). First go and see where he lives and then you will believe and stay with him. But here too nothing is said about what for the disciples is now the fascinating question of Jesus' dwelling. The new element is only that it is suggested that Jesus' abode cannot be made clear by references to the city of his earthly birth, Nazareth, from where he came and from where by human tradition nothing good can come.

In the story there now follows a conversation with Nicodemus, who went by night to seek Jesus in his dwelling. Here we hear something about what was then the very central event of the birth of a child in a Jewish dwelling, but again in a very Johannine way: it is the rebirth of someone who had entered Jesus' house. 'What is born of the flesh is flesh and what is born of the Spirit is Spirit' (3.6). With these elevated but obscure words the question of Jesus' dwelling is mysteriously suggested but at the same time left unclear. A completely new concept of dwelling is suggested, but not expressed in an immediately comprehensible way.

At all events it is already evident from the first three chapters that those who know where Jesus lives 'can bear witness to what they have seen and heard'; they can speak on the basis of an overwhelming experience of their own. That is what is done by John the Baptist (1.19-34; 3.22-30), the disciples (1.35-51), Nicodemus (3.1-21) and especially by Jesus himself (1.13-25; 3.1-21), albeit to begin with very carefully. Where and how Jesus lives we do not discover.

In the next chapter (ch.4), in a conversation with the woman of Samaria, we get a first glimpse of Jesus' dwelling at least in a negative way: 'The hour is coming,' says Jesus, 'when you will not worship the Father on this mountain (the mountain of Samaria) or in Jerusalem' (the Jewish Mount Zion) (4.21). Here it is already evident that where Jesus dwells has to do with the question where God dwells and therefore where he can and may be celebrated. But here too the Johannine Jesus goes against all patterns of expectation, Jewish as well as Samaritan. The dwelling of God himself becomes problematical. It is not on Mount Gerizim nor on Mount Zion. However, when asked the logical question, 'If it is not here or there but everywhere, is God's dwelling in fact anywhere?', Jesus gives a first surprising answer, 'It is I who am speaking with you' (4.26). God's dwelling is to be found only where Jesus is. This exclusivism is characteristic of the Johannine communities. But even this story does not take us further, for it, too, does not seem to say anything about where Jesus himself dwells.

In chapters 5-10 further light is then cast on the identity of the person of Jesus with the help of all kinds of key concepts from the great Jewish festivals. The interest in the question about Jesus' dwelling is here diverted towards his person. And precisely through this it becomes clearer where Jesus lives. For Jesus says, 'Let not your heart be troubled. In my Father's house there are many mansions. Were that not the case I would have told you, for I go to prepare a place for you' (14.1-2). Here the suggestion is suddenly made that Jesus, who has his own as yet unmentioned, mysterious and fascinating place, must first leave his disciples in order to prepare a dwelling for them 'in the great abode of the Father'. It is understandable that this disturbs some people, and that above all Christians who live on the basis of the Synoptic Gospels feel dizzy and unaccustomed to it. This had already become clear in Jesus' discourse about the bread in John's Gospel. Many disciples had left Jesus at that time, but Peter, ignorant and stumbling, yet trusting, could simply say, 'Lord, where else can we go?' (6.68). Here the Gospel of John gives the impression that within our own earthly sphere we really cannot find any true dwelling place, even with the earthly Jesus among us, who first of all must disappear. Jesus seems to have to go away in order to prepare a dwelling in another mysterious 'somewhere'. In this phase of the story this Gospel seems to be saying to us: you are putting the wrong questions about Jesus' dwelling and your own spiritual need for a dwelling. This is further accentuated by the words of Jesus, 'When I have gone away and prepared a dwelling for you, I shall return to take you to me, so that you shall be where I am' (14.3), that is, where Jesus dwells. This is evidently somewhere above.

However, there again follows one of the mysterious Johannine twists to this story. Even the explanation just suggested also does not seem to be right, or at least can be understood in the wrong way. We are not pointed to a dwelling somewhere above, since Jesus makes it more precise: 'On that day (i.e. on Easter Day) we shall come to you and abide with you' (14.23); that is, according to the Greek construction, come and abide with you as a guest. We shall come and abide with you – suddenly in the plural: we, Father and Son together and in the power of the Holy Spirit. 'I shall return to you' (14.18), and 'on that day you shall know that I am in my Father and you are in me and I am in you' (14.20). The place where God is and therefore the place where Jesus is is not somewhere above, but involves a descent from above, in and among us here below, in our familiar worldly sphere. Jesus is therefore consistent in saying that he does not pray that 'the Father shall take us out of the world' (17.15), for that is not dwelling with Jesus the Son of man and it is not a good human way of dwelling. So for Johannine theology the fact that Jesus dwells among us after Easter as a house guest means that the face of God and the face of Jesus shine out in the very faces of our house guests. As one of the Johannine letters has put it: 'No one has seen God, but if we love one another, God dwells with us, and his love is made perfect in us' (I John 4.12). 'For if anyone does not love his brother whom he can see, he cannot love God whom he has never seen' (I John 4.20).

What was first expressed in terms of space must therefore be understood in a different way. Only now does the disciples' first question, to which they get no answer ('Rabbi, where do you live?'), or rather an indirect answer ('Come and see') receive its specific content in the Gospel of John. Jesus does not live 'somewhere'; he *is* 'God dwelling among us'. 'We have found him' (1.41), cry out the first disciples, him, i.e. the dwelling of God among us, and the particular guest is the dwelling of Jesus among us. Not on Mount Gerizim; not in Jerusalem nor even in Rome; not somewhere here or there; and not even everywhere in anonymous universality; not even in the localized abode of Jesus, whether still living in Palestine or after his death in heaven with the Father. He is simply present wherever people believe in Jesus and bear witness to that belief, and wherever people form a 'community of Jesus'. God dwells where we admit him, where a community admits him and does so by believing in Jesus and following him in love for their fellow human beings. That is a good place to live and this living together gives out a light of its own towards others who do not live there. For, as the Johannine Jesus says, ' I have given them the glory which you gave me' (17.22): the glory of living together, but with faces turned outwards.

So in chapter 17 Jesus prays first for himself (17.1-5), then for his first disciples (17.6-19) and finally for all those who will also come to believe in Jesus as the guest through the mediation of these first disciples (17.20-25); this last passage can only be understood in the light of the Johannine notion of dwelling together. For if we are to understand the passage well we must remember that when this Gospel was written, there was some degree of tension between the Johannine communities and the Petrine communities, which were built on Peter and the Eleven. The Johannine communities at that time did not recognize the authority of Peter and the Christian character of the other, non-Johannine Christian communities (John 1.42; John 21; etc.). But in their jealous maintenance of their eccentric peculiarity, the Johannine communities believed that their communities – the communities of the so-called 'beloved disciple' – had a better and deeper insight into the mystery of Jesus than Peter, the bearer of the tradition of the other communities. This is clear from six texts in the Gospel of John which I cannot analyse here (13.23-26; 18.15-16; 20.2-10; 21.7; 21.20-23; 19.26-27). Nevertheless the Johannine sense of superiority and exclusiveness protected by in-groups did not as yet have sectarian tendencies. In chapter 10 Jesus says, 'I have other sheep which are not of this fold' (10.16). That is, outside the Johannine communities there are others, above all the Petrine and Pauline communities, of whom Jesus says, 'Them too must I bring and they shall hearken to my voice and there will be one flock and one shepherd' (10.16b). Thus in this Gospel Jesus prays that the Johannine communities and the Petrine communities may be one, i.e. that they may recognize themselves in each other's different interpretations of Jesus not despite but precisely because of the fact that there are 'many dwellings in the house of the one Father': 'That they may be one as we are one, I in you and you in me, that they may all be made perfectly one so that the world outside may see that you have sent me' (17.23). Then human dwelling together, religious dwelling together, is possible and the community which results will shed its light outside and have the power to attract others.

In the question of the spiritual need for dwelling, the Gospel of John looks above all at the religious aspect of dwelling together; by contrast, the Synoptic Gospels look rather at the human aspect of living in this religious house: at the work of Jesus among us healing people and bringing liberation, when he went round Palestine doing good, when sickness and demons, domination and sin, vanished at his appearance. But for us, the Gospel of John and the Synoptic Gospels together are canonical holy scripture, i.e scripture to inspire and to guide us. Johannine theology by itself is not a norm for us; it is corrected within the New Testament, above all by the Synoptic Gospels. As is evident from their history in the second century, where these Johannine communities did not involve themselves in this wider context of 'many dwellings in the house of the one Father', they turned into Gnostic sects and ultimately disappeared without a name and without a trace from our history. In precisely this respect the tension at that time between the Johannine and the Petrine communities is still a model for the church today in its polarization into different church traditions. No reference to a fragment from the New Testament can bring us to the perfect unity that we desire, but only the New Testament as a whole. And this shows us, without calling one another heretics, that there are indeed many dwellings in the house of the one Father, even for those with a Johannine theology, albeit as corrected by the Synoptics – although now we are perhaps less inclined to accept the supplementation of the Synoptics which the Gospel of John brings.

Be that as it may, in the wider context of the whole of the New Testament the Gospel of John teaches us – who are in search of a worthwhile religious house to live in – that in any case 'good living' is possible only where God has also become a particular source experience, as he has dwelt among us and with us as a guest in Jesus and since Easter in the power of the Spirit in our fellow men. Whenever the human aspect or the religious aspect of this dwelling together disappears into the mist, we mutilate christology, we mutilate our church or our social group, and we mutilate our life together. Where on the other hand a religious community shows a human face and this human face sheds its light from a human community of dwelling, the so-called outside world will see that our living together shows a face of its own, a face that can even be fascinating, indeed seductively beautiful, for others 'outside'.

When other people ask ' Where do you live?', like the first disciples, we must be able to answer them, 'Come and see.' Come to our religious house, and see. What we then go on to do, on the basis of this living, this dwelling together, must not be determined by our needs or our frustrations within the house, but by the needs and wants which prevail in the so-called ' outside' world, which often cannot even begin to raise the question of a house which is good to dwell and to live together in for the simple reason that it does not even have the material for a dwelling. The 'Come and see' can only take credible shape in solidarity with this so-called outside world – at least if we do not want to succumb to the same one-sidedness as a result of which the Johannine communities in the second century went under without leaving a trace.

29

Priests and Religious as Figures for Orientation

(Delivered at the celebration of the fiftieth anniversary of the profession of two religious and the fortieth anniversary of an ordination to the priesthood. The readings were Mark 1.9-11; 4-5.20)

Religious and priests are figures for orientation. They perform this function for a believing community which puts into explicit words, celebrates liturgically, and in differing circumstances gives tangible expression in a praxis commensurate with the kingdom of God to the salvation which God (of whom many people are unaware) is involved in bringing about in the history of our world. A person does not live by abstractions nor even by visions, but by living incarnations in which visions take bodily form. So we can only live fully from God in and through the concrete humanity of Jesus. As an image and metaphor, a likeness and mirror of God, Jesus, the Son, shows in visible human action who and how God is, and what he means for us in his love, in the same way as the face of a human son always shows some of the features of his father or mother. 'You are my dear child, I am depending on you', for I am counting on you to liberate people. That, in the last resort, is Mark's story of Jesus' inauguration.

I believe that, following in Jesus' footsteps, the religious too must be something like this, as must be the priest who presides over the community. They are not the light. They do not have the light, but they bear witness to the light. They have the other's features on their face and are yet themselves, with their own name.

But that attractive and challenging image of what religious and priest may and can betoken as figures of orientation should not make us forget the serious and precarious crisis in which at present both religious life and the priesthood are involved, at least (and we must always bear this in mind) in our prosperous Western countries. It

would be ostrich-like if we were to keep quiet about such a problematical fact on a festival like this one. Let us honestly acknowledge that
over recent years, even in our own Dominican circles, we are celebrating
more golden jubilees of religious or fortieth anniversaries of priesthood
than the first professions of young people or their offering of themselves
for some ministry in the church. Obviously we have reason only to
celebrate the past; the present and the future no longer seem conducive
to celebration and encouragement.

This situation depresses some people and makes them pessimistic.
Among others it encourages thoughts of disaster. Imperceptibly but
inevitably, many people are beginning to become indifferent; or they
are saying, 'We'll see our time out'. More grimly, some are looking
elsewhere for scapegoats for this situation. Let us honestly and frankly
say: all these are fruitless and above all unimaginative attempts,
pseudo-solutions without Christian resourcefulness and without Christian hope.

We are also threatened with another and perhaps more subtle
danger. The situation can provoke nostalgia for the past and encourage
conservative tendencies. Some people in fact want to go back to what
to a great extent can be called the cause of the present crisis. These are
solutions which, after what will probably be a brief success, will
inevitably land us in even greater trouble.

So over against the real crisis I am not arguing in any way for
conservatism. On the other hand, however, what is at stake is the
Christian identity of a messianic community (even of our own little
Dominican community at the Albertinum). The question is whether the
community has enough messianic force to be able to provide religious
and the various ministers that the church needs. Our Christian identity
is at stake, and we need to be critical about that. Tradition is solidified
experience which calls for renewed experiences if it is to become a
living and attractive challenge and call for others. If the original
experience is not to ossify and become the literal repetition of old
experiences and thus empty formulae, it must be handed on as a living
reality. Something of this kind can only happen if the old experience is
handed on to others in and through new experiences. A living
community of God – strong enough to provide volunteers for the
religious life and the ministry of the church – lives only if it does not
live just from traditions but is itself above all in a position to be able to
create new traditions, where yet others can enter it. That means that
the living community of faith, the feeding ground of religious orders
and of ministry in the church, is not so much a message that must be
believed. It is an experience which becomes a message for others and
which as the presentation of a message can become a new possible way
of experiencing life for others who may hear of it (again within other

experiences of their own). That is the way in which the gospel has been handed down over the centuries, above all by the attractive and active praxis of the kingdom of God, in smaller or wider contexts.

Jesus said to his community, the church : 'The gates of hell shall not prevail against it', and, more positively, 'I shall be with you to the end of time.' That means that as Christians we may believe that the content of the good news which makes up the gospel is so powerful and surprising that there will always be enough people, men and women, to join the movement-about-the-gospel and hand on the torch of the messianic movement. What we need to remember is that, within grace, the torch keeps burning with the oil of our own lives. If not here, in Europe, the torch burns in Africa or Latin America. In the last resort Jesus did not give his promises exclusively to Europe!

That is why today we are not pessimistic about our faith. Quite the reverse, though we experience our ups and downs and we must also face our own particular challenges. History teaches us that above all in times of persecution the Christian community becomes rich in religious figures to serve as points of orientation, who, matured by suffering for the good cause (man's concern as God's concern) are able to lead their communities in wisdom, in courage and in surprising resourcefulness. Many New Testament writings came into being in just such situations of persecution.

But our Western churches seem to be weary. They have already endured twenty centuries: times of belief and unbelief, of joy and suffering, suffering sometimes at the hands of others and sometimes through their own failure to understand. Now, however, Western churches no longer undergo persecution. The world does not speak against them as it used to, perhaps because they no longer speak out against today's world but rather allow themselves to be taken over and integrated with this world. However, the Western churches do not see that perhaps a more subtle form of 'persecution' is unmistakably taking them over and enslaving them. What I mean is prosperous Western society which – more subtly than the brutal persecution which rouses opposition – takes them gently by the arm and at the same time hinders them fatally. In that case I sometimes think that we may not ascribe the crisis in the religious life and in the church's ministry exclusively to antiquated church structures or to a church order which not only earlier but now has become insensitive to new situations – although we must concede that a particular form of church leadership can cripple Christian imagination and the resourcefulness of many Christians and lead to indifference. But we cannot close our eyes to the fact that our Western culture also makes us, religious and ministers, stealthily but surely technologists in religious and church affairs. Certainly, in earlier days, on the basis of an unmistakable Christian inspiration, a good deal was done in a slapdash way where now we rightly go to work with more technical skill and insight, even recognizing the significance of appropriate structures. Nevertheless, Western skill and technology can also reify our spirit, our charisma and our inspiration, pauperize it so that it becomes a rational and enlightened planning of means and ends – rock-hard as in a modern business, or efficient as in many kinds of training. In the meantime other non-Christian modern movements, from the right wing or from the left, show more of an eye for and sensitivity to verve and a sense of occasion, inspiration and conviction, even myth and ritual. That is why they are proving so attractive.

In the gospel stories from Mark I was struck above all by Jesus' remark 'Don't be afraid.' In fact people have the most grotesque expectations of their God on the basis of their deepest feelings. They expect that if you give yourself completely to God and as a religious or a minister want to be concerned only with God's concern as man's concern, there can be nothing but God, the great eagle who devours all the smaller birds, and that in that case you must efface yourself and all the world of God's creation. That God's concern is in fact man's concern, just as God makes man's concern his own, and that that is meant by what the gospel stories call 'the kingdom of God' at the same time surpasses all our expectations of God. People often imagine God quite differently from the way in which God sees and imagines himself. 'Does not even the sparrow find a home of its own? Does not the swallow have its own nest?' Do we learn nothing from the seed that grows, from the mustard seed that becomes great by first being small? For human beings to think of God in purely human terms can indeed lead to bizarre and degrading ideas. People offered sacrifices in the past to honour their God. Are things different in our day? Does not a great deal of disaster and suffering happen in our world in God's name? But Jesus says: When you feel God approach, don't be afraid. God is a God of humankind, a God who, as Leviticus says, 'abhors the sacrifices of men' (Lev.18.21-30; 20.1-5). God is a fire, indeed. However, he is a fire which does not consume the burning bush but leaves it intact.

Don't be afraid: that is the great news, the gospel of Jesus which we confess as Christians. Precisely because we believe that the torch of the gospel will always find new bearers, in whatever form, we can and may celebrate without hesitation, truly celebrate, without any sceptical restraint on our joy. It is not as though today we were celebrating the last three Mohicans! Otherwise, we would hear the voice of Jesus' rebuke, not from afar, but from within our own beating hearts: ' O ye of little faith!'

In 1974, in an indescribably terrifying place where hundreds of people had been shut up for months by the victors in a dictatorial coup d'état, a prisoner suddenly began to play his guitar. He sang of the stubborn hope of an enslaved people. A guard came past and with a blow of his sword struck off the singer's hand. The song stopped. But then all the prisoners went on, although they were poor and wavering shadows. At the risk of execution they took up the thread of the song of the singer who was bleeding to death. This is the sharp and acid brilliance of enslaved people who at the risk of their lives sing in a boundless way, the way of the real measure of our astonishing humanity.[1]

This is the way in which we take up the thread of the gospel tradition and make a new tradition which people can live by. 'Forget not the words of old', the gospel.

30

Christian 'to the Death'
(Matt.16.21-27; Jer.20.7-9)

From that time (viz., the time when Peter solemnly confessed that Jesus is the Messiah of God) Jesus began to show his disciples that he must go to Jerusalem and suffer many things from the elders and chief priests and scribes, and be killed, and on the third day be raised. And Peter took him and began to rebuke him, saying, 'God forbid, Lord! This shall never happen to you!' But he turned and said to Peter, 'Get behind me, Satan! You are a hindrance to me; for you are not on the side of God, but of men.' Then Jesus told his disciples, 'If any man would come after me, let him deny himself and take up his cross and follow me. For whoever would save his life will lose it, and whoever loses his life for my sake will find it. For what will it profit a man, if he gains the whole world and forfeits his life? Or what shall a man give in return for his life? For the Son of man is to come with his angels in the glory of his Father, and then he will repay every man for what he has done' (Matt.16.21-27).

Confronted with the Gospel according to Matthew which has just been read, unless we are sceptical, we prosperous people either take it with a pinch of salt, or explain it to ourselves in terms of the offerings which we choose to give in order to ensure ourselves a better place in heaven. Our bourgeois reading of the gospel seems to be able to defend all standpoints.

If we are not to make whatever we choose of the text, before we prosperous Western Christians begin to discover the meaning of this passage from the gospel we must first try to understand what the evangelist Matthew meant to say with these words to the Christians of his time. Otherwise we are not listening to the gospel, but to our own ideas.

After Matthew's story of Peter's solemn messianic confession, that Jesus is the 'Messiah of God', a gospel which was read in the liturgy last Sunday, today, immediately afterwards, we hear Jesus' sharp rebuke to Peter – though Matthew makes Jesus take Peter aside to rebuke him, so that the other disciples do not hear it. To some degree Matthew wants to safeguard the authority of the church, without removing any of Jesus' criticism. Peter is not choosing God's side, so he is choosing the side of the ungodly, Satanic powers. This is a very strong story. On the basis of human convictions, Peter is rejecting a suffering Messiah who would be brought low by secular and religious powers. Peter (who has only just been made the first stone of the church as a messianic community) thinks: 'Surely such a Messiah must triumph over all, even over the powers of hell?' Indeed that is the case, says Matthew, but what you forget is that this does not happen in the way in which non-messianic, all too human people suppose. In an ancient way Matthew subtly interweaves the suffering and the violent death of Jesus with suffering, torture and the violent death of Christians simply because they are Christians: that is, they proclaim God's rule as justice and love among their fellow human beings. In favour of Peter it can be said that it is bewildering when it is the good, the true and the righteous against whom stones are cast. For Jews and the first Christians, 'messianic community' meant, 'Alleluia, we are freed. No more suffering and oppression. Goodbye to all tears, goodbye to all slavery!'

However, on the basis of Jesus' reaction Matthew wants to impress on us that being a Christian does not take so triumphal a human course and does not smoothly produce an experience of being 'high'. This story of Matthew's stands at the end of what for him is Jesus' Galilean mission. From now on Jesus is going to limit himself to the direct training and instruction of his disciples who had followed him from Galilee, the nucleus of the coming community of the church. Matthew sees this teaching by Jesus in the light of what is already his church's belief in the death and resurrection of Jesus. Hence within this story there is the first allusion to the suffering of Jesus as what is really a prophecy of the suffering and persecution of the messianic community.

Earlier Matthew has told of Jesus' founding of his church. This is built on a rock: Peter. For the Jews of that time a messiah without a messianic community (which is also called 'the community of God' just as the messiah is 'of God') was unthinkable. A messiah, Jesus the messiah, also had a following, a community or church. By this Matthew wants us to understand that the community will not fare any differently from the messiah. That is why he speaks, like all the Synoptics and the whole of the New Testament, about the actual historical necessity of the suffering of Jesus and of his messianic community, given the wickedness of this world – even if it is controlled by the sovereignty of God. 'Anyone who wants to be my disciple must deny himself and take up his cross.' These words which are basic to our being Christian, have often been *devalued* in ascetic terms and at the same time have been *over-valued*: by that I mean that they have been stretched beyond their real meaning to present the Christian life as the permanent bearing of a cross, in direct contradiction to what Jesus had called the 'light yoke' of the kingdom of God. Exegesis has drawn a veil of dullness and sobriety over Christianity, a dark cloud of penance, sacrifice and the inflicting of pain, even of self-contempt and self-depreciation. Christianity is said to be at its best when blood flows and people have to suffer pain under a harsh yoke – at least that is what certain Christians said who themselves happened to experience neither pain nor yoke. This interpretation completely forgets the context in which the New Testament – and today the Gospel of Matthew – speaks about the 'messianic need to suffer'. The context in which the Gospels speak of this is always one of persecution and trial, of threats of torture and death. The passage is therefore concerned with extraordinary, indeed extreme situations in the life of a Christian, situations which occur only exceptionally in someone's life. But when it comes, the situation is decisive. So although it is not one which happens every day, the Gospel of Matthew nevertheless makes it clear to us that while many Christians may perhaps never be confronted with this difficult choice, making that choice well and decisively will nevertheless be the result of a daily life which is oriented on it. Precisely because of that, in this pericope Matthew connects the decisive situation with the final verdict of the Son of man on our life (16.27).

In many countries, in Latin America and also behind the Iron Curtain, many Christians do live in this extreme situation. And in the perspective both of these present-day experiences and what the Gospel of Matthew says, we can understand the first reading in the liturgy today, from Jeremiah 20.7ff. In a critical situation of this kind even the prophet Jeremiah, like Peter, is assailed by the temptation to avoid the evil threat – and who would not be? He laments, 'Whenever I speak, I shout "violence and destruction" (i.e. criticize human society in the name of God), but I myself end up simply doing nothing.' 'Sometimes I think', says Jeremiah, 'I will not mention him or speak any more in his name: I will keep quiet' (Jer.20.9). It is precisely when confronted with such extreme situations that what Jesus means strikes home: 'If anyone will be my disciple, let him take up his cross.' Jesus does not say *my* cross; he says *his* cross. Without doubt, in Matthew 'take up his cross' is already coloured by the fact of Jesus' historical crucifixion.

But this in no way excludes the probability that Jesus himself had already used the words 'take up his cross' (see Matt.10.38; 16.24; Mark 8.34; Luke 9.23; 14.27). Long before the time of Jesus, for both Jews and Greeks (see already Plato, *Republic* II,361) the expression 'take up one's cross' meant to have the courage to die a violent death for a particular cause (although for the Romans that was in itself a bad cause). So what Matthew is saying in this story is that Christianity can result in a violent death: an execution, being lynched or a treacherous shot from a mercenary killer. From a Christian perspective, anyone who in these circumstances seeks to save their own skin is lost: 'Whoever will save his life will lose it.' In that case all the former peaceful times of Christianity become meaningless: they are untried and lack the seal of fulfilment. Without Jesus' violent death there would have been no special seal on his message, his life-style and his person, and nothing would have been known of his Galilean mission. Jesus risked all to the death, as did Peter later; Monsignor Romero and many others with him go on risking all today. There are circumstances, like those of Jesus, like those of Bishop Romero, in which one can predict a violent death. This does not call for any extraordinary revelations: what is extraordinary is trust in one's own calling to serve justice in a world of injustice, power and slavery. In that case the dramatic dénouement of trust in one's own calling is obvious. But it is not the last word. There is V day, God's 'third day'. What is the mystery of this complete risk, in trust, Matthew does not state directly in this passage, but today's reading from Jeremiah goes into it. After Jeremiah, like any human being inclined to weariness, had said, ' I've had enough, I'm giving up my prophetic statements', he was restored, encouraged and driven on by something stronger than himself and affirmed: 'But a fire is burning in my heart, it is burning in my bones' (20.9b) – and he remained faithful to his prophetic message. Even being emotionally under the spell of 'the good cause', man's concern as God's concern, cannot be resisted. It has deeper sources than one's own courage or depression: 'O God,' Jeremiah finally says, 'I have put my cause in your hands' (20.12-13), just as Jesus says, 'Father, into your hands I commend my spirit.' That is Matthew's own message, which we can listen to today.

But what does this message mean for us prosperous Christians who do not have to think of martyrdom and torture, and only know the miseries of any human being, small and great, some of which we bring on ourselves?   Briefly, this. First of all, for want of persecution we need not involve ourselves in radical asceticism. This costly sacrifice which we choose for ourselves is often a subtle expression of self-assertion rather than surrender to a good cause.

In that case, what then? This. Within our own surroundings, however small-scale they may be, we must stand up for justice and love, for truth and goodness, even to our own disadvantage. This in itself will bring us persecution and suffering enough, which is what Matthew is ultimately concerned with. And in that case the miseries of the human condition, large and small, often so painful and impossible to understand, will cease to be a real problem.

31

Christian Obedience and its Pathology

It is always worth while recalling great traditions of collective experiences involving both religious and non-religious people with the aim of creating a better future for authentically human life. Such traditions may bring critically to light blind spots in our new, present-day, views and evaluations of many things and relationships, correct though they may be. If our concern is critical, these old traditions can prove both liberating and productive towards the development of the true humanity of mankind.

Among these great human traditions, we find on the one hand pagan witnesses, which Johannine theology calls 'this world' and the Gospel of Mark 'men': present-day Christians call them the modern world. These have always been critical of Christian obedience, and Christian humility, which is closely linked with it. For Christians it is a good thing to listen to this 'pagan' criticism, even when it is no longer completely correct from a historical point of view.

On the other hand we find 'Christian witnesses', people who in their experience of authentic Christian obedience find inspiration and orientation for a criticism of the secular self-sufficiency of those who do not seem to be aware of their loneliness and their lack of solidarity.

The directors of *Spirituality,* the annual November number of *Concilium,* have asked me to give a broad survey of both sides of this mutual criticism. That is in fact a not inconsiderable historical task. Here I can do no more than analyse a few phenomena from history, though they are fundamental. On the one hand is the Graeco-Roman criticism of Christian obedience in antiquity and on the other the revival of this criticism in our modern world, albeit within the new situation which has arisen since the Western Enlightenment. For it is this modern criticism which has drawn a good deal of its inspiration from the Middle Stoa.

1. 'The world's' criticism of Christian obedience

(a) The Greek idea of human grandeur

As the representative of what was already a long Greek tradition, Aristotle expressed a supreme disdain for any servile subjection.[1] We should remember here that at that time this subjection was a reality on a massive social scale, to which the elite owed their privileged position; they did not take this into consideration in their theories of human grandeur. The elite contrasted that grandeur, expressed in the typically Greek and later also Roman view of human 'greatness of soul' (*megalopsychia,* which Cicero translated as *magnanimitas*) with servile subjection. This grandeur consisted in great or fine humanity on the basis of an ethically good attitude to life (*kalokagathia*).

This Graeco-human grandeur went in two different directions, though with the same basic attitude. On the one hand was active and political grandeur, the disposition of people who made great plans and were also able to carry them out. They were able to 'hold the world in contempt' for a great cause, to stand above it through their own human greatness and the veneration of others. On the other hand, there was a contemplative ethical grandeur. Here human greatness lies in ethical excellence, a greatness of which Socrates is regarded as the prototype.[2] The wise Greek was able to transcend all outward vicissitudes of human life through inner self-respect and self-awareness. For this wise contemplative man, the great political figure is a dangerous fool who has to be kept down. Only intrinsic ethical human value transcends the external world.[3]

The Greek could give this ideal various forms within different movements. He could be like Plato, scornfully transcending this shadow world and looking out on the divine world order of ideas, as a model for the right ordering of the earthly world order which had been reduced to a chaos by short-sighted politicians. He could also look for it in the direction of Aristotle, by denying an order transcending this one, excluding God from human life[4] and thus hoping for all salvation from and for mankind only from and through mankind and, moreover, within this earthly life. The maxim that it is better to give than to receive here has a distinctively Greek background.[5] The subject which is ethically active is the one which is superior, the dominantly virile over against whatever or whoever is the receiving subject, the subordinate, dominated, the feminine principle of the receiving subject.[6] Because this magnanimous, typically-male man has virtue in himself, he transcends the earthly world outside, even when this fails him; for he knows that on the basis of his own intrinsic virtue he has the right to be honoured by all other men, the right to all earthly goods. The Aristotelian man of grandeur keeps to the golden mean between vanity or boastfulness and small-mindedness (*mikropsychia; pusillanimitas,* sometimes also called *humilitas* or modesty). These two attitudes are vices, because they imply a mistaken self-knowledge, except in the case of the person who is really lowly; for him such humility is suitable. However, the person who has a sense of grandeur does what is good, not because it is commanded by someone else, even by a God; he does it because he judges it to be good and beautiful in itself.[7] Such a man is autarkic, self-sufficient: he can do without everyone and everything and needs nothing, not even God. In contrast to petty servile men he will laugh scornfully and condescendingly, ironically concealing his own grandeur,[8] and in contrast to those with political power in this world he knows that he is superior, above all in ethical wisdom. All he needs is friends of like mind; he is satisfied in converse with them.[9] Autonomous and free, he is in the service of the one great ethical cause, and regards his own outward life as nothing.[10] This 'humanly great' man should normally be the king of the country;[11] he himself is aware of this, but he is able, autarkically, to renounce the honour which others apparently begrudge him. That was how Aristotle taught and how he lived.

However, the Greek spirit went even further. The Stoics made the views of Aristotle even more radical, though they were already radical in themselves, but at the same time came some way towards meeting the religious needs of men. For example, they denied the Aristotelian view that people need some external goods before their acquisition of virtue. For the Stoic sage, from the beginning it was enough to have a subjective ethical intent. On the basis of that he did not so much condemn the outside world or the world perceived by the senses, as the world in so far as it lies outside human free will and appears as fate in contrast to human freedom. The harmony of the great world order, i.e. the will of God, can require sacrifices from the individual aspirations of human beings. They must voluntarily accede to the law of the universal divine Logos, the reason in all things. Stoic condemnation of the world is therefore purely ethical. In contrast to the human grandeur of Plato and Aristotle, the greatness of the Stoic sage was, moreover, accessible to all men – both to the slave (Epictetus) and the Emperor (Marcus Aurelius). Furthermore, this was the period of Graeco-Roman cosmopolitanism, the so-called great brotherhood of all men: *'Homo, res sacra homini'* (Seneca).

Unlike the original Stoa, the Middle Stoa, somewhat later, was aware of the illusory and utopian character of a direct knowledge of the will of God. Perfect harmony between human reason and the universal divine reason is therefore a chimaera. There must therefore be intermediaries between the will of God and human reason – this was the new wisdom. In this way we are able to know and carry out the will of God with at least a degree of probability, especially through the natural tendencies of the individual things through which universal order is realized. By obeying our private and individual natural aspirations, we translate the universal law in what is a probable and correct way, that is, we are obedient to God. This view was to shape history throughout the Western world, whether Christian or non-Christian.

However, even in this version of the Greek spirit, the dominant norm of human grandeur is the subjection of man to the will of God. Despite this, however, this Greek and also Roman attitude to life (for in the later 'imperial' Stoa the Greek ideal was universally disseminated by Rome) consisted of an exclusive trust in one's own human powers in this struggle to obey the will of God. For these men of grandeur, praying to God is only a prayer of thanksgiving and never a prayer of petition or a supplication for help (see also Cleanthes' Hymn to Zeus). Greeks never kneel before God and ask him for help; that would be against human worth and self-sufficiency. Even when Seneca writes, *'Deo parere, libertas est,'*[12] 'man's freedom consists in obeying God', he is expressing the conviction that man owes himself to God and for that very reason no longer has need of God and can rely only on his own powers.[13] In this pantheistic view, trust in God is possible only in the mode of human self-confidence. Even at the climax of Graeco-Roman pagan spirituality, i.e. in Marcus Aurelius, in whom we can trace something of what Christians call the humble obedience of faith – 'Why should God not help us even in those matters that are within our power?'[14] – and where this magnanimous humanist thus shows some need for God, this humble confession remains within Stoicism, man's self-sufficient autonomy. We could say that for want of a right concept of God and his creation, what Christians would call humility or obedience evidently cannot thrive on pagan soil. However, the pride with which the Greek is human is at the same time a criticism of Christian humility.

This Greek spirit (which was developed in different ways, later also by Neo-Platonism) arose from a certain tragic experience of life. As the Greek looks at himself, at his own intrinsic human powers, he is optimistic and able to cope with life. However, if he looks outside, at the world and society, he becomes pessimistic, believing that man is shattered by the vicissitudes of blind fate. Man's inner worth and happiness can only be destroyed by things outside him. Thus salvation or human redemption must be sought in some technique or other by which man is able to scorn 'the world' and transcend it on the basis of his own self-sufficient, unthreatened grandeur. Freedom here is not privatized, inward independence, which in fact can go hand in hand with a lack of social and political freedom. But even though they were religious, these philosophers never took refuge in a god, imploring him to send them good fortune. By the witness of his own autonomous conscience the magnanimous man knows that as a 'good man' he does not deserve adversity; it is fate, not he, who is wrong. This *contemptus mundi* or scorn of the world is therefore the other side to man's self-sufficient grandeur and has nothing to do with a denial of oneself, a *contemptus sui*.

When this Graeco-Roman attitude came into contact with the humble obedience of Christianity, it was to offer fierce opposition. The Greek spirit saw in Christian obedience a regular attack on human grandeur.

(b) 'Pagan' human grandeur as a criticism of Christian obedience and the reaction of Christians

Pagan wisdom had only scorn for the witness to the death of Christian martyrs, an action which is described by the Acta Martyrum as the most profound force in Christianity. Why this rejection by pagans when the pagan *magnanimus,* the man of great soul, was also ready to lay down his life for a great cause? Furthermore, it is a historical fact that many Stoic sages became martyrs, murdered or banished from Italy for their ideals, which were critical of society. Nevertheless, high-minded pagan figures like Epictetus, Marcus Aurelius and Celsus[15] simply regard the obedience of the Christian martyrs as weak and cowardly pettiness, and even perverse disgust for human life. They certainly did not see it as human grandeur and *magnanimitas*. Their criticism of Christians was that they crept to a god crying for help, and in martyrdom did not trust in their own autonomous powers.

The Greek church fathers almost always begin their arguments by making a distinction between true humility and its many pseudo forms; in the last resort they too are Greeks. For the rest they respond to the pagan arguments with counter-arguments. Humility is the only true human greatness. In so doing they analyse the pagan version of this concept. Nevertheless it is remarkable that with the exception above all of Augustine, the Greek and Latin church fathers (like mediaeval theologians after them), usually start from the view that the pagans too have a concept of humility or lowliness. Christians heard the pagan Celsus say in his anti-Christian polemic[16] that Christian humility is a plagiarism of Plato, but that the Christians had interpreted Plato wrongly. For the Platonic *tapeinos* or humble man always bears witness to a 'well ordered' humility, and according to Celsus the Christians did not have this reasonable ordering:[17] Christians, after all, allowed thieves and prostitutes to enter what they called the kingdom of God first:[18] this was an abomination even for permissive Greeks. Augustine, by contrast, was firmly convinced that humility is an original Christian quality that was unknown among the pagans, who did not have any idea of it.[19] The Greek Christian Origen came to the fore in dealing with the objections made by Celsus. He too points to possible caricatures of humility.[20] For him authentic humility is only a virtue of the great among us, just as for pagans magnanimity was only the privilege of great men. All saints are humble. And only humility can really be called human greatness. In other words, humility does not confront a person with the world or his fellow man, but with God. In that situation the only appropriate attitude for a person is humble obedience. 'To humble oneself', as a patristic Christian virtue, thus means to see oneself in relation to God. He alone is great, and over against him every single person is small. Augustine was to express this general patristic conviction very clearly: *'Tu homo, cognosce quia homo es. Tota humilitas tua, ut cognoscas te.'*[21] To know your own humanity is true humility, for true humanity is (a) God's creation and (b) damaged by sin. Therefore knowing oneself in the light of God brings about humble obedience in faith and – by means of a radical change in the pagan concept – precisely this comes to be called *magnanimitas,* human grandeur.

So over against pagan humanism the church fathers stressed God's greatness and human misery. The patristic and later the mediaeval theologians (up to Thomas Aquinas) could thus identify true humility directly with *magnanimitas.* Here, however, the pagan concept was mystically transformed. Patristic theology was ultimately concerned only with the grandeur of God who has mercy on man in his insignificance. This brought about a fundamental change in the typically pagan concept of the *contemptus mundi* (scorn for the world). For pagans, contempt for the world (*spernere, despicere mundum*) was the obverse of autarkic human self-assertion over the fate which overtakes man from outside: contempt for the world was an expression of self-glorifying human grandeur. However, on the basis of Christian creation faith in patristic theology, this Greek *contemptus mundi* or scorn for the world was fundamentally extended to a *contemptus sui,* self-denial. The *spernere mundum* becomes *spernere seipsum;* in other words, Christians regarded even the human grandeur of the pagans as nothing when confronted with the cosmic and social world outside, particularly in the presence of God. In this way a real confrontation with paganism was avoided and an internal Christian solution was found to the problem. There was no question of a synthesis between pagan grandeur and Christian humility. A legitimate pagan criticism was not elaborated in a Christian sense; it was simply defused within the system. The relationship between man's liberation of himself and salvation from God remains unresolved, though this was the particular pagan contribution which could be made as a criticism of Christianity.

Christians became more aware of this problem in the twelfth century, although the non-religious version of pagan Greek philosophy (Aristotle's own view of human grandeur) was unknown at the time. Christians were at that time confronted above all with the ideas of the Middle Stoa. In the Augustinian tradition of the Middle Ages, St Bernard made a distinction which was to dominate the whole of that period. You could consider man from two points of view: (a) in himself, that is, in what he is in himself and would be without God. In that case the answer is clear: sheer nothingness, shadow and dirt. After all, he is created 'from nothing'. And (b) in relation to God the creator, through whom he is positively what he is, and to whom he therefore owes all his human greatness. But in that case God's greatness is also in man.[22] Even a Stoic sage would perhaps be able to say something to this effect, though his spirituality would still be fundamentally different.

This is very clearly revealed when Bernard goes on to explain this distinction more precisely, in a way which Thomas Aquinas was to oppose. He says that our human share in our humanity is sin and evil, injustice and disaster; God's share in our humanity is goodness and salvation, righteousness and happiness.[23] Our contribution is negative: all that is positive comes from God, so that 'humility' points to man's contribution and *magnanimitas* to God's. A true Greek, however, would never have been able to express himself in this way. Still, even Bernard was to some extent reserved in his belittlement of men. He drew a distinction between *humiliatio,* humility which is imposed from outside, and *humilitas,* which is accepted spontaneously in a happy and friendly personal way. *Humilitas iustificat, non humiliatio,*[24] that is, what justifies us is not humiliation from outside but the humility we have chosen freely. Finally, we can only become humble through ourselves. Here we really see something of the mediaeval spirit. Therefore *humiliari,* keeping oneself humble, has nothing to do with *se humiliari,* humiliate oneself, either in patristic teaching or in the Middle Ages. For Bernard the humble man is authentically autarkic and autonomus: *causa sui.* Although his teaching is obviously in the patristic tradition, it also reveals something of the Greek feeling towards autonomy.[25]

We may conclude that pagan humanism was concerned with human grandeur coming from and through man, though it is also the gift of God, as in the tradition of the imperial Stoa. However, this is a grandeur without real humility. Here human grandeur begins to be coupled with ignorance of God's true divinity. On the other hand, in their recognition of God's true greatness, patristic and mediaeval theologians misunderstood man's secular grandeur and were unable to accord it a proper place. This failure coloured and frequently discoloured the concept of Christian obedience. Therefore we may say that neither the pagans nor Christianity *at that time* succeeded in combining human grandeur and humility: justice was not done to one of the two aspects. Thus reciprocal criticism failed to be achieved on either side.

Only in the thirteenth century was Thomas Aquinas finally to venture a synthesis. This was the century in which people came into contact with the Aristotelian and pagan concept of human grandeur. It was a shock for mediaeval Christians and gave rise to fierce discussion in the years between 1250 and 1277. Several predecessors, notably Albert the Great, had already indicated a particular direction for Thomas to take, but he was the one who after a long period of heart-searching and hesitation arrived at a synthesis in which the pagan criticism of Christian humility and obedience was assimilated and on the other hand the pagan view was criticized (though it glosses over Aristotle and Christianizes him). Despite this baptism of Aristotle into Christianity, Thomas shows a fine sensitivity to his pagan human impulse and in the long run respects it.

So after some hesitation in 1271, Thomas arrived at a synthesis; it is in his *Summa Theologiae,* above all II-II, q.161 and q.129. Without denying the mystical transformation of *magnanimitas* by the church fathers, he nevertheless first accepts the pagan *magnanimitas* and in so doing criticizes the traditional Christian view of man as a heap of misery on which God has mercy.[26]

For Thomas, humility has nothing to do with the outside world or with fellow human beings, but only with the relationship of man to God. The Aristotelian virtue of *magnanimitas* regulates the human passion and desire for grandeur (as a mean between recklessness and despair) in the service of man himself and therefore also in the service of his humanity, whereas humility regulates the same human passion in relation to God. Humility is therefore essentially a religious virtue. In the light of his belief in creation from nothing Thomas can repeat the traditional distinction that man, seen in and from himself, has nothing of his own. (as opposed to God) but sin, but seen in relation to God everything that is positively present in him is the pure gift of God.[27] However, this is only apparently the same as what Bernard had said. For in a Greek way Thomas adds that man has his own worth not only thanks to God's worth but also 'as an inalienable human worth which is peculiarly his own'.[28] He has a grandeur of his own, and that grandeur cannot be made to vanish by mediaeval mysticism. Man is subject, even over against God, and he himself is therefore responsible for his good actions as well as his evil deeds. He alone is responsible and no one else, not even God.[29] As a magnanimous man he measures his own strength and sees what he is capable of doing; he is not afraid to accept his grandeur. But as a humble man he knows that these powers are gifts of God, though this knowledge does not impede his humanistic élan. Thomas is ultimately no longer concerned with the drama of God's grandeur as contrast with puny man. The drama is shifted to man: in man himself it is concerned with the tension between human grandeur and human wretchedness. Magnanimity is a virtue of human hope, to be realized through one's own human strength and directed towards the exaltation of what is human in man.

In this way Thomas succeeds in rehabilitating man's trust in himself, which is in no way contrasted with humility. He presupposes this *magnanimitas* but at the same time takes it up into belief in the Creator God who brings salvation. 'Pagan' humanistic trust in oneself is therefore included in God's grace, which on the one hand heals bruised man and on the other allows him to share in communion with God. Thus Thomas rejects the patristic and mediaeval belittling of man: he restores man's trust in himself, human grandeur, through man and by virtue of human strength. But on the other hand this strength is a divine gift and is often damaged by man. Taken up into the one perspective of salvation that transcends all human powers and to which man can react only with theologal hope, this Christian hope includes man's confidence in himself *sub deo*.[30] Only the man who obeys God in absolute faith and looks for salvation to him alone is the man who may also trust in his own powers to save for good a part of humanity in man and society which is nevertheless confirmed and transcended by God.

Thus Thomas' own Thomism laid the foundations for our 'modern times' which would no longer unfold in accordance with the all-prevailing monastic model of the Middle Ages, but would develop autonomous secular structure. In this sense Thomas no longer belongs to the 'Augustinian middle ages', though on the mystical level he follows the statements of patristic and mediaeval spirituality. However, in the substructure of this mystical dimension he recognizes the autonomous dignity of man who is subject to his own laws. Furthermore, at the end of the thirteenth century, we see how the modern world begins to develop its own secular structures.[31] Thus Thomas lays the foundation for a non-monastic Christian spirituality. At the social level his restoration of humanism to Christian spirituality at the individual level becomes his doctrine of 'social justice'.

The drama of the modern period which followed Thomas was twofold. Some years after Thomas' death the theory of Siger of Brabant, which gave a very one-sided twist to pagan magnanimity and upset the balance in Thomas's synthesis, was condemned by the church because Siger refused to call humility a virtue. The second drama lay in the fact that in the sixteenth and seventeenth centuries, despite the appearance of neo-Stoicism, Christian spirituality retreated to an earlier Augustinianism with the result that it became ineffective in the modern world. People had long forgotten Thomas' Christian humanistic affirmation that 'to minimize the perfection of God's creatures is to minimize the perfection of God's creative power'.[32] The modern world therefore looked outside Christianity for the kind of man it needed. For although Thomas had laid the foundations, within Christian obedience in faith, for man's concern for large-scale undertakings to promote human development, and also provided the foundations for confidence in man's scientific and technical reason in helping to solve the problems of the world, since then this Thomistic humanistic concern has become an effective reality above all outside the Christian churches (albeit here often without a theologal perspective). The Enlightenment can therefore be understood as a reaction against the 'Augustinianism' of the sixteenth and seventeenth centuries. This reaction was inevitable.

2. 'Modern man' and Christian obedience

(a) Modern man's criticism

Descartes already criticized humility in a new way. He too stressed human self-affirmation in *magnanimitas* (which was now called *génerosité*).[33] He was fundamentally concerned with the inalienable ego as the subject of free will. This ego is opposed to all servile humility. A new protest based on man's will-to-power and directed against Christian submissiveness is expressed here. Human consciousness takes over control; man is master of his own heart. Descartes contrasts the Christian 'Your will, not mine, be done' with the superiority complex of the 'generous' consciousness, full of the rediscovery of human grandeur.

Spinoza, who is less inhibited by Christian traditions than Descartes, regards man's proud assertion of himself as the heart of all virtue. He sees humility and arrogance as twins, both of them the daughters of an illusory imagination or of dreams.[34] Man has to find his place and his true greatness in the identity of the universe with himself.

Kant is vigorously opposed to *humilitas spuria* or cringing humility.[35] Although 'phenomenal man' is only an exchangable value for him, 'noumenal man', the person, is an end in itself. Man is rightly conscious of his insignificance and real humility over against the law, but he himself is the one who makes and supports the law; so the only proper attitude for him is an assertion of his own ethical dignity. Thus servile submission is improper for him. He is autonomous and does not need grace and forgiveness or privilege; he is the servant of no one. The maker of the law does not humiliate himself, 'even to Seraphim'. Kant mocks the piety of the Psalmist who said, 'I am a worm and no man', saying that 'anyone who makes himself a worm should not complain of being trodden on'. However, Kant is not as naive as Descartes and

Spinoza, neither of whom seemed to be aware of man's evil intentions. He sees through man's deceitfulness, which damages man's dignity as an end in itself. Kant discovers a new ethical pride specifically in negative experiences of humiliation.

Of course we must remember that the Enlightenment had been preceded by religious wars among Christians. In the light of the divisions in Christianity there was a growing awareness among both Catholics and Protestants that from now on the political unity of the state could no longer be guaranteed by religion as the basis and expression of social life. If it was to survive as a state it had to be emancipated from religion, which had become a disintegrating force. From this time onwards the integrating principle was to be Enlightened Reason. But this Enlightened Reason was in fact a 'bourgeois' reason, concerned with what was quantifiable, with what had an exchange value in the public sense; everything else was relegated to the purely private sphere of personal convictions. According to Kant the Enlightenment was 'man's exodus from the state in which he has not yet come of age and which is his own fault': in other words from his inability to use his own reason without the direction of others. Authority must be legitimated; it must be open to public discussion and not just imposed by the sheer force of its 'being there' historically. Otherwise it produces only servants and slaves. If authority loses its structures of social credibility it becomes inhuman coercion. The Enlightenment therefore sees authority as a relic from feudal times. The new awareness sees society as being based on a 'contract' and this presupposes the equality of all men and their freedom to enter into a contract. The only form of authority that the Enlightenment regarded as valid was the authority of autonomous knowledge or cognitive competence.

B.Groethuysen[36] and others have analysed the way in which this history of freedom in the Enlightenment was in fact a very limited and curtailed history of freedom. The specific class characteristics of 'the citizen' (that is, not as *citoyen* but as a member of a particular economic class) are proclaimed as universal human values (something that in the end had also been done by most of the old Greek elitist views). Specifically middle-class norms were regarded as universal human norms.

The new view was not so much a consequence of a new way of looking at life; on the contrary, a new praxis, dominated by the economic principle of exchange, produced this new perspective. Life took priority over ideas. Ultimately even God was made bourgeois; he is just the one who rewards the good and punishes the evil – the guarantor of a middle-class society. This also led to a break with nature and with the universal order, which was not really a Stoic action.

Nature, it was thought, was dominated by God's natural laws, but man was sovereign in the human sphere. God was obliged only to give man his due, also in accordance with a kind of contract. Modern man looks for guarantees so that he knows that his zealous efforts will not remain unrewarded. Commercialism even works through to religion! God's power stops as it were where freedom begins: God and man are rivals. God simply becomes the final judge: he is 'the executive power of middle-class consciousness in the hereafter'.[37] Virtue and ethics are thus divorced from their relationship with God. Truth, honesty and good manners become the foundation of Enlightened life. Religion is reduced to ethics and thus deprived of both its mystical and its political potential. The separation of religion and politics, redemption and liberation, mysticism and politics are essential features of this individualistic and ultimately 'bourgeois' religion. Furthermore, religion undergoes a process of sentimentalizing; religion is a separate private sphere of emotion and sentiment. Man, in his subjectivity, becomes the measure of all things. However, this subject is purely individual self-assertion and in no way an affirmation in solidarity of another man's freedom. Thus middle-class religion ultimately becomes a means of reconciling people to misery and the injustice caused by others. The man who is not a middle-class citizen is the victim of this, and becomes servile man.

Later, Nietzsche[38] was to condemn humility as a product of Judaism and Christianity, a complex of resentment. The good news of Jesus to slaves was bad news for the strong and the powerful. For Nietzsche, Christian humility is a servile and vindictive distortion of a plebeian consciousness which denies itself for the moment in the expectation of an eschatological reversal. *Magnanimitas,* now the Superman, again becomes the privilege of a ruling class which creates its own values and then makes them into universal human norms.

(b) Christian criticism of the privatized autonomy of Enlightened reason

Christians today are much more clearly aware that the will of God can only be made known to us through the mediation of history. There are dangerous ways of talking about 'the will of God'. If God's will can be made known to us only through the medium of human experiences in the world – a process in which the Christian community and its leaders have their own interpretative function – then it follows that we can never be confronted 'unambiguously' with the will of God.

Furthermore, ethics is a different language game from the language of religion. Religion is not just ethics and it cannot be reduced to ethics, although on the other hand there is an intrinsic connection between religion and the ethical life. The understanding of the difference between good and evil is logically prior to the understanding of God and his will. This means that in the first instance we should not define our moral obligations in terms of God's will, but in terms of what is directed towards the dignity of human life. On the other hand, someone who believes in God may and should interpret what he regards here and now as urgently worthy of man as an expression of God's will, without sacrificing any of the serious purpose of that will or reducing God himself in a middle-class way to the level of a purely eschatological judge of man's use of his autonomy.

Thus historical mediations of God's will, including those which come through the authorities in the world or the church, introduce a dialectic into Christian obedience. In this sense, in certain circumstances 'illegality' can be interpreted from a Christian perspective as a higher form of trust in God which is not to be reduced to obedience to church authority. Christians' eyes may have been opened to this by the Enlightenment!

On the other hand, the Christian view of authority and obedience can simply represent a protest against the purely 'cognitive competence' of all authority, as Enlightened reason interpreted it. Authority also has a liberating function with regard to man's true humanity precisely because his critical memory of certain liberating traditions which have yet to be assimilated is part of the constitution of critical reason and an instrinsic element of it.[39] Furthermore, the fact that man is a subject in solidarity, his recognition above all of the fact that the other man is free and is a subject, is part of the social constitution of the subject in a fully human and a theological sense.[40] The autonomous middle-class subject is thoroughly criticized from this position because of his individualistic, utilitarian and unbiblical conception of his 'autonomous freedom' which is above all to the disadvantage of others. In particular the principle of exchange, which is reflected in the Enlightenment conception of freedom and autonomy, is revealed in the light of the Christian tradition of freedom to be only half-freedom, which in fact makes others (indeed the major part of the world's population) the victim of its own concept of freedom. However, given the difficulties that Christians rightly have with the feudal and patriarchal way of exercising authority (a practice which was rightly criticized by the Enlightenment), we must consider whether the discomfort some modern Christians feel about 'religious authority' has not to do with a liberal, middle-class view of human freedom and autonomy. We ourselves, at least in the West, are after all products of this middle-class culture. Here the recollection of the freedom of the gospel has not assimilated sufficiently the latter's criticism of the autarky of the Enlightenment, so that we ourselves often identify middle-class freedom with the freedom of the gospel.

Without denying the gains made by the Enlightenment in achieving freedom, Christians should above all transcend its half-freedom, in a dialectical way. They should follow the direction which J.B.Metz rightly called solidarity with the freedom of the other man.[41] Only if they do this will Thomas Aquinas' original view of human grandeur and *magnanimitas* be taken up again into Christian spirituality in a post-bourgeois way. For unless there is this dialectical transcending of the Enlightenment, there is a grave danger that a misunderstanding of Thomas Aquinas' *magnanimitas* will encourage only the optimistic belief in progress and the ideology of development, thus strengthening and furthering the enslavement of two-thirds of the population of the world.

Finally, Christian obedience is above all a matter of listening and watching out for the *kairos,* the opportune moment in our time, especially listening obediently to the howls and cries of two-thirds of the world's population for liberation and redemption, following this up by acting in conformity to this 'voice of God'. This too is a fundamental form of human obedience and one that is derived from the authority of suffering man.

32

Messianic or Christian Anti-Messianism

Over the past decade all kinds of neo-mystical religions and beliefs centred on experience have developed in Oceania, Africa, Latin America and somewhat more recently in North America: the Jesus People is only a particular Christian variant of them. This is a movement which criticizes our instrumental society and is even revolutionary, although it is of a purely inward and religious kind. A characteristic of this movement is its anti-rational effect, expressed among the Jesus people in biblical fundamentalism and a rejection of reason, in which science and technology are almost condemned as heresies. Liberation from an unjust world is expected from a purely gracious and mighty act of God which produces inward conversion. In this experience of inward liberation one experiences a new world, a psychological and inter-personal earthly paradise, a kingdom of peace, justice and love, while the world with its socio-political and bureaucratic power structures is left as it is: they are thought to be completely invulnerable to structural change.

Inward liberation, in loving co-humanity and brotherliness to one another, is a free and liberated oasis in the midst of a world of inhuman structures. This is a religion of the conversion of the heart, experienced as the beginning of God's kingdom on earth. The degree of joy, even of intoxication, with which these young people celebrate their inward liberation, their almost too childish delight at their inexpressible happiness, in fact makes us wonder how deep their hopelessness and lack of redemption, their suffering must have been before their conversion, how anxious, meaningless and lonely the noisy beat generation of our welfare society must have felt itself to be. In this sense this phenomenon of radicalism is a fundamental criticism of our competitive society, which leaves almost no room for inwardness, for tranquillity and human enjoyment, for just *living* together with brothers and sisters. Now they have abandoned this prosperity with its loneliness and have experienced a meaningful content to their lives, a happiness that 'the dead still live', that neither evil structures nor injustice can separate them from the love of God in Jesus Christ, at the same time they show something of the eschatological joy which characterized the mood of the first Christians. In the midst of an old world they live as though they were in a new one.

Here without doubt we are confronted with a radical form of the religion of inwardness and co-humanity which by-passes the social and political dimensions of human and religious life and furthermore the social and political conditions which make possible truly inward, creative freedom: the kingdom of God in them and in their midst, in their brotherliness together. In their experience this radical inner liberation completely relativizes the expectation of liberation from alienating social and political structures which do away with people's freedom, but at the same time their emotional irrationality makes them – perhaps unconsciously – extremely vulnerable to manipulation, above all by conservative political forces which of course (at least in America) subsidize them, because they see these religious movements as a way of systematically neutralizing potential political revolutionaries who are dangerous to the *status quo*. In their protest against society they seek their revolution only in the conversion of the heart, and such an undertaking is gladly supported with delighted opportunism by a liberal establishment based on the *status quo,* which in America has put millions of dollars at the disposal of a Jesus-crusade on the campus of American universities and colleges – a royal gesture which at first sight indicates nothing but the concern of the authorities for the religious dimension of the people.

The second form in which the freedom movement manifests itself is what we might call political radicalism. In my view, this form of freedom movement, which looks for freedom only through liberation from social and political structural violence, has – albeit somewhat paradoxically – the same basic religious and messianic pattern as the neo-mystical messianic movements. The so-called political and ethical Jesus movement, with its slogan 'Jesus the political contestant', is simply a milder Christian variant of it.

This political and radical movement also wants a better world, a kingdom of righteousness and peace, but it expects it only from a radical change in society and liberation from the old structures. It, too, looks for the beginning of a 'new world' from a sudden and powerful intervention, this time, however, not from God or from a gracious gift of Jesus but through a committed revolutionary action which does away with the 'old world' and builds up a new one. This radicalism has been expressed most sharply in the revolts among university students, above all in American and French universities. At the peak of this rebellion, when university buildings were occupied by students and they were in charge for a time, such liberation was expressed in an apotheosis of delight, a feast of freedom.

Professor John Searle, who has given quite a sympathetic account of this phenomenon in his book *The Campus War,* describes this experience after a successful occupation in the following words, taken from the particular experience of those who were involved: 'It was incredible, it was total. And what was so wonderful was that everyone felt the same thing...It was a festival of life, a liturgical celebration of humanity' (*The Campus War,* Penguin Books 1969, 202). It was in a mood of this kind that after several days' occupation of university buildings the now famous ecumenical celebration of the eucharist took place in the presence of people with many different views of life. Elsewhere, at Columbia University, in Harvard and Berkeley, people hugged one another, laughing and crying in sheer delight. People experienced liberation, a new world (35-36). Furthermore, the statistics of this time have shown that in those days and months of a sense of liberation, the visits of students to psychiatrists ceased almost completely.

Apart from the specific significance of this revolution, at all events it had a therapeutic function for everyone concerned. People felt that in fact they had experienced a foretaste of a new and better world. Professor Searle terms the deepest basis of the student liberations a 'religious' impulse, meaning by 'religious' an experience of liberated freedom, but in the form of a total experience of the holy in terms of human wholeness and being healed; for him the experience of freedom also has an emotional and irrational character, the illogical language of which he – Oxford analytic philosopher that he is – has ungraciously analysed as the 'correct logic of philosophically illogical arguments'.

In my view it is impossible to find a difference between the eschatological experience of freedom, 'inner freedom', and the experience of freedom as liberation from structural alienation. The basic difference is to be found only in the totalitarian experience on the one hand of 'inner liberation' by virtue of a mighty act of God's grace and on the other hand of freedom from structural violence by means of a mighty act of revolutionary intervention. Only in their final experience of liberation do people recognize the same 'religious' characteristics, which moreover in both cases tend of themselves towards liturgical celebration.

Thus a totalitarian experience of freedom manifests itself in a kind of 'Arcadian experience of delight' and an inward drive towards liturgical celebration of the feast of universal brotherhood, by virtue of either inner liberation or liberation from structural alienation. Thus what at the moment are the two most explicit and radically divergent liberation movements are rooted in a protest against what is felt to be inhuman and alienating in the world and society: both are supported by a powerful desire for a new and better world, a kingdom of justice and peace; the only radical difference is in the interpretation of what must make up a kingdom of brotherliness, and how this condition must be achieved.

We might be able to conclude that both radical movements in fact coincide in what we could call the 'basic messianic pattern' of all liberation movements, an expression of an expectation of universal reconciliation, a final kingdom of peace, joy and justice, which is already celebrated liturgically in a first radical experience of freedom on the one hand as joyful thanks over a freedom which has already been received or achieved, and on the other hand as an expression of hope for the final liberation to come. It is striking that despite the fundamental difference between the inner and the socio-political conception of liberation, these differences fall away completely in the one great liturgical feast of freedom and universal reconciliation.

Now this basic messianic pattern is far from being a new phenomenon in our human history. It is as old as history. Even before the two radical movements in our time were known or at least analysed, sociologists of religion had paid attention to an occasional phenomenon which (on the basis of Judaism) they had called 'the messianic pattern'. In particular, the famous French sociologist Henri Desroche had analysed this historical phenomenon in sociological terms. It has emerged from this study in the sociology of religion that in extreme situations of social and political *malaise* the rise of radical movements with a messianic attraction are to be found as part of the warp and weft of most people's history. In these radical messianic movements one discovers an almost unchanging basic pattern, above all of a socio-political or a mystical and inward character, despite variations of colouring and despite differences in scope, namely whether they are universal or nationalistic.

Simplified to form a pattern, the basic messianic approach looks something like this. Socio-political situations of economic and above all of cultural and spiritual helplessness and loss of identity have always been times in which radical movements with a messianic attraction arise, movements which dream of a radically new world which is to come directly, because the old world has become intolerable. Liberated and redeemed life is imminent. In such situations of malaise, imagination flourishes: utopian pictures of a completely new world emerge, pictures of an unheard-of kingdom of peace, justice and love. The focal point of such a movement is usually a figure who comes forward to bring salvation and who is expected to usher it in. He is usually thought to have an extraordinary, indeed divinely providential mission and power: he becomes the liberator, the one who solves all problems, the redeemer and saviour. You only have to think of such people as Che Guevara, Fidel Castro, or the many African liberation figures who have been or are revered with an aura of religious power. Or of the Bagwhan.

In some instances, as in the critical rationalism of Popper, Albert and Lenk, the messianic qualities of liberation are not ascribed to an individual but to human critical language, just as for his part Jürgen Habermas ascribes clearly messianic, all-encompassing qualities of liberation to what he calls pure 'critical-rational dialogue'. In my view we should therefore speak of two kinds of radicalism: on the one hand irrational, 'religious' or 'quasi-religious', whether inner or socio-political liberation, and on the other hand, following the Enlightenment, of the positivistic or at least technological and rational messianism of the pure 'critical discourse' as the only authority of liberation.

Historically it is the case that the appearance of Jesus of Nazareth in Palestine took place in a period which had all the characteristics of a collective feeling of a loss of cultural and religious identity. Moreover in Galilee it was a time of socio-political and economic malaise, the breeding ground of all kinds of messianic movements which in the time of Jesus were to be found in abundance, either of a political Zealot kind or with pre-Gnostic inwardness. The unique thing about the Jesus event is that Jesus himself refuses to accede to the Messianic expectations of his contemporaries and even of his followers. He breaks through the basic messianic pattern and is essentially the anti-Messiah; he refuses to make the unjust world a kingdom of justice, peace and love with a reference to God's mighty arm or to radical political action, though nevertheless a new and better world was the one theme of his preaching and the whole of his life-style.

The New Testament story of the three temptations in the wilderness expresses trends in the radical messianic movement which were then prevailing. But although Jesus found a certain human plausibility in these messianic expectations of people who were enslaved both inwardly and in social and political terms – at any rate the New Testament presents them as three temptations for Jesus himself – he resolutely refuses to succumb to them: for him they are satanic possibilities, not possibilities of a rule of God who is concerned for humanity, or the power of love. Jesus is essentially the anti-Messiah, that is he refuses to change the course of history, which in fact robs men of their freedom and oppresses them, into a new and better history by an act of power whether of God or of man, though he nevertheless fights to the death in word and deed, at the same time fiercely attacking all injustice. As a result the church after him can apply a purified concept of the Messiah to him, though in a radically new sense which breaks through the sociological pattern: what is messianic is Jesus' unjust suffering and death, which is avenged by God in his resurrection. His execution was the intrinsic consequence of his refusal to rely on divine or human power. That made him the victim of the ruling powers; he was sacrificed to powers to which he nevertheless refused to succumb. He was concerned with the human history of suffering caused by personal and structural power. But in contrast to the attitude of critical negativity on the basis of utopia, which knows no other standards than those which are close at hand, Jesus' impulse and strength against the domination of existing circumstances comes from a very particular life-style which strives for freedom only by being concerned for human freedom. In the face of the existing situation he sets out a new praxis of the good life which frees others and restores them to themselves. For an irrational radicalism Jesus substitutes the provisional realization of what is sought, and in so doing gives us a guideline for our own creative action, which is to refuse to implement human freedom by force. Jesus does not press a better world on people if they themselves do not want it, because unforced communication can only be instigated through freedom from compulsion.

Anyone concerned to discover the ultimate motive of Jesus' specific praxis of liberating goodness comes up against his underivable relationship to his Father. In Jesus, in a personal human figure, in a man, we can see the way in which God is concerned for all humanity and a better world. In Jesus' concern we see the practical identity between God's concern and man's concern: a kingdom of God concerned for humanity (although this was of course expressed in what were then still theocratic conceptions in which we can no longer share). Jesus died, not with a longing for resurrection, but for love of his brethren, hoping that here this love and not his death would have the last word. Jesus' resurrection is the divine confirmation of this hope, in which he stood out for a better and juster world.

The nucleus of this hope was both the living God and the incomprehensible, unrationalizable fact that the human person is not subject to control, but only comes to fulfilment in free acceptance of the other. Jesus refused to manipulate the freedom of others, whether through human or divine power or through structural manipulation. He transcends the sphere of functionality, efficiency and purely critical and rational dialogue, though he respects them in their place. He knows the limits of emancipation as self-liberation and opens these up to the sphere of redemption which is under no one's control, the sphere in which the other is accepted as other and not as a function, not even with an eye to achieving a communal goal of liberation. In this sense, the gospel of Christ desacralizes politics, science and technology by removing them from a totalitarian sacral sphere and entrusting them to mankind, men and women who are to build up a more human world on an empirical basis by honest and practical historical means. The relationship of Jesus to our history therefore implies the dialectic between the promise of the kingdom of God and our rational and practical concerns – love which directs us towards a new rationality.

For Christianity the conversion of the heart is essential, but being manipulated politically by merely inner liberation and a religion which would limit itself to an appeal to inner conversion without stating the conditions (above all a realistic definition of the subject who is being changed, the human being, who is not just a logical subject but also an active subject) threatens idealistically to reduce men and women by taking no notice of the need of liberation from social and political alienation. Although the man who is inwardly sanctified has a certain invulnerability to structural violence – Jesus is an example of this – structural violence nevertheless hampers and restricts complete freedom; Jesus' execution on the cross is also a clear example of this and at the same time a living protest against it. Human freedom should always consist in an indissoluble *dialectic* between inward liberation and structures which, while bringing freedom, are nevertheless always to a certain degree alienating because they are objectified. In their onesidedness, the two forms of present-day radicalism, each in its own way, heedlessly and unrealistically by-pass this dialectic. As a result, on the one hand they reduce the significance of inner liberation and meaningfulness, and on the other minimize the importance of socio-political liberation. In their one-sided radicalism they are in fact a clear symptom of the social crisis in the world and in the church.

Reinhold Niebuhr was able to express something of this permanent dialectic when he said these words as a prayer addressed to God: 'God, grant me the serenity to accept the things I cannot change, the courage to change the things that I can change, and the wisdom to know the difference.'

33

A Saint: Albert the Great

15 November 1980 was the seven hundredth anniversary of the death of the Dominican Albert the Great. This fact was the occasion for Pope John Paul II to pay a visit to Cologne, the city closely associated with Albert the Great. This seven hundredth anniversary was comme- morated at the Albertinum in Nijmegen and the following sermon was delivered there.

The South German Albert, short in stature, being at the most just over four feet nine inches, is called Albert *the Great*. Scholars later named him *doctor universalis*. That speaks volumes. This man lived on in the popular imagination of the Middle Ages, then, as the Great, without peer in Europe. After his death a number of popular poems were composed, up to twenty-eight verses long, which celebrated in all kinds of ways the acts and wisdom of this freeman of Cologne, a mendicant monk. There may be a good deal of legend in all this, but you must take note of legends: they do not arise without good cause.

What is historically certain is this: he was a man who made it his life's work to introduce Arabic and Aristotelian philosophy in terms which could be understood throughout the West.[1] At the same time he was Prior of a Monastery, Provincial of the German province of his Order, Bishop of Regensburg, Papal legate and penitential preacher throughout Germany and Bohemia: a man who three times was able to settle a bloody conflict between the prince bishop of Cologne and its free citizens, and moreover played a not insignificant part in the nomination of Rudolf of Habsburg after the long miseries of the interregnum. He was a man who, old in years, went to the Council of Lyons, not so much to help to solve theological problems as finally to make the Pope revoke the papal interdict which for seven years had wrought havoc in Cologne, pauperizing the city. He was the great

political peacemaker, called to help wherever something went basically
wrong in Germany; the man who on his apostolic journeys began to
study mines, analysed minerals, explained how chalk become marble
and how this marble can begin to show all kinds of figures, even human
ones, as it comes into being by cooling – just as, he added, you can also
see certain figures formed in the clouds. He was the person who studied
the ancient Roman remains when the cathedral of Cologne was rebuilt,
who knew how to train falcons, taught gardeners how to grow things
better and could advise nurserymen and farmers how to improve the
breeding of their cattle. By his knowledge of nature and observation of
flies he was able to rid a convent, where they had settled in the rafters,
of a plague of them. He was the tranquil mystic, the only one in the
Middle Ages who wrote commentaries on all the works of Pseudo-
Dionysius, and who as a result of this became the teacher of Eckhardt
and, two hundred years later, at the beginning of modern times, also
inspired Nicolas of Cusa. Finally, he was the innocent and sometimes
naive man with an inward, childlike devotion to Mary and the human
passion of Jesus. That historically he became such a legendary figure in
popular imagination indicates precisely what he was.

Here today we are celebrating the liturgy; we are not gathered
together for a theological seminar. In the last resort we are not
commemorating a theologian or scholar but a saint, a consistent
Christian. However, one is a always a Christian – as people put it
nowadays – in a contextual way. For Albert this context was nature,
people and their political and social problems, his Dominican community, and God. However, for him that meant that nature with its trees,
stones, minerals and animals, society with its good people and intri-
guers, is itself God's own world. Furthermore, Albert is very much less
precise in defining the boundaries between nature and grace than is
Thomas Aquinas. For Albert, any phenomenon – and he was a good
observer – in nature, in social structures and among human beings, was
also God's concern. For him, politics, mysticism, episcopal finances,
getting hold of an authentic text of Aristotle, was all an expression of
one and the same spirituality. It was from him that Meister Eckhardt
learnt that it is not the contemplative Mary but the active Martha who
is the model of the true mystic.

The chroniclers say little about Albert's youth, but in his own
tractates 'On the Animals' and 'On Meteorology' we learn a good deal
about it. He came from a family of officers or officials, one of the
better classes in his time, but he did not have the noble, upper-class
refinement of a Thomas. Albert's rougher and sometimes aggressive
language betrays his status and is completely alien to Thomas. With
his people he spoke the local dialect of Cologne. Albert came from a
small town, Lauingen, on the Danube in the region of Augsburg. He

often went the rounds in the country with his father's servant. He observed everything. Thus for a whole two hours he watched a fight between a swan and an eagle and was able to say that swans are very musical but very thrifty with their singing; 'what I mean,' he says, 'is that they sing only when another swan dies.' He traced the journeys of fish in the Danube and once must have seen a kind of whale there. He gives all the details, even about the use of whale blubber for certain illnesses. He does not say anything about his schooling, though as the son of an official he will have gone to school in one or other of the large cities in the neighbourhood.

After the death of his father we find him with his uncle in Padua, first of all not yet at the university there. To begin with he evidently did not know what he wanted to study. For the moment he continued to read in 'the book of nature'. In 1222 he experienced the great earthquake which wrought havoc throughout northern Italy and flattened the city of Brescia. He tells how in this way he came upon a long-hidden well: a worker went down into it, was suffocated, and died. The people called down vengeance on the water spirits. 'Nonsense,' said Albert, and explained how gases can build up in a closed well; it was only necessary to air the well, and after a short time they would have fresh drinking water. And so they did. Albert enrolled for the university, founded in Padua from Bologna. There was no theological faculty there, but only law, philosophy and free arts. Albert chose the last, evidently not entirely of his own free will.

One day the Dominican Jordan of Saxony, one of the greatest persuaders of young people who ever lived, came to give the university sermons in Padua. Wherever this magnetic figure appeared, after his sermons dozens of students. and sometimes even their professors, would come forward as candidates for the Dominican *vita apostolica,* coupled with a life of academic study. After only two years in the order he was the successor of St Dominic as Magister General. This man's incredible power of persuasion lay in his knowledge of people, above all his knowledge of mediaeval students. When someone once said to him, 'How comes it that you can capture so many philosophy students, but not the theologians and canonists?', Jordan answered, 'You have to know that philosophers drink the water of Aristotle all the week; so when on Sundays they drink the wine of the word of God, they soon become drunk and can be caught; but the theologians and canonists sniff the word of God all the week as well. They're rather like vergers in church; they run round the altar too much to be able to kneel before it.'

However, Albert resisted the charm of this skilled fisher of men. He wanted above all to be a Dominican, but he feared that he would not be able to go through with it to the end, and thought that in that case he should not begin. In a later sermon Jordan analysed exactly the psychology of the young person who wants to venture something but fears that he cannot go through with it. Albert felt that he was being psychoanalysed, and after the sermon offered himself as a Dominican. Jordan promptly sent him to Cologne in his own fatherland to begin his novitiate and his studies there.

At that time Cologne was the most important city in mediaeval Germany, though it had no universities. Albert's first training was traditionally monastic. After his studies he became adviser to a monastery as lector in theology: alongside the Prior there had to be a theologian in every monastery for the permanent training of the fathers in the apostolate. This had been the wish of Dominic.

In the meanwhile, from 25 January to April 1240 the whole of northern Germany had been terrified by a great new comet in the firmament. Among his other commitments Albert studied this pheno- menon closely, made notes and did not bother at all about the rumours of disaster which were sweeping over Germany.

He was about thirty-one when he was sent to Strasbourg, where for the first time he really had an academic position. During his five years there he began his great theological works. While at Strasbourg he already acquired the reputation of being the greatest scholar in the the West. This became known in Paris, the academic centre of the world at that time. The Magister General appointed him to Paris, to be the first non-Frenchman there. As yet he still had no doctorate (which at that time was not a title but the official admission to teaching as an independent professor). Of course Albert had already of course heard of a certain Aristotle, and knew his *Logic,* but in Paris he was confronted with the fashion of the new theology of the time. Confronted with the giant Aristotle he felt himself to be the puny David, but after a few years he was to write: I want to introduce Aristotle throughout the West. More than Thomas at that time he became an authority in the interpretation of Aristotle. Roger Bacon, a chagrined opponent of Albert, had to acknowledge that it had never yet come about that anyone had become a university *auctoritas* during his lifetime, and against all university practice he mentioned Albert, both first name and surname.

However, after three years, with his doctorate, Albert had to leave Paris. The Magister General had established five theological faculties in Europe. Cologne was one of them, and Albert had to become the first 'Regnens Studiorum' there. Thomas became one of his pupils. After six years teaching, Albert became Provincial. He had then almost finished his formal academic career, though he continued to work on his publications. He became an administrator, visiting all the monaster- ies in Germany and settling political disputes. However, during his apostolic journeys (for as a Dominican, like the Franciscans, he had to travel on foot) he could not resist studying mines on the way. For him everything was God's world, and he used what he had seen in nature in his expositions of the Trinity or of transsubstantiation in the eucharist. In this way he was even able to demonstrate to the people of Cologne quite clearly that wine and not beer is the most appropriate material for the eucharist.

Well known for his upright way of living, based on the *aequum et bonum,* on fairness and the common good, he was nominated by the Pope to be Bishop of Regensburg, a problematical see all of the finances of which his predecessor had appropriated for his own benefit and use. The Magister General begged him not to be obedient to those whom in his letter he called 'the lords of the curia'; he also added that sometimes a holy disobedience is the only appropriate attitude. Albert was squeezed between two conflicting orders, that of the Pope and that of the Magister General. But the letter from the General only came when Albert had already gone too far in his commitment to Rome. He was consecrated bishop, and then asked to be relieved after a year: the finances of the see were again in order and he had chosen a good successor. He had been to Rome to ask for his release and to give the Pope advice about a good successor. And so it came about that Albert had obeyed both the Pope and his Magister General according to his own lights. The Order never completely forgot and forgave this fact.

As an ex-bishop he was now 'le seigneur' Albert. He eventually returned to the monastery but now had a greater degree of personal freedom. In the meantime he continued to work on his philosophical and theological works, while at the same time he travelled throughout Germany, Flanders and the Netherlands. Thomas did not reach fifty, but Albert lived to be more than sixty-five – which for the Middle Ages was an exorbitantly long lifetime.

Who was this many-sided Albert? In the first place he was a pastoral man. He did not want to follow Thomas and the Paris trend, which regarded theology as an academic specialism, albeit also with a pastoral dimension. You must study theology, said Albert, *ut boni fiamus,*[2] in order to become a good man, a better Christian. All his pupils vie with one another in praise of their master; the only one who does not is Thomas. He never mentions Thomas in his writings, though he sometimes quotes him word for word: that was Thomas' mute homage to his great teacher.

It was Albert who tried to draw Thomas' attention to the need for theologians to study the 'modernist' literature of the time. For Albert and Thomas the order was traditionally theological in the style of Saint Bernard and the Victorines. There was even a reaction against the use of Aristotle in theology, and three popes had forbidden study of his works, with the exception of his Logic. But Albert said, 'There are some people even among us Dominicans – I call them imbecile obscurantists – who want to use philosophical muzzles and no one opposes them. They are brute beasts who call down anathemas on things of which they do not have the slightest idea;'[3] such people murdered Socrates in former times, drove Plato out of Athens and intrigued to reject Aristotle.[4] That is the way Albert talks. Thomas perhaps thought the same, but he would never have expressed himself so boldly. Some years later, the General Chapter of the Order made the reading of Aristotle compulsory in Dominican houses of study.

Albert had impressed on his students, *in dulcedine societatis quaerere veritatem*:[5] to look for the truth must be the teamwork of brothers who live together in a brotherly way in a religious community. Thomas had often heard that from Albert and he himself writes (here quoting him almost word for word): that young Dominican theological students need not fast and undertake heavy obligations, *sed magis in quadam dulcedine vivere, in amore*:[6] they must live in the comfort of a loving brotherly community and seek the truth in that way. That is their fasting. For monks of the time that was half way to heresy.

Seven hundred years ago today, on Friday 15 November 1280, Albert of Cologne, as the people of that city continued to call him, died. He was probably seventy-four. In the last years of his life he was very withdrawn: although he was not really in his dotage, his enjoyment of life left him. No one had anything to do with the miserable old man. In those days Albert must have experienced the feeling of being 'out of sight, out of mind'. The chronicles, which if not historical are nevertheless close to reality, say that one day a good old friend of his knocked on the door of his cell in Cologne and asked, 'Albert, are you there?' Albert is said to have replied, 'No, Albert is no longer here. He used to be here.' A gentle complaint from an already forgotten old man in the midst of a life which was bubbling up again with other visions? Or was he already immersed in God? – for it was when praying that he had formerly climbed mountains to begin to study particular kinds of iron ore.

As far as I know Albert from a more detailed study of just some of his tractates, I would want to sum up his spirituality like this: a man only has full possession of himself in nature and society as a human being in the very act of his living community with God. That is why he was declared a saint in 1931 by Pius XI (God knows why this was almost six hundred years after St Thomas). His fellow citizens of Cologne, the whole of Germany, Brabant and Flanders, and also the Netherlands, had already declared him a saint during his lifetime, as a man of justice and love, the peacemaker, the great administrator of his time. And even during his lifetime his favourite pupil – not Thomas, but Ulrich of Strasbourg – called him *nostri temporis stupor et miraculum,* the dumb amazement and living wonder of the thirteenth century.

34

Dominican Spirituality

For the most part people live by stories. I myself live by my own story. When I became a Dominican I linked my life story with the family story of the Dominicans; as a result, my life story took on a new orientation and I picked up the thread of the story of the Order in my own way. So my own life has become part of the Dominican family story: a chapter in it. Through the story of the Order I have attained my own identity. Stories of the Dominican Order keep us together as Dominicans. Without stories we should be deprived of remembrance, fail to find our own place in the present and remain without hope or expectation for the future. Thus as Dominicans we form a group precisely as our own storytelling community, which hands down its own traditions within the wider story of the many religious communities, within the all-embracing story of the great community of the church, and within the even greater community of mankind. This makes us our own special family, recognizable from all kinds of family characteristics, some major, some minor, but none of which can be hidden.

In saying this, I have already said something about 'Dominican spirituality'. This can only be my own life story in so far as it has become a chapter of the Dominican family story. My own life story extends and enriches the history of Dominican spirituality, while as a small – almost infinitesimally small – chapter in it, it is at the same time relativized and criticized by the already older and wider story of the Dominican family. This makes me ask whether I really am not distorting this family story. So I am already sceptical towards all those who would suggest 'one's own insight' or 'one's own experience' to others as a norm for Dominican spirituality. Furthermore, thank God, there are still Dominicans alive today. In other words, our story is not yet exhausted, completely told; there is still something to be said.

A first conclusion already follows from this: a definitive all-round definition of Dominican spirituality cannot be given. You cannot make a final judgment on a story which is still in full swing. We can only trace some of the main lines in the plot of the story, which has now been handed down for seven centuries in constantly different ways: the one basic story has been told in countless other languages and tongues with a view to constantly different listeners, and especially with a view to their cultural, historical circumstances and the nature of their church.

The basic story which stands at the beginning of our own Dominican storytelling community is of fundamental importance here. But the origin of any relevant story usually blurs into an obscure past which is difficult to reconstruct historically. Dominic (1170-1223), the origin of the Dominican family story, did not write any books. Through laborious historical reconstruction which extracts the 'real Dominic' from all kinds of legends (so typical of the Middle Ages), we nevertheless have sufficient firm ground under our feet. In particular, though Dominic may not have left behind any books or documents, what he did leave behind as a living legacy was the Dominican movement, the Order, a group of people who wanted to carry on Dominic's work in his footsteps. The Dominican story therefore begins with Dominic and his first companions; together they stand at the beginning of what is to become the Dominican family story. They gave the story its theme: they set its tone.

However, this story, often retold and sometimes rewritten, is in itself a particular way in which the thread of an already older story, that of Jesus of Nazareth, is taken up and continued in a new manner. This already brings us to a second conclusion. Dominican spirituality is only valid in so far as it takes up the story of Jesus and brings it up to date in its own way. In its Decree on the Renewal of Religious Life, the Second Vatican Council said that 'to follow Jesus' is the ultimate and supreme norm of any form of religious life (*suprema regula,* no.2). Dominican spirituality is therefore subject to the criterion of the sources of all Christian life. This also means that even the 'Dominican spirituality' of Dominic and his first followers is not directly an absolute law for Dominicans. A fuller and more sophisticated knowledge of the 'story of Jesus' which has become possible since then (e.g. through new devotional experiences based on the Bible or through more refined exegesis of scripture) may therefore lead us to different emphases from those of Dominic and his followers. For according to the Council's Decree on Religious Renewal, this renewal must happen in the first place through a return 'to the sources of all Christian life' (no.2), the Gospel of Jesus Christ (Mark 1.1), and this is the source which is never exhausted and always offers new possiblities, for which even Dominic himself did not know the all-embracing 'Open Sesame'.

At the same time this implies that the story of every Order must be judged as a part, or better as a modulation, of the greater story of the 'community of God', the church ('a participation in the life of the church': ibid., no. 2). Here the Council points to the 'present-day projects' of the church: biblical, liturgical, dogmatic, pastoral, ecumenical, missionary and social. That is, Dominican spirituality essentially presupposes a critical involvement in the very specific needs and problems of today's church in its historical circumstances; it cannot be an isolated cultivation of our own 'Dominican' garden alongside the ongoing life of the world and the church.

Given all this, however, as governed by the gospel and subjected to the constant historical criticism that it exercises, and at the same time as a concrete historical feature of the necessary major projects of the church in the world here and now, in fact 'the original inspiration of one's own religious institution' (thus the Council's Decree on Religious Life, no.2) is the basic theme of the Dominican family story, and is therefore normative. Here the Council Decree points not only to the original 'specific project' (*propria proposita*) of the founder, but also to the order's 'own religious traditions', at least in so far as these are sound (*sanae traditiones*), that is, to the 'spiritual heritage' of a religious order: its spirituality.

The third conclusion may therefore run: Dominican spirituality is valid as a special modality of the church's task 'to follow Jesus', especially – for us – in the footsteps and the inspiration of Dominic, as this inspiration has constantly provided new light and direction in the best moments of the history of the Order. Therefore we must clearly bring this basic historical story to mind, for in the course of time the Dominican community has also had a broken relationship to its own origins. When the Inquisition brought, for example, Joan of Arc to the stake, the Dominicans involved were essentially contradicting Dominic's inspiration and orientation. People had become deaf and blind to the origin of new charismata: this was an essentially un-Dominican attitude.

As a third criterion for renewed religious life, the same Decree of the Council gives the relationship of the story of Jesus and the original basic story (for us, of the Dominicans) to the altered circumstances of the time (no. 22). This implies that Dominican spirituality cannot be defined purely by a reference to the original story or purely by a reference to the further modulations and updating of this basic story in the course of the history of the Order, though this is presupposed. Dominican spirituality also involves the way in which we live out this Dominican family story here and now, in our time. Dominican spirituality does not indicate simply how things were 'at the beginning' or in the course of the history of the Order. In that case we would simply be writing a historical report of the way in which Dominicans were inspired in former times. But historical knowledge is not yet spirituality. Thus someone who was a good historian but not a Dominican could reconstruct it better than we could. If it is not to be purely the 'history' of a spirituality (and furthermore, if it is not to become an empty ideology), Dominican spirituality is a living reality today; it is handed on (or distorted) by Dominicans living now, who reshape the Dominican family story here and now with an eye to the situation in the world and the church, the cultural historical situation of the moment.

Thus the fourth conclusion runs as follows: without a living relationship to the present, any talk about Dominican spirituality remains a purely historical preoccupation with the past of the Order (often an excuse for neglecting tasks which are urgent now). Dominican spirituality is a living reality which is to be realized among us now. Otherwise we simply repeat stories which others have told for a long time, as though we ourselves did not have to write our own chapter in what is of course a story which had already begun before us. Whereas now we do have to write a new chapter which is still unpublished, if after us anyone else is going to think it worth taking up the thread of this Dominican story again. If in fact we can, may and will write that new living chapter, I am certain that many young people, men and women, will again be drawn to continue the Dominican tradition after us. For any meaningful story has a power of attraction; it is retold, and no one can stop its snowball effect. Whether that happens, however, depends on the tone in which we write our chapter in the great Dominican family story and the tension it contains. Will it be a dull, unread little paragraph? Or will it be an alien story which does not take up the thread of the family story that has already begun, and so allows the Dominican story to die out, perhaps for good? Or will it become an attractive episode, attractive perhaps only because all that the hearer notices is that we are zealously in search of the real thread of the story, which for the moment we have lost track of? That too can also be an important part of the already old Dominican family story.

Should you now reread my previous 1954 duplicated article on 'Dominican Spirituality' in the spirit which I have just described, I think that you may find that it still provides sufficient inspiration and orientation in its historical reference to the 'golden thread' which runs through the Dominican family story from Dominic down to the present day. As may become evident, this golden thread sometimes runs across the fabric of Christianity – a fact that we may not obscure when we are writing our share in the great history of the Order. Provided that this golden thread is woven into our life story, however different it may be in content, we have in fact realized Dominican spirituality. 'Spirituality' is not spirituality so long as it is only described, whether in an assertive or an authoritarian tone. It is spirituality to the degree that it is realized in practice – as a completely new rendering of an older Dominican melody.

How does this older melody go, this constantly recurring theme, this basic story?

I would say that it is a cross-grained story! In the twelfth century and at the beginning of the thirteenth there were two burning points at issue: a need for renewal in the priestly life and a need for renewal in the monastic life. The Fourth Lateran Council in 1215 dealt with these two problems separately, without any relation between them, and without connecting the two. This Council was not without its influence on Dominic who, as an Augustinian canon of Osma, on a journey to the south of France had already gathered round him a group of fellow workers to provide for the pressing needs of priestly care in the see of Toulouse, which had severe pastoral problems. Dominic saw the signs of the times. In the twelfth century, religious movements had arisen: a great many lay people joined them. The basic tendency of these movements was to combine gospel poverty with preaching, but they often had an anti-clerical tone. All kinds of clerical abuses had prompted the question: does Christian preaching require the permission of the church (the bishop), and involve commissioning and sending by the church? Or is not religious life, and life according to the gospel in the footsteps of the apostles (at that time called the *vita apostolica*) itself a qualification for Christian preaching? This last view was the standpoint of many religious movements, whereas it was officially regarded as 'heresy' by the Councils. We could say that the heretical movements of that time were inspired by the gospel and Christ, while the official preachers, though orthodox, did not lead a life in accordance with the gospel – at least to all outward appearances – and were completely embedded in feudal structures. All manifestations of this new religious movement – above all in France, Italy, Germany and the Netherlands (the rich countries of that time) show striking common features (independently of each other): living out the gospel *sine glossa* (without compromises). Its spirituality was characterized by a deep devotion to the humanity of Jesus: following the poor Jesus. (This happened under the influence of the Cistercian movement and the Gregorian reform.)

At the same time there was clear influence from the contemplative, Greek Byzantine East (through the crusaders and cloth merchants). The situation became more serious when these gospel movements came into contact with dualistic Eastern movements which arrived in the West through the Slav lands of the Danube; they were called Cathari, a collective term for Gnostic and dualistic trends. As a result the whole of the 'gospel movement' became even more suspect to the church. The problem became that of saving the gospel movement for the church and mobilizing it against heresy. We must set the phenomenon of Dominic against this historical background of all kinds of enthusiastic revivals of evangelism, but on the periphery of the official church. Dominic was not alone in seeing the problems in the situation: Pope Innocent III, Bishop Diego, with whom Dominic travelled to the south, and Francis of Assisi also saw it. With outspoken realism, Dominic formulated a clear rescue programme. He saw that an enormous potential for the gospel was being lost to the church. Though trained in the already traditional canonical priestly life, he was nevertheless sympathetic to these new counter-experiments. But he saw quite clearly why they either kept failing (splitting off into 'heretical' sects), or came to be incorporated once again into traditional monastic life (e.g. the Premonstratensians). He wanted to make these counter-movements authentic alternative forms of the church's evangelism, a church movement: he wanted as it were to 'live like the heretics' but 'teach like the church'.

Evangelism must be a challenge within the church; in other words it must be the church and not a sect. Dominic's own vision came near to this in that he saw the solution of the problems of the time in the combination – in one institution – of apostolic preaching (that is, preaching with a critical remembrance of the need for a proclamation endorsed by the Pope or by the episcopate), and the *vita apostolica* (that is, radical evangelism: following Jesus like the apostles). He brought together organically, in one programme, the themes treated separately by the Fourth Lateran Council. Because this same Council, to some extent contrary to the personal views of Pope Innocent III, had forbidden all new forms of religious life (Mansi 22, 1002) and 'banned' unauthorized preaching (Mansi, ibid., 990), Dominic combined the best of traditional monastic life with the basic trends of the new counter-movements which had arisen all over Europe and which, to make the Christian proclamation credible, required a life commensurate with the gospel from those who proclaimed it. In so doing he broke down the feudal structures of the old monastic life: thus there arose a new form of religious life, the Order of Preachers, the Dominicans. Hence our earliest constitutions are largely made up of elements from the constitutions of traditional religious life, especially from the Norbertines and Cistercians (at that time the most lively religious institutions). However, Dominic and his first followers transformed these elements by the very purpose of the Order: apostolic itinerant preaching; that is, the new spirit of what were then modern, experimental gospel movements brought into the perspective of the church.

Dominic had been caught up in this spirit through his contact in the south of France with all this heretical gospel enthusiasm, which was shared by a broad spectrum of people, high and low. Through the structure of his Order, Dominic had weakened the economic stability which had been the basic principle of the older monastic institutions. On the basis of a *religious* criticism Dominic thus attacked the foundations of the feudal system (in church and society). Furthermore, the association of the contemplative monastic element with itinerant preaching resulted in a basic difference from the traditional form of monastic life. The new 'corporative' idea (a particular form of organization, as in the official guilds) was adapted to the religious institution: no 'monarchical' authority from above but a democratic form of government with a range of choices (democratic and personal). Paradoxically, Dominic's evangelism led to a new incarnation in secular structures, especially those of the rising democratic mediaeval bourgeoisie.

By thread and cross-thread, Dominic wove a new fabric, created a new religious programme. Thus the Dominican order was born from the charisma of the combination of admonitory and critical recollection of the spiritual heritage of the old monastic and canonical religious life with the 'modernistic' religious experiment of the thirteenth century. Dominic had a fine sensitivity both to religious values from the past and to the religious promise for the future emanating from the modern experiments of his time. The Dominican Order was born out of this two-fold charisma. With Pere Cormier, a modern Magister General of our Order (see my 1954 duplicated article, p.7), I would say that this is our *gratia originalis,* the grace at the origin of our Order.

Dominican spirituality is therefore in the first instance to be defined as a spirituality which, on the basis of admonitory and critical reflection on the heritage left behind by the past religious tradition, takes up critically and positively the cross-thread provided by whatever new religious possibilities for the future keep emerging among us. Therefore it can never be a *material* repetition of what our Dominican forebears have themselves done admirably; nor, however, can it be an *uncritical* acceptance of whatever 'new movements'(in the mystical or political sense) are now evident in our midst. For Dominic, the essential thing was the question of truth. In his heart Dominic was ultimately one hundred per cent behind the new apostolic experiments of *preaching* combined with poverty, but – remembering the good achievements of the previous patterns of religious life – he unconditionally observed the guidelines laid down by the Fourth Lateran Council (1215) for any renewal of both priestly and religious life. His charisma was organically to combine two divergent guidelines and thus personally to extend the aims of this Council.

On the basis of this spirituality, which found expression in our very first Dominican Constitutions, the further history of the spirituality becomes understandable. This brings the historical, changing, cross-grained, new element into the very heart of Dominican spirituality. For example, the Constitutions from the years 1221-1231 said: 'Our brothers may not study the books of pagan writers (referring above all to Aristotle) and philosophers (what is meant is Arabic philosophy, the great modernism in the Middle Ages); far less may they study the secular sciences.' However, only about twenty years later, Albert the Great and Thomas Aquinas were to regard the study of secular sciences and the 'pagan philosophers' as a necessary condition of the preparation and formation of an appropriate Dominican apostolate. Thus on the basis of an authentic Dominican spirituality these two Dominican saints boldly went against a Dominican constitution set up in earlier times and were therefore in opposition to what was then in fact called official 'Dominican spirituality'. They did this – inspired by what Dominic did in his time – so successfully that the definition was later removed from the Constitutions by a General Chapter; indeed, later Constitutions urged Thomas as a model (Raymond of Penafort had centres for the study of Arabic built in Nursia and Tunis). That is an authentically Dominican development, after the heart of St Dominic, who himself tried to reconcile 'the past' and new 'possibilities for the future'. (This brought with it the new danger that Thomas would later cease to be a beacon pointing towards the future and would become a closed frontier.) If no cross-thread can be seen in the story that the Dominican perceives and takes up again himself, there is every chance that Dominican spirituality will fade; worse still, that on the basis of an 'established' Dominican spirituality – a contradiction in terms – we shall wrongly write off as apocryphal talk new attempts at a truly Dominican spirituality. The greatest moments in the history of our Order are when at the same time this history becomes anti-history or a cross-thread: Dominic himself, Albert and Thomas, Savonarola, Eckhardt, de las Casas, Lacordaire, Lagrange, Chenu, Congar, to name a few. However, at the same time Dominicans have sometimes (in the first instance at least) run into difficulties with the already established Dominican story when in an un-Dominican way it has refused to take up the new cross-thread. Without mistaking the fundamental worth, by which we are all supported, of the many anonymous Dominicans who have quietly lived a successful Dominican religious life (though their tranquillity can have a broad influence and produce cross-grained stories within the Order), nevertheless it only becomes clear what is typically Dominican when Dominicans sometimes, following the example of Dominic, reshape 'the old' and combine it with the dynamism of constantly new and different forms. If this does not happen at regular intervals, then there is every chance that the well-known Dominican concern for truth is dishonoured in an Inquisition and the new 'Dominican possibilities' are rejected. They may then come to life outside the Dominican family. I would not want to include this less rosy story – which is also part of our Order – in the golden thread of our family story, which is always in a state of constantly taking up the cross-thread again. However, the cross-thread sometimes ensures the continuity! The history of this cross-thread is the golden thread of the Dominican family story, woven into a broader, as it were more serene, whole. That St Ignatius of Loyola was shut up in the cellars of one of our monasteries because he shocked the people of his time with a new charisma is one of the many stories in which 'Dominican spirituality' has perversely become its opposite; it now shows us to be guilty of un-Dominican chauvinism. In other words, this is typical of times in which the Dominicans were no longer 'Dominican' and on the basis of their own 'established' position had already dubbed the new counter-thread heretical. The constantly new forms which Dominican spirituality must take in accordance with Dominic's basic story will emerge even more clearly precisely through the moments in which we have failed in the past.

It is essential for Dominican spirituality to attend to God as he has already revealed himself to us in the past and to attend to the present-day 'signs of the time' in which the same God, who is faithful to us, makes his appeal. Any onesidedness – in one-track, uncritical judgment either of the past or of what prove to be symptoms of the future in the present – is un-Dominican. Dominic submits the present, with its own possibilities of experiment, to comparison with the dangerous recollection of certain events and legacies from the past, just as at the same time he opens up the global past and gives it the stamp of the cross-grained experimental present: it is out of this kind of attitude that the Order was born. This must remain its 'genius'. The *présence à Dieu* and the *présence au monde* (as Lacordaire puts it) describe the very nature of Dominican spirituality throughout the history of the Order. And perhaps today we are going to see clearly that – in recollection of the religious past – the *'présence au monde'* or critical solidarity with the human world is the only possible mode of our *présence à Dieu*. At the same time this insight confirms the need for a critical recollection of the religious past in which the same *présence à Dieu* is always revealed in the communication of what were then the contemporary signs of the time. The 'modernism' of the Dominican order lives on dangerous memories from the past. After what was almost a centuries-long sleep, it was Père Lacordaire and Magister General Jandel who in the nineteenth century recalled the Dominican Order to its original charisma and brought about a break with the serene traditionalism to which the 'established order' had fallen victim. 'Lacordaire' (and everything connected with that within our Dominican history) was in fact the rediscovery of the Order by itself. For the Lacordaire movement was nourished by the original charisma of the order and as a result again raised the problem of 'Dominican spirituality'.

Some consequences of Dominican spirituality are clear from this (see my 1954 paper).

1. Belief in the absolute priority of God's grace in any human action: the theologal direction of the Dominican life and its programme in relation to ethics, the world, society and the betterment of people. No cramped self-concern but trust in God: I can trust God more than myself. Therefore a tranquil and happy spirituality. God still gives an unexpected future to the limited meaning and scope of my own actions.

2. Religious life in the light of the gospel (*vita apostolica*) as the atmosphere in which the Dominican is *apostolic* (*salus animarum*, salvation as the aim of the activity of the Order): through preaching in all its forms. The result of that is *contemplari* and *contemplata aliis tradere* (i.e. the agreement between what a person proclaims and their own life, see Thomas, II-II, q.188, a.6 and a.7, in which he contrasts the character of the Mendicants with that of other religious institutions and at the same time connects this with 'poverty': being free from financial worries). This general Mendicant view became typically Dominican through the essential insertion of study into the structure of this Dominican evangelism. This particular element was not character-istic of the mediaeval evangelical movements. 'Study is not the aim of the order but an essential instrument for this work' (says Humbertus of Romani in his commentary on the Constitutions). The failure of many gospel movements was also brought about by a lack of thoughtfulness. Furthermore, while the universities, which were only established at that time, had intensified the element of scientific study, at the same time they had concentrated it and centralized it so that there were no intellectuals in the dioceses. Dominic saw this, and therefore he incorporated study as an institutional element in the very organization of his order. He would not have any monastery founded 'without a doctor in theology', and any monastery had to be a 'school of theology': a Dominican monastery is 'permanent instruction'. The distinction between study monasteries and pastoral monasteries is un-Dominican; both must be monasteries for study *and* pastoral ministry. (See Thomas' defence of a religious institution 'founded for study': II-II, q.188, a.5.)

3. The 'Jesus spirituality' of the order – the 'humanity of Jesus' (Albert, Thomas, Eckhardt, Tauler, Susa, etc.)(here directly connected

with the only two Dominican devotions, to Mary and to Joseph), but this humanity experienced as a personal manifestation of God's love for mankind – is the centre of Dominican spirituality and mysticism without any predilection for 'derivative devotions'. All this is typically twelfth-century; along with all the other characteristics it is also typically Dominican.

4. *Présence au monde* (*la grâce d'entendre ce siècle,* as Père Lacordaire says): openness for constantly new charismata which the different circumstances require of us. Hence the need for structures which do not hem us in but are democratic and flexible, through which it becomes possible for Dominicans to accept the rise of new stories which go against the grain. It is characteristic that the Dominicans never had their Constitutions approved by the Pope, so that they themselves could adapt them to new circumstacnes (see P.Mandonnet, *Saint Dominique,* Paris 1937, I, 237; L.Moulin, 'Les formes du gouvernement local et provincial dans les ordres religieux', in *Revue Internationale des Sciences Administratives,* nos.1-3, 1955, 9 n.1).

5. (As a consequence of 4.): Since Albert and Thomas, Dominican spirituality has been inwardly enriched by the inclusion of the Christian principle of secularization within the essentially religious, gospel trend (Dominicans at first rejected this, but soon they generally accepted it): this involves first coming to know things (objects, inter-personal relationships, society) in their intrinsic characteristics and their own structures rather than prematurely defining their relationship to God. In modern times this has enormous consequences over against all kinds of forms of pseudo-mystical supernaturalism, which often ends up as a sense of superiority masquerading as piety.

To begin with, the Order agonized over the introduction of 'natural sources' into Dominican evangelism. The traditional rejection of the 'profane sciences' by the monks continued to have its effect, though this was limited by the Dominican principle of dispensation. The first Dominicans were 'anti-philosophical' (thus running the risk of an evangelical supernaturalism). The *Vitae Fratrum* (G.Frachet) reeked of 'holy naivety'. Albert and Thomas changed the direction, Albert even arguing fiercely against fellow-brethren 'who thus again want to become the murderers of Socrates'. The dispute was over the consequences of integral evangelism which Albert and Thomas wanted to be enlightened, not naive. In the Chapter of Valenciennes (1259), the trend supported by Albert and Thomas won through: the study of the 'profane sciences' became obligatory in Dominican training.

6. The other elements: a liturgical choral office, monastic observances and community life, are traditional and generally religious, and in this sense not typically Dominican. That was the dangerous recollection of the monastic and canonical past to which Dominic continued to give

expression in his new religious and apostolic programme – albeit in critical, reduced and more modest form.

7. The 'principle of dispensation' (historically this seems to go back to Dominic himself in person), i.e. respect for the particular personal charisma of a fellow Dominican within the Dominican community, bearing in mind the purpose of the order. Of course this is an extremely dangerous principle, which has been abused to disastrous effect. However, Dominic would rather take that risk than give up the human and Christian significance of the dispensation principle because of the threat of abuse. As a general principle this was a completely new Dominican discovery in the Middle Ages. In furtherance of study in the service of the 'salvation of men' (*salus animarum*) and in furtherance of the apostolate, it is, paradoxically, possible to be a Dominican (if necessary) on your own. This presupposes having been trained as a Dominican, but it is in no way understood as a matter of standing outside the law: on the contrary, dispensation is a constitutional Dominican law. Conformity is alien to original Dominican legislation. Even now, this original Dominican principle opens up broad possibilities for 'modern experiments' in our time, even experiments which some people accustomed to an 'established' Dominican spirituality cannot stand. (However, these experiments also always need to happen from and within the dangerous recollection of a tradition which is already centuries old. This tradition prefigures permanent perspectives which are always worth thinking about – without it all experiments seem doomed to religious failure.) Although there are countless examples of this characteristic from our rich family archives, I want to point to just one event in the first redactions of our Dominican Constitutions. The striking 'democratic structure' of our Order has been said by experts in administration to be unique among Catholic monastic institutions. This feature can be understood precisely as a result of the typical cross-grained spirituality of the Order (along with its respect for all that is good in the tradition). The Constitutions were 'reformulated' during a revision at a time when great canon lawyers from the universities of the time had entered the Order (for example, Raymond of 'Penafort). This reformulation took place at a General Chapter in Bologna. Shortly before and during this Chapter, social protests were voiced in the university and city of Bologna, and in addition there was already a dispute between the Ghibellines (the conservatives) and the Guelphs (the progressive popular party). Dominicans were involved as advisers throughout this conflict. The 'co-responsibility of all' required by the progressive party had its influence on our Dominican Constitutions. 'What affects all must also be resolved on by all.' This new civic principle called for at that time was also supported by the Dominicans and later sanctioned in our

Dominican Constitutions (under the influence and as a result of the civic experiences in Bologna). New 'secular experiences' thus came to exercise a substantial influence on our earliest Constitutions. The emancipatory social movements of that time left a substantial mark on our Constitutions, differing completely from the traditional administrative model then current. Following the example of Dominic, these Dominicans did not just raise a warning finger and point to what had been the custom from earliest times, but at the same time listened to the voice of God in what came out of the human secular emancipatory movements of the time (however turbulently). As a result of these experiences they rewrote the Dominican monastic structure, barely twenty years after Dominic. That is just one case of the cross-thread that the Dominican family story keeps showing as its 'own theme' down the ages.

I have only recalled a few Dominican characteristics: more could be mentioned. Furthermore, I should point out explicitly that I am in no way denying that perhaps non-Dominicans do the same things. In that case Dominican spirituality can simply say with delight: all the better! It is not our concern to maintain an unparalleled exclusiveness. It is a question of what we, as Dominicans, do here in any case, and do in the strength of the charisma of the Order and our Dominican commitment (through our profession). If others also do the same thing, this can simply confirm the validity, the correct intuition of our view. When a typical view is universalized, it in no way loses its value: quite the opposite.

The man who was once an Augustinian canon, Domingo de Guzman, while trusting in the original direction of his life nevertheless gave it a new course (which became the beginning of the Dominican Order), thanks to a living contact with the needs of people and of the church of which he was unaware when he was first called. One cannot accuse Dominic of betraying his first calling, which was meant to be irrevocable. His change of course was a new way of life (in contact with what then appeared to him to be better possibilities), in order to remain faithful to the deepest sense of his calling, when confronted with new needs. (According to Dominic's earliest biographers he could be moved to tears at the sight of the needs of others. Hence the desire of this realistic organizer – which remained with him all his life – to go to the Cumani, somewhere in the Balkans, evidently the place where the dualistic heresy crossed from East to West.) The Order came into being from such an amazing change of course *in trust*. A change of course in trust is therefore part of the essence of the Dominican charisma.

No theologian, canon lawyer, professional psychologist or sociologist can work out at his study desk or in his armchair what we must do now. This must be tried by way of concrete experiment, by charismatically inspired religious, albeit bearing in mind the sometimes dangerously cross-grained element – the golden thread – in our Dominican family story. In so doing it will adopt, with due criticism, the successful attempts in the context of our past, gratefully rethinking them and making them fruitful in the context of the new programme. With Thomas Aquinas, who clearly followed the matter-of-fact and brilliant temperament of Dominic here, we can say, 'The excellence of a religious institution does not lie so much in the strictness of its observances as in the fact that these observances are designed with greater skill towards the purpose of the religious life' (II-II, q.188, a.6, ad 3). And in the circumstances of our time this calls for a renewed and skilled religious decision in which all have a share, both high and low, so that the structures themselves remain open to this new cross-thread.

This question is our duty. For in our profession we also opt for a particular community, a Dominican community and its ideals. There can be such faults and defects in a particular community (whether through betrayal of the Dominican family story or because this story is no longer alive there and has become ossified and dead) that *out of faithfulness* to his or her Dominican ideal the professed religious is ethically permitted (and in some cases may even be obliged) to leave the Dominican community because it does not give him or her the support to which they have a right by virtue of their profession. For paradoxically, here we expose ourselves to the danger that as Dominicans we may expel a 'Dominican charisma' from our ranks. The Dominican family story gives us adequate pointers if we also listen to God's voice in the characteristics of contemporary movements and trace their lines of force, so as to enrich this story with a new chapter which is still to be published. Many people think that the Dominican family story is exhausted, because hardly anyone still comes under its spell. All of us who are Dominicans today, men and women, are the only ones who can give it a new twist so that the story flourishes again (not as a stunt or a sensation but as an authentic Dominican family story), so that others in turn will join the Dominican storytelling community and continue to hand the story on. Here we may also happily pass on the folklore which each Order has alongside its own great story: that simply points to the fact that the great Dominican family story is made up of, and told by, ordinary, very human, people, though they transcend themselves through the strength of God's unmerited and loving grace. However, it would be fatal for the Dominican family story if this greater story eventually became narrower and was reduced to the story of the folklore of Dominican houses.

I am aware that I have said a great deal and very little. That is perhaps the most appropriate thing for the chapter which we are all adding, here and now, to the story of a great family tradition. I hope that it will become a serial which lasts longer than the stories which have entranced the whole world on television, but which have not in any way renewed the face of the earth: Peyton Place, the Forsyte Saga or Dallas. May the Dominican story be a parable which in an unspoken, but compelling, way ends with the words of Jesus: 'Go and do likewise' (Luke 10.37).

In 1206, even before Dominic was thinking of a Dominican Order, he had founded a convent at Prouille. However, the aim of this convent was on the same lines: Dominic wanted to make the evangelical religious movement, which many women had also joined, into a church movement – that is, to bring the gospel to the church and to bring the church to sectarian gospel movements. Evangelism without the church or the church without evangelism is essentially un-Dominican, that is, it goes against the original charisma which brought the Order into being.

In Dominic's time, gospel inspiration was almost always to be found in 'deviant' movements. Hence Dominic's own preaching among the 'heretics'. From among such women (Waldensians who remained orthodox, the 'Catholic Poor') Dominic recruited the first occupants of Prouille: he gave a church atmosphere to the gospel they had experienced outside the church. In 1219 he also founded convents in Madrid and Rome (S.Sisto), to which he gave Constitutions (which would later also form the basis of the Dominican Order). After many difficulties the convent of S.Agnese was founded at Bologna with the financial support of an eighteen-year-old girl, Diana of Andalo (later the friend of the second General, Jordan of Saxony), but only after Dominic's death,

However, it is typical that at the end of his life Dominic, and after his death, the whole male side of the Order, systematically began to oppose the incorporation of new convents into the Order. This opposition would involve them in fights with Popes until 1259. It is evident from the archives that this opposition was motivated by the aim of the Order itself: the care of the sisters hindered the Dominicans in their task of preaching elsewhere. At a special Chapter in 1228 (in Paris) all Dominicans were prohibited from involvement in spiritual direction and pastoral care in our convents (with the exception of the first four great convents), on pain of exclusion from the Order. In northern areas, however, the growing Dominican movement had encountered the very lively evangelical women's movement there: all of a sudden this became Dominican (or sometimes Franciscan). After a time there were hundreds of convents, each with more than a hundred evangelical Dominican women. No one had planned this: it was a spontaneous consequence of the encounter between Dominican preaching and the evangelical women's movement of the time. After that, the male Dominicans came to be fundamentally opposed to having to care for the sisters, which hindered the purpose of their own Order. Time and again, papal bulls enjoined the Order against its will to provide both financial and spiritual care for these sisters. In 1252, at the Chapter of Bologna, the Order opposed the repeated papal bulls (occasioned by an appeal from our sisters to Rome). In a bull of 15 July 1252, Innocent IV made some concessions: Rome would stop issuing the bulls for the moment but the existing convents had to be taken into the care of the Dominicans. However, the Dominicans would not accept this, and in the end they secured a retraction from the same Pope, who said: 'I have allowed myself to be convinced that preaching is the most essential task of the Order. This aim must have priority and is hindered by the care of the women's convents. Therefore the Pope resolves to release the Order from all obligations towards the convents... with the exceptions of Prouille and San Sisto in Rome.'

However, all the convents stormed the papal Curia with heartfelt pleas. The Pope was caught between two Dominican fronts: the men and the women. He knew that the men were opposed in principle. Then the Magister General, Johannes Teutonicus, died (in 1252). Cardinal Hugo a Sancto Caro, who had become a Dominican and was himself enthusiastic about the evangelical women's movement, was given full authority by the Pope to come to an arrangement with the Order. First he wanted to break the opposition of the men 'with quiet measures': until the election of the new General (Humbertus of Romani), the Dominicans had at least to take over the spiritual care of the sisters. The Order remained obstinate and at the Chapter of Milan in 1255 it was resolved that (in contrast to the monasteries) three successive General Chapters would be needed to come to a decision as to whether a convent was to come under Dominican direction. This first resolution was endorsed in Paris (1256) and Florence (1257) and thus became a Dominican ruling. In 1259 a definitive resolution was passed that all convents already established had the right to the pastoral care of Dominican priests. (This ending of resistance by the Order was the result of the mediation of the Dominican cardinal Hugo a Sancto Caro, who combined both the official Dominican standpoint and that of the church in his own person. In the Order, from Dominic onwards, the specific Dominican character was often a compromise between the papal perspective and the views of the Dominicans; both parties knew

how to secure the essentials of their position.) After about thirty years
of opposition the Order capitulated: for new convents, the Dominican
resolution, passed by three Chapters, remained in force. The combination of papal Curia and Dominican sisters had won the argument.
Furthermore, the Order was obliged to make Constitutions for the
whole of the women's side. In the General Chapter of 1259 at
Valenciennes, Humbertus of Romani approved the Dominican Constitutions as adapted for sisters. All this also gave the sisters economic
security, so that they could devote themselves to a life of study and
contemplation (since left to themselves, the sisters often lived in very
real poverty – as a result of over-population). The close collaboration
of male and female Dominicans that now took place resulted in the
Dominican mystical movement which arose in the fourteenth century.
This followed from the theological and mystical direction of women by
Dominican lectors and the women's response to the direction (1300-
1480). It was in the time of the Great Plague which also affected
thousands of Dominicans and had broken their first élan. Furthermore,
the Order was divided by the schism: Avignon and the two Popes.

Later, above all in the nineteenth century, many congregations of
sisters were founded outside the Order, so that the Order did not have
any responsibility for them and no one was concerned for a truly
Dominican spirituality: this spirit was often that of normal nineteenth-
century religious life with its caritative inspiration.

As Dominicans, therefore, we need to remember that at present
many developments have taken place in which men and women together
seek a form of Dominican spirituality in a modern revival of life in
accordance with the gospel, combined with social criticism. Although
this is still a search, we may not exclude this Dominican possibility out
of hand. A Dominican community spirit and the collaboration of
Dominican brothers and sisters may perhaps help us to understand the
mystical Dominican movement in the fourteenth century (a high point
of Dominican spirituality). Taught by our own history, we may not
exclude possible new charismata out of hand. 'Dominican options'
which are new and at first sight disconcerting are possibilities for the
future and may not be suppressed *per se,* though we must pay attention
to the danger of references to the religious past.

35

Speech of Thanks on Receiving the Erasmus Prize

The honour done to me by Your Royal Highness fills me with profound gratitude.

First of all, I am grateful to you that the Foundation of the Erasmus Prize, which since 1958 has each year brought distinction to philosophers and architects, musicians and other artists eminent in choreography, film and ballet, painters and sculptors, journalists and finally specialists in both the human and the natural sciences, has decided – in 1982, for the first time – to celebrate theology. Indeed, since theology has renounced its mediaeval status of 'queen of the sciences', as a result of which *a priori* it enjoyed royal privileges, so that it has come to regard itself as just one particular way of coming to know reality alongside many others, it too can take its turn as a candidate for royal distinction alongside those many other disciplines which make a positive and critical contribution to a culture or a society which cries out for more humanity.

I am also grateful to you for having chosen me from among the theologians of Europe to receive the Erasmus prize. This also makes me embarrassed when I see how much theology I myself have learnt from my fellow theologians. In particular I would like to remind you of the reasons why the Foundation chose me to receive this prize. According to Article 2 of the statutes of this Foundation the prize is awarded each year 'to a person or an institution which has made an eminent contribution to European culture in respect of culture, social sciences or other social questions'. It seems to me a particularly happy touch that you should mention as a reason for the award of this prize not only my contribution to the furtherance of European values, but also my critical views on the way in which these values function in the world. We certainly cannot forget that the ideological short- sightedness of all traditional Western forms of humanism in modern times has robbed foreign cultures of their own humanism. The many forms of what has understood itself to be humanism, albeit with many qualifications, have seldom been liberating and truly philanthropic in the fullest sense of the term. In the autumn of 1492, Giovanni Pico della Mirandola, translating the creation story into modern terms, sketched out in advance in an almost prophetic way the future of Christian humanism with all its later forms, Christian and non-Christian:

> God was pleased to create man as a being whose form is indefinite. He put him in the centre of the universe and said to him: 'We have not assigned you a particular place to dwell in, a particular appearance; we have not given you a special gift, O Adam, so that you can appropriate for yourself any dwelling place, any appearance, any gift that you desire, according to your own powers and your own views. As to the other creatures, their nature obeys laws which we have prescribed for them and which mark out their limits. As for you, no impassable frontier will bar your way, but you will determine your own nature in accordance with your own free will, to which I have entrusted your destiny. We have not created you celestial or terrestrial, mortal or immortal; you shall be your own free sculptor and poet of your own image, to give yourself freely the form in which you desire to live' (*De dignitate hominis,* ed. E.Garin, Florence 1942).

The past decades have taught us, not without pain and grief, that this arbitrary and unbridled Western concern for self-realization has not brought men salvation either personally or in the social and political sphere. Furthermore, our unrestrained economic expansion nurtured on a nineteenth-century myth of limitless progress has been achieved at the expense of people from other parts of the world and has threatened the environment in which we live to such a degree that the whole of mankind is endangered as a result. The programme of a total liberation of man by man at present seems to be the greatest threat to all humanity. The 'modern Western world' is in particular need of salvation today, for liberation and redemption precisely from those dark powers which modern man has himself called to life. The demonic in our culture and society has taken on a different name and content from the demons of the ancient world and the Middle Ages, but it is no less real and just as threatening. I am not criticizing science, technology or industrialization in any way here, but rather those who have these powers and use them for their own personal, national and continental profit – and so much the worse for those who do not have the good fortune to live in a prosperous country or who are at best tolerated as immigrant workers. Is it not a supreme irony of history that science and technology, which since the seventeenth century we have hailed as the cultural forces which will finally deliver mankind from all those things from which religion has failed to deliver us – hunger, poverty, tyranny, war and historical destiny – at this moment represent, in the hands of men, the greatest threat to our future? 'Knowledge is power,' said Francis Bacon. But our domination over nature has led to the beginnings of the destruction of fundamental elements of life; our unrestrained economic growth threatens our human survival; control over genetic structures and the manipulation of them conjure up disturbing prospects for the future; and finally, the nuclear arms spiral twists higher and higher above our heads and given that a strategy of deterrence makes sense only if one is determined to use nuclear weapons if need be, this necessary determination in itself is enough to make this strategy inhuman and ethically indefensible. Neither science nor technology are to blame, but man. Once one gives these means an absolute character; once one invests them with a sacrality and an immunity characteristic of our modern world, they cease to contribute towards our freedom and become a threat to man and society. The sciences are children of their time and in their own intrinsic autonomy reflect the hesitations, the blind spots and even the sicknesses of their time. Science is no more purely objective than the other forms of knowledge; so it certainly does not have any letters patent by which in a legitimate way it can lay claim to the dominant role which it in fact exercises in Western society, at the expense of other kinds of cognitive relations with reality. The applied sciences are also an instrument of human will and are thus subject to the same distortions which affect it. Knowledge is power, but power delivered into the hands of an unfree liberty, itself the slave of greed, lust for power and personal or collective egoism and the uncontrolled need for security, is in fact power on the way towards corruption. It is a fact that science and technology cannot bring men their authentic salvation: 'holiness' and wisdom. What they can do is to make us considerably more competent, and that in itself is a blessing. Science and technology work miracles when they are used to bring about the freedom of others, solidarity among men and women. But in fact the sciences function as an instrument of power: power over nature, power over society and also power over men and women, even extending to power over their masculinity and femininity. Science is the key to the military power of nations; it is the secret of their economic and social prosperity – also at the expense of others. The trust placed in verifiable and falsifiable knowledge and in technological know-how as unique ways of removing human misery dominates the present-day cultural world, whether we look at Europe and North America, Russia and India, Japan or China.

Towards the end of the eighteenth century science seemed to be announcing the end of all religions, which was innocently thought to be a period of childlike ignorance in the history of humanity. Now that the year 2000 is approaching it is in fact science and technology themselves which compel us to raise more necessarily and more urgently than ever the religious question – if the question of human salvation is to retain any meaning at all. It is not science and technology which make us anxious, but their absolute claim to bring us salvation. We have come to see that human creativity implies the possibility of self-destruction. Science and technology, once acclaimed as the liberators of mankind, have subjected us to a new kind of social and historical fatalism. This historical irony is biting when we see how the East is seizing hold of Western technology and science for its material prosperity, while the West is looking to the East for its lost inwardness. Is it then our creative power itself which threatens the meaning of our history? Or is it that the finite creature is never in a position to understand and free itself? Is not the acceptance of a living relationship with the transcendent the deepest dimension of our finite human creativity and, as a result, the deepest and most extreme possibility of all humanism?

Now it is theology which seeks to preserve this faith and this hope in a liberating and saving power which overcomes evil and therefore refuses to be hypnotized by a catastrophic vision of things, despite the inextricable mixture of sense and nonsense at the heart of which we live. History can teach us that a humanism which in any society is founded exclusively or at least predominantly on science and technology, poses the threat of inhumanity to human beings and their society.

But if religion here has its irreplacable word to say, this must be a religion concerned for man in the world, a religion which begins from faith in a liberating God and is interested in the human being in his specific historical and social context. Might there be another humanism, neither dogmatic nor threatening, and more universal, more humanist than the humanism of God himself, a God concerned for humanity who wants men to be concerned for humanity as well? But if the religions and the Christian churches want to proclaim this message with some credibility, they should begin by confessing that they have often obscured and even mutilated the face of God's humanity. Where religion or science is made absolute, rather than God himself, not only the image of God but mankind itself is disfigured: *ecce homo* – on the cross and on the many crosses which men have set up and keep setting up. Theology has also played its part here in the past. But whatever one thinks of contemporary theologians, one thing should be granted them: by means of a historical praxis of commitment to mysticism and politics, they are trying to discover the human face of God and, starting from there, to revive hope in a society, a humanity with a more human face. Despite all its failings and hesitations, I personally see this perspective opened up above all through the diverse and richly varied group which finds expression in *Concilium,* the international review of theology the idea for which came to birth in the country of Erasmus.

For all these reasons, it is greatly to the honour of the Erasmus Prize Foundation that it has chosen this year to give its prize to theology. Because the main task of theology is to preserve the transcendence of the God who loves men, hidden and yet so near, in the face of the idols which human beings set up, it must always be opposed to the positivistic claims that might be made by the sciences, no matter how valuable or how necessary they might be, to be the only relevant cognitive relationship to reality, and their claims to provide the only effective solution to vital human problems. But this very theology must in turn accept that unless it adopts a truly interdisciplinary approach, it is reduced to being an ideology.

The fact that in paying homage to theology as a distinctive factor in culture you have awarded this prize in 1982 to me personally, I regard as an incidental pleasure.

Notes

7 *The Free Man Jesus and his Conflict*

1. Mark's composition (a) in stereotyped fashion also has an appearance of 'disciples of the Pharisees'; (b) adds two new images (vv.21,22); (c) puts the whole pericope (2.18-22) in a wider group of 'shocking actions' of Jesus (2.1-3.5) ending with the words 'and they sought to do away with Jesus' (3.6).

17 *I Believe in the Man Jesus*

1. That is why I usually talk of 'Christian creation faith' without separating the Christian and the philosophical aspects.

2. I have deliberately used the rather pedantic word 'relational' to avoid the ambiguity of 'relative'. Relative is contrasted with absolute; that need not be the case with the word relational.

3. See E.Schillebeeckx, *Christ,* New York and London 1980, 229-34.

24 *Christian Identity and Human Integrity*

1. Thomas Aquinas, *Summa contra Gentiles* I, 4.

2. Ignatius, *Romans* 6.2.

27 *How Shall We Sing the Lord's Song in a Strange Land?*

1. As one of many possibilities I have taken in this article the parable of Luke 18.9-14. But what Jesus means to say in it is in fact expressed in almost all his parables. See the parable of the prodigal son (Luke 15.11-32), the parable of the good Samaritan (Luke 10.30-37), the parable of the rich man and Lazarus (Luke 16.19-27), of the great banquet (Matt.22.1-10), of the places at table (Luke 14.7-14) and so on. The basic theme is always that God's love is gratuitous, free; it presents no conditions to men. It does have consequences. Therefore this love is essentially criticism of any discrimination and exclusive attitudes on the part of people to their fellow human beings: that in no way implies ethical indifferentism, but makes a

demand to act in accordance with the life-style of the kingdom of God, which calls for community.

29 *Priests and Religious as Figures for Orientation*

1. G.Bessières, *Les acrobates de Dieu: Eloge de la prière,* Paris 1975, 32f.

31 *Christian Obedience and its Pathology*

1. *Nicomachean Ethics,* 1124.20 – 1125a.
2. See e.g. A.J.Festugière, *La sainteté,* Paris 1942; id, *Contemplation et vie contemplative selon Platon,* Paris 1936; M.Pohlenz, *Griechische Freiheit,* Heidelberg 1955.
3. The last version of Aristotle's teaching on *magnanimitas* is to be found in *Nicomachean Ethics* 1123a.34 – 1124b.6.
4. *Nic.Eth.* 1099b.11-14.
5. *Nic.Eth.* 1167b.16 – 1168a.34; 1124b. 10-23.
6. *Nic.Eth.* 1167b.30 – 1168a.34; 1124b. 5-12.
7. *Nic.Eth.* 1116a.17-29.
8. *Nic.Eth.* 1124b.18-23 and b.30-31.
9. *Nic.Eth.* 1169b.23-28.
10. *Nic.Eth.* 1169a.18-20.
11. *Politics* III.13: 1284.3ff.
12. Seneca, *De clementia* 15.7. See M.Pohlenz, *Die Stoa,* two vols., Göttingen 1959.
13. Seneca, *Letters* 4.1; Epictetus, *Dissertations* II, 16.11-15.
14. Marcus Aurelius, *Meditations (Ta eis heauton),* IX, 40.
15. Epictetus, *Dissertations* IV, 7.6; Marcus Aurelius, *Meditations* XI, 3; Celsus, in Origen, *Contra Celsum* VII, 53; VI, 75.
16. P. de Labriolle, *La réaction païenne. Etude sur la polémique antichrétienne du premier au sixième siècle,* Paris² 1942; W. Nestle, 'Die Haupteinwände des antiken Denkens gegen das Christentum', in *Archiv für Religionswissenschaft* 37, 1941, 51-100; E.Dekkers, ' "Humilitas". Een bijdrage tot de geschiedenis van het begrip "humilitas" ', in *Horae Monasticae,* Tielt 1974, 67-80, and N.I.Herescu, 'Homo – Humus – Humanitas', *Bulletin de l'Association G. Bude,* Paris, June 1948, 68ff.
17. Origen, *Contra Celsum* VI,15.
18. *Contra Celsum* III, 61.
19. Augustine, *Enarrationes in Ps.31.18*: PL 36, 270; *Tractatus in Johannem* 25, chs.16,19: PL 35, 1604.
20. Origen, *Contra Celsum* VI, 15; III, 62.
21. Augustine, *Tractatus in Johannem 25.16*: PL 35, 1604.
22. Bernard, *Sermon* V: PL 183, 530-2, 534.
23. Id., *De consideratione* II, 11: PL 182, 754.
24. Id., *Sermones in Cantica* 34; *Sermones de diversis* 20; *Sermo de conversione ad clericos* 7. See esp. PL 182, 841.
25. This aspect has been neglected in the studies of R.Bultot, *La Doctrine du mépris du monde, IV-1 and IV-2: Le XIe siècle,* Louvain-Paris 1963.

26. R.A.Gauthier, *Magnanimité. L'idéal de la grandeur dans la philosophie païenne et la théologie chrétienne*, Paris 1951.

27. '*Omnis creatura est tenebra vel falsa vel nihil*, in se *considerata; (hoc dictum) non est intellegendum quod essentia sua sit tenebra vel falsitas, sed quia non habet nec esse nec lucem nec veritatum* nisi ab Alio *(De veritate*, q.8, a.7 ad 2; I-II, q.109, a 2. ad 2).

28. When Augustine says, '*omnia sunt bona bonitate divina*' (PL 40,30), Thomas corrects this as follows: '*Unumquodque dicitur bonum bonitate divina, sicut primo principio exemplari, effectivo et finali totius bonitatis.* Nihilominus *tamen unumquodque dicitur bonum similitudine divinae bonitatis* sibi inhaerente, *quae est formaliter* sua *bonitas denominans ipsum*'(I, q.6, a.4).

29. See a sharp text in Thomas' commentary on Job, in which man is seen as the ultimate subject. Here Thomas defends Job's words to God: 'Thus it seems as though a discussion between man and God is unthinkable because of the eminence with which God transcends man. But in that case we must remember that the truth is not different depending on who speaks it; therefore the one who speaks the truth can never be put in the wrong, *no matter who he is speaking with*' *(Expositio in Job*, ch.13, lect.2).

30. '*Spes, qua quis de Deo confidit, ponitur virtus theologica;...sed per fiduciam, quae nunc ponitur fortitudinis pars, homo* habet spem in seipso, *tamen* sub Deo' (II-II, q.128, art. unic., ad 2).

31. See e.g. G. de Lagarde, *La naissance de l'esprit laïque au déclin du moyen age*, 4 vols., Paris 1956-1962.

32. *Summa contra Gentiles* III, 69.

33. Descartes, *Traité des passions*, III, art.155-60.

34. Spinoza, *Ethics* III, 26, 55; IV, 52, 53, 55, 57.

35. Kant, *Der Metaphysik der Sitten. Ethische Elementarlehre*, I, Frankfurt² 1978, 553-84, esp. 568-71.

36. B.Groethuysen, *Origines de l'esprit bourgeois en France*, Paris 1927, and (with more critical apparatus), *Die Entstehung der bürgerlichen Welt- und Lebensanschauung in Frankreich*, 2 vols., Hildesheim and New York 1927, 1973. Also dependent on him are e.g. L.Goldmann, *Der christliche Bürger und die Aufklärung*, Neuwied 1968, and D.Schellong, *Bürgertum und christliche Religion*, Munich 1975. See also 'Christendom en burgerlijkheid', *Concilium* 15, 1979, no.5. Cf. T. Lemaire, *Over de waarde van kulturen*, Baarn 1976.

37. 'Le pouvoir exécutif de la conscience bourgeoise pour l'au-delà'(Groethuysen, *Origines*, 123).

38. F. Nietzsche, *Beyond Good and Evil*, Penguin Classics 1973, nos. 260, 261, 267.

39. J.-B. Metz, *Glaube in Geschichte und Gegenwart*, Mainz 1977, passim.

40. Edward Schillebeeckx, *Christ*, London and New York 1980, 736f.

41. J.-B.Metz, 'Produktive Ungleichzeitigkeit' in *Stichworte zur 'Geistigen Situation der Zeit'*, ed. J. Habermas, two vols., Frankfurt 1979, Vol.2, 529-38; see also id., 'Wenn die Betreuten sich ändern', *Publik-Forum* 13, 27 June 1980, 19-21.

33 *A Saint: Albert the Great*

1. *In 1 libr. Physicorum,* tr.1, c.1.
2. *In 1 Sent.,* 1, a 4c et ad 4: ed. Borgnet, Vol.25,18.
3. *In Epist.Dionys.,Epist.* VIII, n.2.
4. *In libr.VIII Politicorum,* c.6: ed. Parma VIII, 803f.
5. *In libr.VIII Politicorum,* c.6: ed. Parma VIII, 804.
6. *In Matth.,* c.9 n.3.